BEHAVIORAL PRIMATOLOGY

Advances in Research and Theory

VOLUME 1

BEHAVIORAL PRIMATOLOGY

Advances in Research and Theory

VOLUME 1

Edited by

ALLAN M. SCHRIER

Brown University

Psychology Press
Taylor & Francis Group

New York London

First Published by
Lawrence Erlbaum Associates, Inc., Publishers
62 Maria Drive
Hillsdale, New Jersey 07642

Transferred to Digital Printing 2009 by Psychology Press
270 Madison Ave, New York NY 10016
27 Church Road, Hove, East Sussex, BN3 2FA

ISBN 0-89859-139-2

Library of Congress Catalog Card Number: 77-82269

Publisher's Note

The publisher has gone to great lengths to ensure the quality of this reprint but points out that some imperfections in the original may be apparent.

Contents

Preface

This series of volumes deals with scientific studies of the behavior of nonhuman primates—apes, monkeys, and prosimians. The behavior of these animals is, of course, of interest in its own right. But, then, so is that of the many other orders of animals. Behavior of nonhuman primates is of special interest because these animals are more closely related to human beings structurally, physiologically, and, beyond doubt, behaviorally, than are any other living animals. Hence, we expect to learn more about ourselves by studying the behavior of these animals than by studying other animals. There are very serious technical and theoretical problems facing anyone interested in generalizing from one species to another, as a number of people have pointed out by now. It is difficult, however, to believe that there is any group of nonhuman animals whose behavior can in general be expected to tell us *more* about ourselves.

It is the editor's aim that the chapters in this series both review and integrate a given line or area of behavioral research. The purpose of these volumes is not to provide a forum for authors to present details of their latest series of experiments (such details belong in journals or monographs) or article-by-article summaries of the literature, nor is it intended to cover all there is to know about the topic (this is not a handbook). In other words, the emphasis in this series is on critical summaries or syntheses of selected lines or areas of current research. This goal is easier to accomplish for some topics than for others. To the extent that chapters approximate this goal, the editor counts each volume a success.

The volume of research on nonhuman primates has expanded tremendously during the past 20 years and researchers' familiarity with them has increased correspondingly. Unfortunately, correct identification of the animals is still a serious problem, at least once we go beyond the familiar rhesus (*Macaca mulatta*) and squirrel monkeys (*Saimiri sciureus*). Excellent research could be worthless 10 or 20 years from now simply because it is not clear what species or subspecies of animal was used. This is why the first chapter in this series is one dealing with names of nonhuman primates and the rules for their use.

The binomial scientific name is the most desirable means of identification of an animal. However, the fact remains that (again, once we go beyond the animals named above) investigators are still more familiar and comfortable with the vernacular names. For this reason, this series follows the widely used procedure of indicating the scientific name of a nonhuman primate in parentheses the first time the vernacular name is given in each chapter, with the latter used alone thereafter. One problem in this connection is that taxonomy, the field formally concerned with classification of animals, is an ongoing research discipline. Revisions in taxonomic grouping and, as a consequence, in nomenclature, are often suggested by new accumulations of data. Controversy exists about other groupings. The vast majority of those writing and reading (as well as editing!) these chapters cannot be expected to keep up with the very latest in the taxonomic literature, so they have to do the next best thing–and that is to be consistent. In general, this will be accomplished in this series by using the nomenclature of J. R. Napier and P. H. Napier, whose book, *A handbook of living primates* (London: Academic Press, 1967), is a source of information about the classification of nonhuman primates, which, though beginning to become outdated (see Chapter 1), still has the advantage of being both comprehensive and convenient.

There was no special plan in choosing the chapters for the present volume, the basis for the choice in each case being the editor's judgement that the amount of research and conceptual activity in the area created a need for an integrative review.

ALLAN M. SCHRIER

These volumes are dedicated to the past chairmen of the Psychology Department at Brown University whose support and understanding made my professional as well as personal life easier and happier: Harold Schlosberg, Jake Kling, and Don Blough.

BEHAVIORAL PRIMATOLOGY

Advances in Research and Theory

VOLUME 1

1

Use of Common and Scientific Nomenclature to Designate Laboratory Primates[1]

Maryeva W. Terry

Regional Primate Research Center at the University of Washington

I. INTRODUCTION

The only satisfactory means of identifying a monkey or ape used in experiments is by its taxonomic species name, i.e., its scientific, Latin, or Linnaean binomen. In some instances, the common name has seemed more stable, leading laboratory workers to disregard the taxonomic designations. But such stability is often illusory: because common names pass mostly by word-of-mouth, their meanings and synonymy are rarely defined precisely, and new meanings easily become attached through simple misunderstandings. In contrast, scientific names change only according to established rules, and their relationships to previous names must be recorded.

Above all, the description of experimental animals only as "monkeys," with no indication of genus or species, is indefensible. The use of such a general term can be justified with dogs, cats, or guinea pigs, but the correct identification of a monkey can be very important. For example, malaria research was retarded at a critical time during World War II by the mistaken designation of the monkey in which *Plasmodium knowlesi,* similar to the human parasite *P. malariae,* was first observed. The increasing use of automated citation retrieval systems that can be

[1] The original draft of this chapter was written about 15 years ago for "The Laboratory Primate" by Theodore C. Ruch. That work circulated in manuscript but was not formally published, because of the press of his other responsibilities. Although the present draft has been revised to reflect the apparent state-of-the-art in naming laboratory primates today, many problems discussed in the earlier version remain unsolved.

addressed by species of animal as well as by research topics makes precise identification more and more important, since articles in which the kind of primate is not clearly identified are likely to become lost in the literature.

There are basic anatomical and physiological differences between primate genera; e.g., the convolution of the cerebral cortex is greater in *Macaca* than in *Saimiri.* There are also some sharp species differences within genera; e.g., *Macaca fascicularis* is relatively more susceptible than are other macaques to poliomyelitis, a fact of practical significance in the testing of vaccines. Since generic and specific differences may affect other functions in ways not now appreciated, the future value of current research can depend upon accurate identification of species even if species is not presently known to be a significant factor. The same argument can be, and has been, extended to include identification of subspecies as well. This step is clearly desirable, but it is questionable whether the information available on the average wild-caught laboratory monkey is sufficient for this purpose. Certainly, institutions planning to undertake breeding should attempt to identify subspecies and to avoid inadvertent interbreeding of them.

II. GENERAL AND COMMON NAMES

Most common names for the larger taxonomic groups have been drawn from the general English vocabulary. Consequently, the connotations and denotations of such words as "monkey" and "ape" are confused by the inexactitudes of common understanding, inconsistencies in British and American usage, and conflicts between a constantly changing living language and arbitrarily defined scientific vocabularies. Even further complications have been introduced by translations from other languages.

A. "Primates"

Many problems of primate nomenclature are epitomized in those surrounding the word describing the Order. "Primates," derived from the Latin word for "first," was used by Linnaeus as the name of the zoological Order, in which he included man as well as monkeys. The English-speaking people, with their great talent for naturalizing words, derived from Latin the noun "primate," to designate an animal of this group on the one hand and a high official of the Anglican church on the other. Because "primate" is an English word, its plural is formed by the addition of *s.* Thus, except for the obligatory capital *P* on the zoological term, the formal name of the Order and the common designation for several individuals of the group are spelled the same, although they are pronounced differently. In the taxonomic term all three vowels are pronounced, prĭ-mȧt-ēz, but in the English plural only the first two are pronounced, prī-māts. "Primate" is also an acceptable adjective, and this form is preferable to "primatal" or "primatial" in biological writing.

Often it is convenient to divide Primates into three major groups: modern and fossil man, monkeys and apes, and lemurs and other lower forms. Since, unlike "Affe," its German cousin, the English word "ape" has taken on a restricted meaning, the language is left without a group name for monkeys and apes. Some fill this gap with "monkeys," but use of the same word for both a group and a part of it can lead to ambiguities. Combining "infrahuman," "subhuman," or "nonhuman"[2] with "primate" does not solve this problem since these terms literally and usefully include the lower forms as well. "Simian primates," however, seems to be both sufficiently general and sufficiently specific.

The use of "primate" alone in the sense of "nonhuman primates" is sometimes the only alternative to unbearably cumbersome locution. To speak of "Regional Nonhuman Primate Research Centers" would be horrendous. In the same way, "laboratory primate" is acceptable, even though the usage ignores studies of human subjects. Phrases such as "human and primate," however, do violence to both science and language and should not be tolerated.

B. "Simian"

Linnaeus used "*Simia,*" a Latin word meaning monkey or ape, as the generic name for most monkeys and apes. As man's knowledge of the animals increased, some of the diverse groups within this omnibus category were removed to new genera, but "*Simia*" was still applied to animals in several different groups. The continual confusion and controversy arising from this situation led the International Commission on Zoological Nomenclature to suppress "*Simia*" by fiat in 1929.

Even though taxonomists no longer use "*Simia,*" its English derivative, "simian," remains potentially useful as both a noun and an adjective. The only primates that it does not denote are man on the one hand and the prosimians (tarsiers, lemurs, lorises, galagos, and tree shrews–if they are primates) on the other.

C. "Ape"

This word has a long and confused history. Evolved from Old Teutonic,[3] "ape" was originally a word for simian primates, and its cognates in the Continental languages retain this general meaning. As the word "monkey" was assimilated into English, the meaning of "ape" was gradually restricted to manlike simians. At first, taillessness was the accepted criterion for classification as manlike.

[2] Since "infrahuman primate" and "subhuman primate" are subject to criticism as anthropocentric, "nonhuman primate" is the preferable form. T. C. Ruch has attributed coinage of "nonhuman primate" to A. H. Schultz.

[3] "Old Teutonic" is the name philologists have given the language spoken by the Germanic tribes before their dispersion across Europe. Since Old Teutonic was unwritten, it has not survived, but many traces of it occur in its descendents: German, Dutch, Anglo-Saxon, etc.

Pennant (1771) defined the ape as a monkey without a tail. Tyson (1699) presented the following division: apes, no tails; baboons, short tails; monkeys, long tails. This stage survives in the name "Barbary ape," a virtually tailless macaque. Today, the anthropocentric significance of lack of a tail has been lost, and increased knowledge of the truly manlike creatures has given "ape" the general connotation of largeness and semi-erectness. The word "ape" is now rarely used for monkeys except by dealers, who like to sell monkeys with small tails as "apes."

D. "Anthropoid"

This word entered English primate terminology through a case of mistaken identity. The obvious relationship between "Affe" and "ape" led to the translation of "anthropoid Affe" as "anthropoid ape," even though apes are anthropoid by definition; the use of "anthropoide singe" in French undoubtedly supported this tendency. Perhaps the tautology is justified so long as "ape" is sometimes abused. "Anthropoid" is an acceptable English noun, as well as an adjective, and can be used as a synonym for "ape."

E. "Orang"

Today, the originally Malayan words "orang" and "orangutan" designate only animals belonging to the genus *Pongo,* but historically "orang" was a general term for anthropoids. The confusion arose because so little was known of these animals that chimpanzees and orangutans were presumed to be members of the same genus. The chimpanzee was thus called the "black orang." This situation persisted into the nineteenth century, and it is not always possible to determine just what animal is discussed in early writings. There is even a suspicion that some humans with developmental or endocrine disorders were mistaken for orangs.

F. "Chimpanzee"

This word is derived from a native African name for members of the genus *Pan.* The name has been abused by some dealers who have used the superficial similarity in the arrangement of the head hair on some true chimpanzees and the young stump-tailed macaque (*Macaca arctoides*) as an excuse to call the latter a "miniature chimpanzee." This misleading designation should not be confused with "pygmy chimpanzee," a common name for the rare *Pan paniscus.* (Efforts to sell monkeys as "apes" or "chimpanzees" were most common in the pet trade. Perhaps a side benefit of the recent ban on the sale of monkeys as pets will be purification of our terminology.)

Some authors reporting laboratory studies have the habit of treating "chimpanzee" as if it referred only to *Pan troglodytes,* the usual subject of research with apes. Since *P. paniscus* does exist in captivity and may be more manlike than *P. troglodytes,* the few extra letters needed for taxonomic identification are necessary insurance of intelligibility to future scientists.

G. "Monkey"

The origin of this word is unknown. It is probably a combination of the diminutive "kin" with either "mona" (a Romance word for monkey) or, as some believe, "man." The English imported this word from the Continent during the sixteenth century. As mentioned above, "monkey" has been used to designate those animals classified between *man* and prosimians and, simultaneously, those classified between *apes* and prosimians. In general usage, at least in the United States, the second and more restricted definition is the more common and would seem to preserve a valuable distinction.

In recent years, translators of Russian have unintentionally produced a new source of confusion by using "lower monkeys" in contexts in which "monkeys" would be sufficient. This tautology comes about because the Russians resolve the problem of distinguishing between apes and monkeys by using the adjectives for "higher" and "lower" with the noun "obez'yana," which is usually defined as "monkey" in Russian-English dictionaries.

H. "Platyrrhine," "Catarrhine," "New World," and "Old World"

The higher primates are sometimes divided into two groups, the Platyrrhini (broad-nosed) and the Catarrhini (narrow-nosed).[4] These taxonomic terms have given origin to the English adjectives "platyrrhine" and "catarrhine." "Platyrrhine primates" and "New World monkeys" may be used interchangeably in referring to all living families in Central and South America. "Catarrhine," however, encompasses man and the African and Asian apes and monkeys. Thus, "catarrhine primates" refers to these three groups, and "catarrhine monkeys" and "Old World monkeys" are synonyms of "Cercopithecidae," the family to which all African and Asian monkeys belong. "Old World primates" has a broader meaning than "catarrhine primates" because all living prosimians occur in the Old World. It is, of course, proper to use the singular forms "catarrhine primate" and "Old World primate" to refer to individual species.

I. "Baboon"

This word entered English from French, and its French cognate was applied to grotesque carvings before it became a name for monkeys. As implied earlier, the factor thought to identify a baboon has migrated from one end of the animal to

[4]These terms are frequently omitted from taxonomic classifications. The level of this division has been given as both Suborder and Infraorder.

the other, from short tail to long muzzle. The name is routinely applied to members of the genus *Theropithecus* and to the savannah-dwelling members of the genus *Papio.* The forest-dwelling members of the latter genus are, however, more usually called "mandrills" and "drills," although "forest baboons" is not unknown. Unfortunately, when animals appearing intermediate between olive and yellow baboons, previously considered the separate species *Papio anubis* and *P. cynocephalus,* were received by laboratories in the early 1960s, some recipients impatiently described all animals in these shipments as "baboons." Since another baboon, *P. hamadryas,* is also used in laboratories, this supposed solution to one confusion paved the way for another. Although a need to communicate biomedical results before taxonomists had had time to consider the evidence may have justified use of "baboon" as a temporary expedient ten years ago, its continued use cannot be defended on these grounds. Taxonomists have long since identified the olive and yellow baboons, and their intergrades, as members of a single species, *P. cynocephalus,* with the large, dark animal being a subspecies, *P. cynocephalus anubis.*

Some people, expecting too much sophistication in the common language, have assumed that the existence of both "baboon" and "monkey" means that baboons are not monkeys but are at a higher evolutionary level. Although baboons do have attributes making them particularly desirable for some experiments, their affinity to other Old World monkeys is well established. In fact, they are members of the same taxonomic tribe as the macaques.

J. "Marmoset"

Like "baboon," "marmoset" was originally a name for strange faces in medieval carvings, particularly those decorating the outlets of downspouts. Now this noun is generally understood to mean any New World monkey of the family Callithricidae. One point of occasional confusion is whether "tamarin" and "marmoset" are mutually exclusive. They are not, tamarins being a subcategory of marmosets, just as marmosets are a subcategory of monkeys. "Tamarin" is a common name for marmosets other than those belonging to the genera *Callithrix* and *Cebuella.* It has special affinity for the genus *Saguinus,* several species of which were, at one time or another, assigned the invalid generic names "*Tamarin*" and "*Tamarinus.*" "Tamarin" is believed to have originated in a native language. The phrases "marmoset monkey" and "tamarin monkey" are technically tautologies but may well be justified to insure retrieval of the article in computer systems based on keywords.

A strange misuse of "marmoset" appears in some translations from the Russian. Although "martysheka" means either "marmoset" or "monkey," only "marmoset" is given as a synonym in several Russian-English glossaries and dictionaries. As a consequence, "zelenych martyshek" is often translated "green marmoset" rather than "green monkey," i.e., *Cercopithecus aethiops.*

K. "Lemur"

In the taxonomic nomenclature, this word, meaning "nocturnal spirit" in Latin, is a valid name for a genus of Malagasy primates and is also incorporated in their family name. In more general usage, "lemur" and "lemurine" have sometimes designated only the Malagasy group and at other times have included any and all primate families classified below monkeys. Since the relationship between these families is not as close as once thought, restriction of "lemur" and "lemurine" to Malagasy species and substitution of "prosimian"[5] or "prosimian primate" in the more general meaning seems a clearer usage. Dealers advertising "lemurs" should be questioned about the origin of the animals. Galagos or pottos are sometimes sold as "African lemurs."

L. Common Names for Genera and Species

Common words of this type are notoriously unsatisfactory as the sole identification of monkeys, being subject to national, linguistic, and local variation in usage.

Nothing better exemplifies the instability and inaccuracy of meaning that can be masked by the stability of a common name than the commonest name of all, "rhesus macaque" or "monkey." The noun "macaque" is naturalized from French and is the obvious cognate of "*Macaca,*" the taxonomic name for the genus. The adjective "rhesus" is an adoption of an invalid taxonomic synonym for "*mulatta*" and had no other meanings or antecedent uses in English to lead to misinterpretation. Initially, then, the English "rhesus macaque" was a full synonym of the Linnaean "*Macaca mulatta*" and an equally precise designation. After general usage for 50 years or so, however, the words have lost even their grammatical identities, "rhesus" often being used as a noun and "macaque" as an adjective. More significantly, the meaning of "rhesus" has steadily broadened to include not only other species of *Macaca* but, on occasion, species of other genera. Probably because "rhesus monkey" seemed as meaningful as "rhesus macaque," the latter form was used relatively rarely, but "macaque" has recently been revived as a supposedly specific name for *M. mulatta* among persons seemingly unaware of such a common usage as "stump-tailed macaque." In their vocabularies, then, a macaque monkey is a species of the genus rhesus.[6] What this reversal signifies is that even scientists cannot maintain the precision of a

[5] "Prosimian" is derived from "Prosimii," a taxonomic name for the Suborder. As with "simian," use of the anglicized form is not dependent upon the validity of its taxonomic cognate.

[6] Fiedler (1956) listed *Rhesus* as a subgenus of *Macaca.* Since expansion of common understanding of "rhesus" has generally involved species other than those he assigned to this subgenus, his publication was not a major factor in the destabilization of the common term. Certainly nothing in his work would justify "macaque rhesus" or "*Rhesus macacus.*"

common name for a familiar animal. It is easy to point a finger at dealers as contributors to this confusion; at least one advertised *M. nemestrina* as "giant rhesus." The ultimate responsibility, though, lies with the scientists who have published such casually acquired names without question and in preference to the taxonomic vocabulary. It is sometimes bemusing that a researcher will spend months learning a technique like computer programming to be certain it is done correctly, but is too busy to learn to designate his experimental subjects scientifically.

Once the taxonomic name has been given in an article, the use of the common name is permissible and, from a stylistic viewpoint, even desirable. The greater ease of forming adjectives and possessives from common names makes for greater readability. Most works on systematics include common as well as taxonomic synonyms. Napier and Napier (1967) provide a list of common names with their taxonomic equivalents.

In this context, the choice of common name is largely a matter of authorial privilege, but some argument can be made for retaining the adjective-plus-noun form, with the noun reflecting the general affinities and the adjective the specific or subspecific name of the animal. Although a name such as "berok" (*Macaca nemestrina*) is correct, it is in truth a name based on a particular population that may or may not be of the same subspecies as the animals being described. On the other hand, "pig-tailed macaque," although only vaguely descriptive of the animal's caudal appendage, does indicate its generic status.[7]

Renewed interest in *Macaca fascicularis* as a laboratory monkey has raised some disagreement on an appropriate vernacular name—"cynomolgus," "irus," "kra," "crab-eating" and "long-tailed" macaque all being in common use. "Cynomolgus" is, like "rhesus," an appositive previously used taxonomically. Its literal meaning, "dog milkers," has nothing to do with the monkeys. The derivation is from an appellation the ancient Greeks gave certain human residents of North Africa; as discussed below in relation to the scientific name, "*cynomolgus*" originally referred to an African rather than an Asian primate. "*Cynamolgos,*" a transliteration of the Greek, was initially used for the African animal but was not the form transferred to the Asian as an appositive. The variant "*Cynamolgus*" was introduced into the scientific nomenclature in the nineteenth century as a generic name for several species of macaques, and Hill (1974) used this form as a subgeneric name for *M. fascicularis.* Since "cynomolgus" is misspelled as often as not, and since the scientific generations familiar

[7] The forms "pig-tailed," "long-tailed," etc., have been purposely used here in preference to "pigtail," "longtail" and other such forms now in vogue. Since English already has the adjective "tailed," use of the noun "tail" in these compounds is unnecessary and thus poor usage. More important, use of the noun reinforces the tendency to use the modifier alone; e.g., "pigtails" instead of "pig-tailed macaques" or "pig-tailed langurs" (*Simias concolor*). In print, a nude modifier such as "pigtail" becomes even more ambiguous because it may also be a common name for members of other Orders.

with its taxonomic use are being succeeded by ones to which its source is obscure, there seems no compelling reason to perpetuate it. Of the alternatives, "long-tailed macaque" is not the best choice because of the inherent danger of its being corrupted to "long-tailed *monkey*." "Long-tailed monkey" is the literal meaning of "*Cercopithecus*," which has been naturalized to some languages, Japanese for example, in forms with that meaning. Ambiguity in translations from or to English would be inevitable. Also, while *M. radiata* has another widely used common name, "bonnet macaque," it is indeed a laboratory macaque with a long tail. The groundwork would thus be laid for a confusion like that now surrounding "stump-tailed macaque."

To most laboratory workers, "stump-tailed macaque" is a specific name for *Macaca arctoides* (formerly *M. speciosa;* vide infra), and this usage was recognized by Napier and Napier (1967) in their list of nomenclatural equivalents. *M. arctoides* is not, however, the only macaque with a stubby tail. For example, Fooden (1969) applied this common name to the macaques of the Celebes. It seems necessary to emphasize that his usage does not imply any special biological affinity between these monkeys and *M. arctoides*. The alternate common name for *M. arctoides* is "bear macaque," a translation of "*Macaca arctoides.*" As "bear" and "bearlike" have been applied to several other primates, and "bear" is also a literal translation of "*ursinus*" (the subspecific name for the South African baboon), the alternate is scarcely a clarification.

Since English is a language hospitable to words of foreign origin, the practice of transferring the adjectival portion of the Linnaean species or subspecies name could do much to resolve the incongruence of such words as "baboon," "tamarin," and "marmoset" with the biological realities underlying current taxonomic thinking. Use of the appositives in latinate form is preferable to their translation into English. In some instances, Latin and Greek roots with the same meaning have been used in binomina for different species, e.g., "*arctoides*" and "*ursinus.*" Furthermore, the presence in English of many words ultimately derived from Latin and Greek opens the way for confabulation. For example, a correct English equivalent of "arctoides" is "ursine." Use of the common name with a latinate adjective would also provide a ready-made solution to the problem of coining common names when a genus such as *Aotus*, previously thought to be monospecific, so that the common name attaches to the genus, is found not to be (Brumback, 1976). Thus, while "owl monkey" describes any *Aotus*, the rubric "azarae owl monkey" would be automatically available to describe this species.

There is no good common name for the genus *Cercopithecus*. "Guenon," which is actually the modern French word for a female monkey of any genus, is sometimes applied to species other than *C. aethiops*. Since "grivet," "vervet," and "green monkey" were originally coined to describe particular regional varieties of *C. aethiops*, extension of any of these names to the group as a whole carries some risk of ambiguity. "Green monkey" also can be misleading to a novice. Not all *C. aethiops* are the vivid green of *C. aethiops sabaeus,* and several other monkeys, both within and without the genus *Cercopithecus,* have a greenish cast to their pelage. Some of these problems could be avoided if "cercopitheque," the French cognate of "*Cercopithecus,*" were adopted into English and used in association with the appositive from the Linnaean name.

One other genus of laboratory primates lacking a satisfactory common name is *Cebus.* "Capuchin" is sometimes used, but there is some uncertainty whether it refers to the genus or to the single species *C. capucinus.* "Cebid monkey" is needed to refer to the family Cebidae, and "organ-grinder's monkey" is a little out-of-date. Some authors have resolved this dilemma by naturalizing "*Cebus*" as "cebus," a reasonable solution. Another alternative is "ring-tailed monkey," which refers to the monkey's habit of holding its tail curled, often in in a complete ring. Unfortunately, "ring-tailed lemur" is descriptive of the colored bands about the animal's tail rather than its posture, so misunderstanding is theoretically possible.

III. SCIENTIFIC NAMES

A. General Considerations

It is unfortunate that the accelerated use of simian primates for experimental purposes has coincided with, rather than followed, a period of great activity by primate taxonomists. Until early in this century, the scientific naming of animals depended on too few specimens and sometimes simply on national prejudice or personal preference. Thus, a given species might have two or more scientific names in use simultaneously, or the same name might be applied to more than one species.

In 1904 the Sixth International Congress of Zoology adopted uniform rules of nomenclature that incorporated the Law of Priority: "The valid name of a taxon is the oldest available name applied to it. . . ." Unfortunately, in Elliot's "Review of the Primates" (1912), which appeared just before monkeys and apes became popular laboratory animals, the priority rule was applied with excessive zeal and insufficient scholarship. Thus, this work had the effect of disturbing the names of some common laboratory primates. The situation was much clarified by the activity of taxonomists and by the International Commission's suppressing by fiat certain names, especially "*Simia*" and "*Pithecus,*" that were causing inextricable confusion. All this resulted in a series of nomenclatural changes that led some laboratory workers to ignore the whole problem. Specifically, in the 1930s the changing of the name "*Macacus rhesus*" to "*Macaca mulatta*" was resented and resisted by laboratory scientists. Now the correct name is widely used and sounds right to the ear. It is a sign of progress that 30 years later the changes from "*M. speciosa*" to "*M. arctoides*" and from "*M. irus*" to "*M. fascicularis*" were accepted peaceably by the laboratory community, even though both species were in fairly widespread use.

In 1958 the Law of Priority was amended so that names which have been in "current use" for at least 50 years will continue to be valid even if an earlier name, a senior synonym, is discovered. This amendment promotes stability so long as an animal is correctly named, but is not a guarantee that changes will never occur. Detection of errors in scholarship or additions to biological knowledge can, and should, result in changes in nomenclature.

1. Typographic and Grammatical Conventions

In formal taxonomic tables the names of the higher taxonomic groups are usually printed in capital letters, with large capital letters being used for names above superfamilies and small capitals for the three types of family name. Capitalization of the first letter is sufficient for ordinary text; italics should not be used. Superfamily names end in -OIDEA, family names in -IDAE, and subfamily names in -INAE. Suprageneric names are treated as plurals when used in sentences.

The names of genera and species are italicized. The first letter of the generic name is capitalized and the word is treated as a singular noun; thus, "*Papio* is. . . ." If a subgenus is recognized, the subgeneric name is also capitalized and is enclosed in parentheses immediately following the generic name, e.g., "*Papio (Choeropithecus) hamadryas.*" Outside the taxonomic literature, however, subgeneric names rarely need be included in the designation of the animal. Even more important, the subgeneric name should not be substituted for the generic; "*Papio hamadryas,*" not "*Choeropithecus hamadryas,*" is correct.

Strictly, specific names are two words, the first being the generic name and the second being treated as an adjective, a noun in apposition, or a noun in the genitive modifying the generic name. The first letter of the second work should not be capitalized even if it is derived from a proper noun, e.g., "*grayi*" from "Gray," "*philippinensis*" from "Philippines." The specific name may be used with either a singular or a plural verb, depending on the emphasis to be conveyed. Thus, "*Macaca mulatta* is" connotes the species as a group and "*Macaca mulatta* are" connotes all individuals composing the species. The constructions "a *Macaca mulatta* was" and "25 *Macaca mulatta* were" are also correct. Three words are used to designate subspecies: the generic name, the modifier denoting the species, and the modifier denoting the subspecies; e.g., "*Macaca fascicularis mordax,*" not "*Macaca mordax,*" is the proper name for the Javan macaque. The rules governing the specific modifier also govern the subspecific modifier.

The second word of a binomen is a modifier and should not stand alone in a sentence to denote the species. In references to *Macaca mulatta,* for example, "mulatta" should be followed by "monkey" or "macaque." An alternative is to use the modifier preceded by the initial of the generic name and to italicize both (e.g., "*M. mulatta*"), but this should be done only after the generic name has been spelled out and only if there is no danger of confusion with another genus. Thus, if both *Cercocebus* and *Cercopithecus* species are discussed in the same article, "*C. nictitans*" should not be used; abbreviations or contractions can be coined, as there is no standardization in this respect.

Although it is usually not necessary outside the taxonomic literature, one may wish to include the name of the first author to use a zoological name and the year of its first use. The author's name is set in roman type (not italics) and follows the zoological name without intervening punctuation. A comma is placed between the author's name and the date (e.g., *Macaca* Lacépède, 1799).

2. *The Linnaean (binomial) system*

Further explanation of the way animals are named will clarify the following discussion of the scientific names of common laboratory primates and the reason why scientific names occasionally change. The currently accepted system of nomenclature is adopted from the 10th edition of Linnaeus's epochal work, *Systema naturae,* published in 1758. Therefore no names published before 1758, even by Linnaeus, are considered valid. Any definitely Linnaean, i.e., binomial, names originated after that date must be considered.

The valid name of a genus or species is the binomen under which it was first designated in a publication including sufficient indication of what group was intended.[8] The binomial form and adequate indentification are the only requirements. The name need not be latinized. Native names or even meaningless words, latinized or not, have status. If a species is found to belong to a genus other than the one to which it was originally assigned, the modifier is retained so long as the species has not been described previously and the modifier is not preoccupied within the new genus.

A name can be invalidated because it is antedated or preoccupied, or it can be suppressed by a fiat ruling of the International Commission on Zoological Nomenclature. A name is a synonym, or is said to be antedated, if another name for the same group was published at an earlier date. Synonyms can be revived and again become valid if it is later decided that they do, after all, refer to distinguishable groups. A generic name is a homonym, or is said to be preoccupied, if it has previously been used for another zoological genus. Although binomial nomenclatures are also used by botanists, bacteriologists, and virologists, their use of a word does not make it invalid in zoological nomenclature, and vice versa.

A specific modifier is preoccupied if it has been used for a different species in the same genus. A homonym is completely dead. Names suppressed by the Commission are also dead unless additional evidence can be addued to justify a new decision. A senior synonym becomes a nomen oblitum, a forgotten name,

[8] A name introduced without description is a nomum nudam.

under the amendment to the Law of Priority protecting junior synonyms long in use.

Despite some difficulties in application, the Rules of Zoological Nomenclature are the only widely recognized standard, and deliberate contravention of them can lead only to worse confusion.

B. Old World Monkeys

1. "Macaca"

According to G. S. Miller (1933), the French word "macaque" is derived from the Portuguese word "macaquo," in turn a form of a Congolese name for some African monkey. Since the macaques are not indigenous to the Congo, some other monkey must have been so designated. Over 200 years ago Buffon mistook a crab-eating monkey from Malaya for the Congolese "macaquo" and incorrectly used the common name. Some 10 years later Lacépède used the latinized version, " *Macaca,*" in a binomen to distinguish a genus of monkeys. Previously they were grouped with other genera either under *Simia,* as in Linnaeus, or under *Cercopithecus,* as in Zimmermann. Two decades later Desmarest altered the name, probably for linguistic reasons, to "*Macacus,*" and this name came into fairly general use. Miller suggests that the greater popularity of the improper form came about because Desmarest's work was the better known. The popularity of this form among laboratory workers may have resulted partly from the euphony when combined with "*rhesus.*"

The generic name "*Pithecus*" was for a time commonly used in scientific literature in place of "*Macaca.*" This name was introduced by Elliot in a mistaken application of the priority rule. Because "*Pithecus*" has an inextricably confused history, the International Commission on Zoological Nomenclature suppressed the name in 1929 on the grounds that its application to any primate "will produce greater confusion than uniformity."

This decision leaves "*Macaca*" the approved name, and it has stood as the sole name of this group for more than 40 years. It is likely to continue in this form unless the group is no longer considered a true genus and is either split or combined with another.

It is perhaps of some help in reading early literature to know that certain macaques have at times been described under the following generic names, the second word of the species name being the clue to the true identity: *Cynamolgus, Gymnopyga, Inuus, Magus, Pithecus, Silenus, and Simia.*

1. "*M. mulatta*" (syn. "*M. rhesus*"). (See Figure 1.1.) Although known scientifically by Pennant (1771), who called it the "Tawny Monkey," and by Buffon (1789), who called it the "macaque à queue courte," to distinguish it from the crab-eating macaque, this monkey received a binomen from neither. The first binomial adjective applied to this animal was "*mulatta,*" meaning

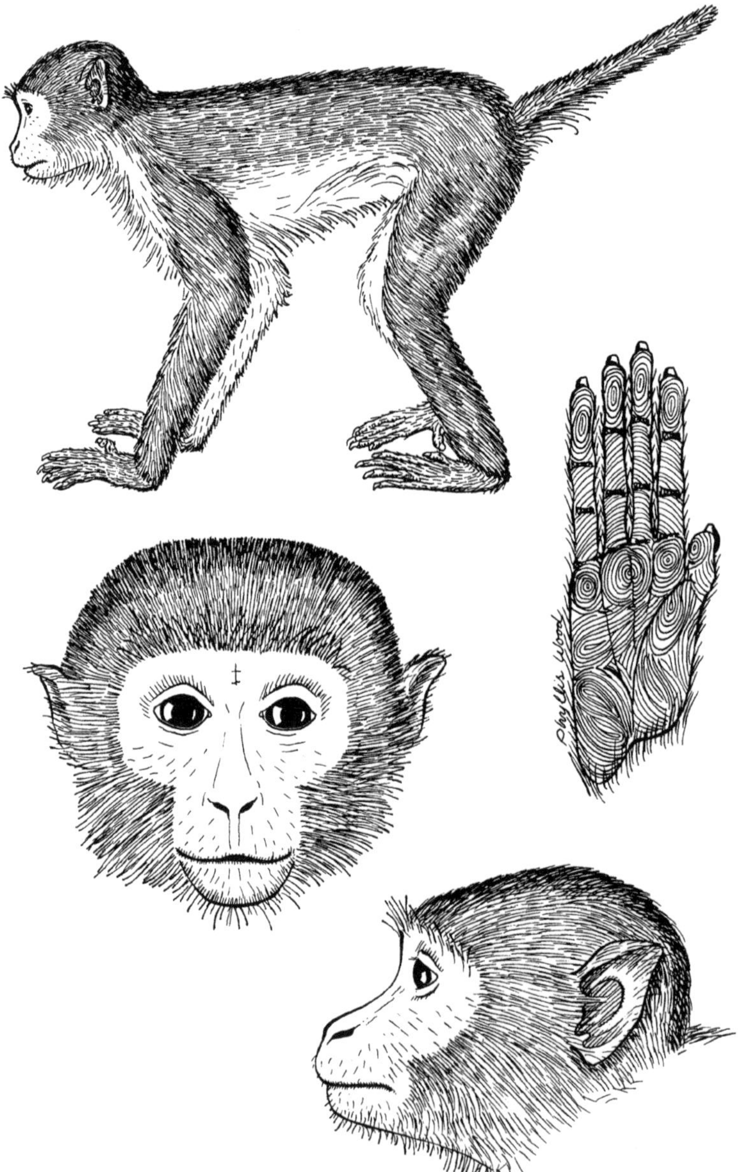

FIG. 1.1 *Macaca mulatta;* this and the following illustrations show animals of common laboratory age.

FIG. 1.2 *Macaca fascicularis.*

yellow, used by Zimmermann (1780) as a direct translation of Pennant. Audebert (1797) used the word "*rhesus*"[9] in a binomen for the monkey which Buffon had described. For some reason, the identity of the Tawny Monkey and the macaque à queue courte was not realized, and "*M. rhesus*" came into use as the species name. Part of this blindness may have arisen because Pennant's original description was based on a living animal, which was not the monkey in his illustration of the Tawny Monkey. The animal in the picture was undoubtedly not a mulatta macaque, but Pennant's verbal description of the Tawny monkey clearly depicts the physical appearance, habitat, and disposition of that species.

b. "M. fascicularis" (syn. *"M. cynomolgus"* and *"M. irus")* (see Figure 1.2.) "*Cynomolgus*" was used by Linnaeus himself as a name for an African baboon.

[9] Although Rhesus was a character in Greek mythology, Audebert (1797) said that his use of the name for the monkey had no significance.

The name was erroneously transferred to the Asiatic crab-eating macaque in the mistaken belief that this animal, as described by Buffon (1766), was African and the same as that described by Linnaeus. Application of the name to the eastern macaque survived for a century. In 1910 the error was detected, and "*M. irus,*" attributed to Cuvier, was substituted. Subsequent review of Cuvier's work has led taxonomists to question the validity of this use of "*irus.*" Thus, "*M. irus*" is not protected by the current use rule, and "*M. fascicularis*" is now being listed by most taxonomists (Fooden, 1964; Kuhn, 1967; Napier & Napier, 1967; Thorington & Groves, 1970).

The subspecies of *M. fascicularis* have more than usual significance because several are island populations. The subspecies that have been used in laboratories most often are:

M. fascicularis fascicularis (Sumatra, Malaya)
M. fascicularis mordax (Java)
M. fascicularis philippinensis (Philippines)

Note that Indonesian law requires export of *M. fascicularis* from Sumatra, and other islands in that country, through Jakarta. Consequently, shipment from Java does not necessarily mean the animals are *M. fascicularis mordax.*

c. "M. arctoides" (previously known as "*M. speciosa*"). (See Figure 1.3.) The association of "*M. speciosa*" with the stump-tailed macaque was an inexplicable error. There is no doubt that the name was originally applied to the Japanese macaque and was used in that sense in the medical as well as the taxonomic literature. When Fooden (1967) discovered this error, the next available name, "*M. arctoides,*" became the correct one for this species. The long-established name of "*M. fuscata*" for the Japanese macaque was not disturbed, however, and "*M. speciosa*" became a nomen oblitum.

d. "M. nemestrina." (See Figure 1.4.) This has been a stable name throughout the time this species has been a laboratory animal. It should be noted, however, that two subspecies, *M. nemestrina nemestrina* and *M. nemestrina leonina,* were intermingled in shipments received from Singapore. It is thus probable that some studies reported in the literature were performed on mixed groups. Fooden (1975) has recently reviewed the taxonomy of this species.

e. "Macaca nigra." The present taxonomic discussion over the level at which to recognize the differences between the simian populations in the Celebes is of practical import to some laboratory scientists. The traditional view, reflected in the listings by Napier and Napier (1967) and Hill (1974), was to recognize a generic distinction: "*Cynopithecus niger*" (sometimes called the black, crested "ape" or "baboon" of the Celebes) was used for the northern animals and "*Macaca maura*" (sometimes called the moor macaque) for the southern group. In the early 1960s, additional biological information, including chromosome studies, indicated that the monkeys are congeneric, and both members of the

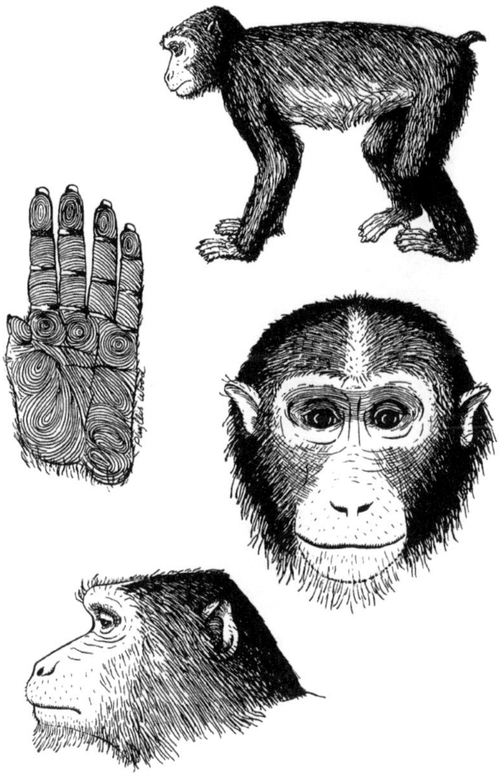

FIG. 1.3 *Macaca arctoides.*

genus *Macaca.* Fooden (1969) supported this viewpoint, but he also elevated to specific status a number of groups previously considered subspecies of *M. maura.* Thorington and Groves (1970) took the position that all the Celebes monkeys are not only congeneric but also conspecific; i.e., all members of the species *M. nigra.* This decision leaves persons working with laboratory colonies of the black, crested variety no choice but to use "*M. nigra nigra*" for the sake of clarity.

2. "Papio"

The taxonomic problems–most manifest to laboratory scientist as nomenclatural problems–presented by Primates are typified by those involving the ground-dwelling members of this genus. (See Figure 1.5.) A species is defined zoologically as a naturally interbreeding population.[10] Any species tends to

[10]The interbreeding need not be absolutely contemporary. If the range of a species is disrupted, the separated populations remain conspecific so long as characteristics typical of the species predominate.

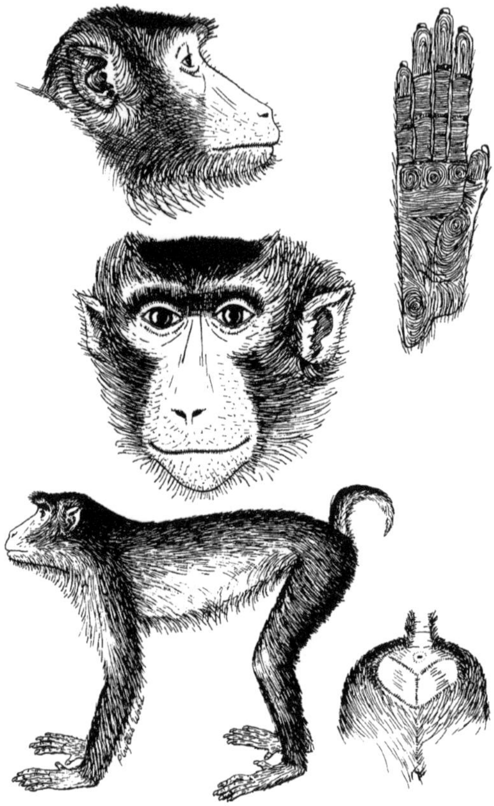

FIG. 1.4 *Macaca nemestrina.*

expand its range until it encounters insurmountable geographic or ecological barriers. An adaptable species, which many primates tend to be, can thus have wide distribution. In time, local populations may develop distinctiveness in average size, coloration, etc., without becoming genetically isolated, but populations at the margins of the range may appear greatly different from each other and somewhat different from populations at the center of the range. Thus, the specimens available for taxonomic examination could, and did, suggest that local populations were individual species. On this basis, five species of African savannah baboons were recognized: the red or Guinea baboon, *P. papio,* in the West; the brown or chacma baboon, *P. ursinus,* in the South; the yellow baboon, *P. cynocephalus,* in Central areas; the olive baboon, *P. anubis,* in North Central areas; and the mantled or sacred baboon, *P. hamadryas,* in the Northeast, with its range extending into western Asia. Beginning in the early 1960s, an extensive series of field studies, plus the accelerated importation of the animals for

FIG. 1.5 *Papio cynocephalus anubis.*

laboratory use, revealed current or recent interbreeding, so that reconsideration of the taxonomic classification was needed.

"*P. cynocephalus*" is the appropriate species name for the first four groups listed above (Kuhn, 1967; Thorington & Groves, 1970); the older group names are preserved as subspecies designations. Most baboons used in American laboratories have been imported from areas, particularly Kenya, where the ranges of *P. c. cynocephalus* and *P. c. anubis* meet. The species name is probably the safest designation unless the animals are very typical of one of these subspecies. South African laboratories have traditionally used the indigenous subspecies, *P. c. ursinus*, as a utility primate. Their papers continue to identify these animals by the older name, "*P. ursinus*" ("*P. porcarius*" in early papers). The long-standing association of France with West Africa has led to use of *P. c. papio* in French laboratories. Again, the older name ("*P. papio*") is persisting in reports.

P. hamadryas continues to be recognized as a separate species, although its relationship to *P. cynocephalus* is quite close. Differences in social structure affecting mating behavior seemingly act to restrict gene flow between the two populations.

3. "Cercocebus"

This word is compounded of Greek words for "tail" and "monkey," so its literal meaning is much the same as that of "*Cercopithecus.*" Although Geoffroy distinguished the mangabeys from the cercopitheques in 1812, his classification was not always observed during the nineteenth century, and "*Cercopithecus*" rather than "*Cercocebus*" was used by some experimental workers. Fortunately, most of these animals were sooty mangabeys and were called "*Cercopithecus fuliginosus.*" Perhaps it is regrettable that taxonomic scholarship has caused the nicely desctiptive "*fuliginosus*" to give way to "*torquatus atys,*" meaning "adorned Adonis."

4. "Cercopithecus"

In the early era of scientific nomenclature, "*Cercopithecus*" was used somewhat indiscriminately as a generic name for monkeys with long tails, including some New World monkeys, but its meaning was gradually restricted to denote tailed monkeys from Africa. The only real disturbance of the nomenclatural stability for this genus was Elliot's choice of "*Lasiopyga*" as the genus for the cercopitheques. The International Commission published an Opinion making "*Cercopithecus* Linnaeus" the official name for this genus.

a. "C. aethiops." (See Figure 1.6.) More than 20 kinds of savannah or grass monkeys belonging to the genus *Cercopithecus* have been assigned taxonomic names, largely on the basis of differences in color. These animals thus present a picture similar to that discussed in relation to savannah baboons—a widely distributed group with regional variations in appearance. Although recognition of relationships within the group at a superspecific level has been suggested on occasion (Hill, 1966; Napier & Napier, 1967), recent field observations suggest a single species (Struhsaker, 1970; Thorington & Groves, 1970).

b. Other species. It is suggested that readers interested in the other cercopitheques, which are somewhat exotic laboratory primates, consult Thorington and Groves (1970) for a review of taxonomic thinking on these animals.

5. "Erythrocebus"

A genus for red monkeys (see Figure 1.7), the meaning of the taxonomic name, was not established until 1897. Before that time, and frequently since, its generic name has been given as "*Cercopithecus.*" The genus is monospecific, *E. patas* being the only species recognized.

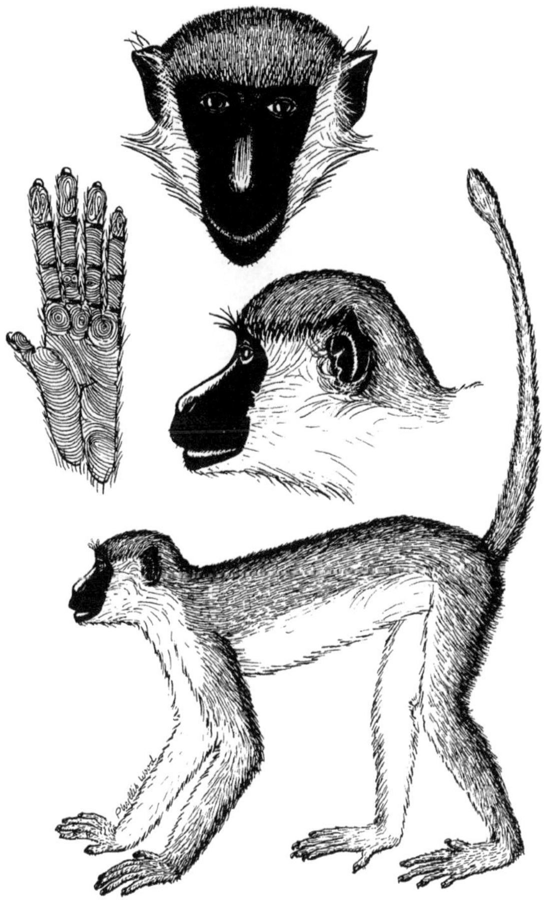

FIG. 1.6 *Ceropithecus aethiops sabaeus.*

C. New World Monkeys

As more than a century was needed to sort out the Asian and African primates, which were available in considerable numbers to European taxonomists, it is not surprising that developing a rational scheme of classification for the animals from the incompletely explored jungles of Central and South America has taken longer. Even now, the organization is considered "provisional" (Hershkovitz, 1972). Thus, future changes are more likely for these families than for any other living group. For example, De Boer (1974) has reported several variations in karyotype not completely in accord with present taxonomy.

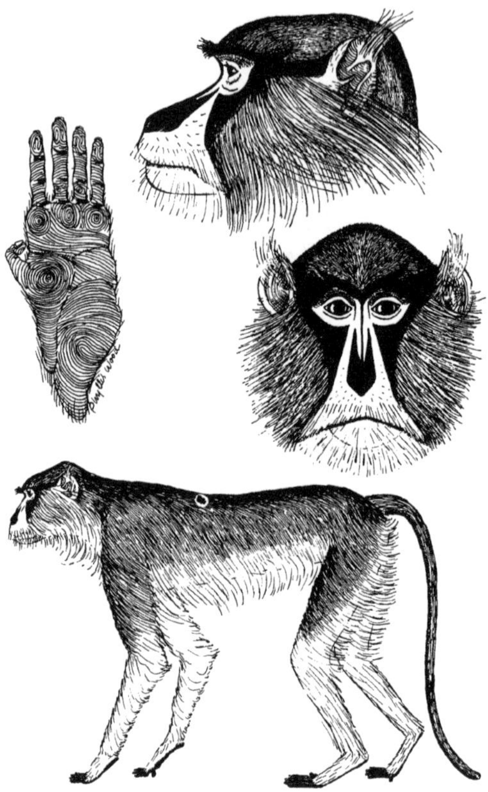

FIG. 1.7 *Erythrocebus patas.*

1. "Cebus"

This generic name, meaning simply "monkey," has been quite stable, but confusion, beginning with Linnaeus himself, long surrounded the number and naming of the species within the genus. The number is now well established at four, as opposed to the 20 species listed by Elliot, for example. "*C. albifrons*" is the valid name for the so-called cinnamon ring-tails (Figure 1.8) and "*C. capucinus*" for the black, white-headed monkey. "*C. apella,*" which at one time or another has been used to designate practically every species of this genus, is properly the name of the tufted species from South America (Figure 1.9). Perhaps it should be pointed out that "*C. fatuellus,*" also applied in the past to a variety of species, has no standing as a specific name; the original specimen given this name was a member of a subspecies of *C. apella.* The fourth species is the so-called weeper capuchin, also from South America, *C. nigrivittatus.*

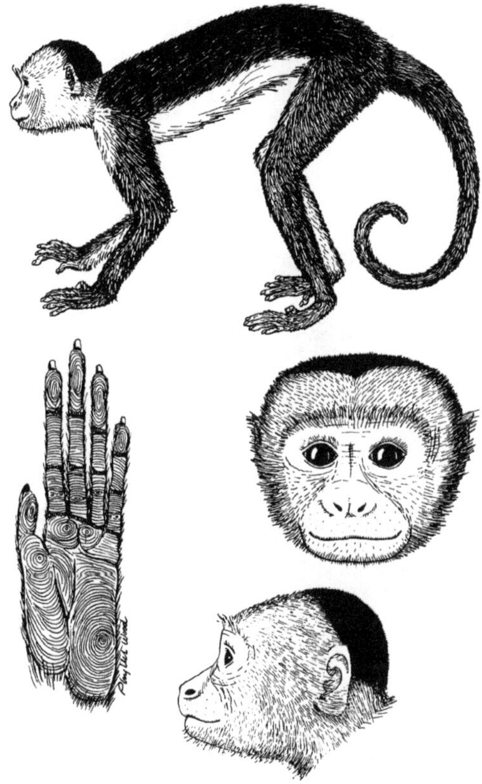

FIG. 1.8 *Cebus albifrons.*

2. "Saimiri"

The generic name of squirrel monkeys (see Figure 1.10) is a native word for "small monkey." The genus has also been called "*Chrysothrix*," yellow-haired. A single species, *S. sciureus,* is now recognized. (The Central American red-backed squirrel monkey, listed as *S. oerstedii* in Appendix I to the Convention on Trade in Endangered Species, is *S. sciureus oerstedii* by this view.) As a widely distributed monkey, *S. sciureus* shows many regional variations. Some of these differences undoubtedly have subspecific significance, but the relation between the variations noted by laboratory scientists and those significant to taxonomists is not always certain. The situation is further obscured by the fact that Jones, Thorington, Hu, Adams, and Cooper (1973) and De Boer (1974) have identified three karyotypes, two of which occur in animals appearing to be the typical subspecies *S. sciureus sciureus.* These variations are not in the number of

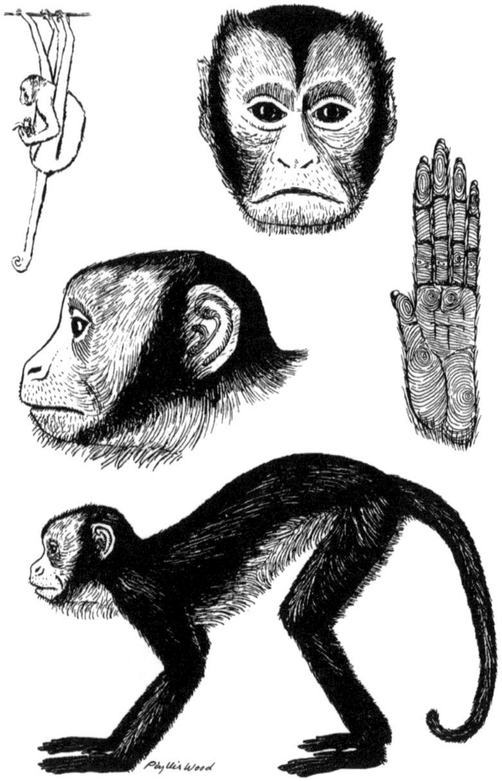

FIG. 1.9 *Cebus apella.*

chromosomes ($2n$=44), but in the number of acrocentric autosomes present. Offspring of mating between different subspecies with different karyotypes had an intermediate number of acrocentric autosomes (Jones et al., 1973).

3. "Aotus"

Except for the variant spelling a-o-t-e-s and an occasional use of the descriptive "*Nyctipithecus*" (night monkey), the generic name has been stable. Traditionally, this genus has been considered to have only one species, *A. trivirgatus,* although a number of subspecies representing geographic variants were recognized. Between 1971 and 1974, different karyotypes were identified in three taxonomically recognized subspecies (Brumback, 1973, 1974, 1975, 1976; Brumback, Staton, Benjamin, & Lang, 1971). These differences involve both the diploid number and the kinds of chromosomes present, and appear great enough to warrant elevating these subspecies to species. They thus become: *A. azarae, A.*

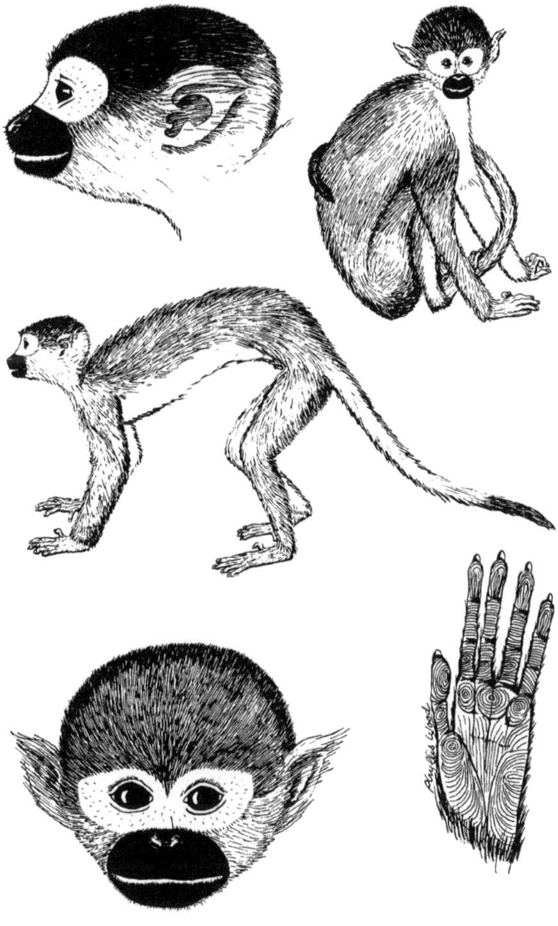

FIG. 1.10. *Saimiri sciureus.*

griseimembra, and *A. trivirgatus.* The three karyotypes and the geographic distributions have been illustrated by Brumback (1974). This is the first time that karyology has fulfilled its promise of providing an objective laboratory test, within the competence of at least some clinical laboratories, to assist non-taxonomists in the identification of nonhuman primates.

4. Callithricidae

The nomenclature of this family has been the most frustrating of all to laboratory scientists. For many years taxonomic uncertainties led to frequent changes in generic designations, transfer of species from one genus to another, and shifts from specific to subspecific rank or vice versa. The family was truly so little known that the common language offered no refuge even to the most impatient. For example, there were two "Geoffroy's marmosets," members of different genera; "cotton-topped" and "cotton-eared" were sometimes interchanged, again a confusion involving members of two genera. In the following discussion of laboratory species, the arrangement provided by Hershkovitz (1972) has been used as the authority.

The name of the type genus, "*Callithrix,*" meaning "beautiful hair," has been disturbed intermittently by substitution of "*Hapale.*" The species names of *C. jacchus* (cotton-eared or common marmoset) and *C. argentata*[11] (silver marmoset) have been quite stable, being traceable back to Linnaeus. Hershkovitz's arrangement indicates "*C. jacchus penicillata*" rather than "*C. penicillata*" for the third member of this genus sometimes cited in the experimental literature.

Except for the disagreement over inclusion in or exclusion from the genus *Callithrix,* the name of *Cebuella pygmaea,* the pygmy marmoset, has been stable.

The greatest difficulty in correlating recent with older research will undoubtedly involve *Saguinus oedipus,* the cotton-topped marmoset or pinché. Among the synonyms known to occur in the biomedical literature are: *Oedipomidas oedipus, O. spixi, O. geoffroyi, Marikina geoffroyi,* and *Saguinus geoffroyi.* The last four usually referred to the subspecies *S. oedipus geoffroyi.*

For the most part, laboratory use of other tamarins developed after fairly general adoption of "*Saguinus*" as the generic name, although a few uses of "*Tamarinus,*" following Hill (1957), may be found. Unfortunately, the numerous variations in coloration within single shipments led many investigators to abandon efforts at identification of species as well as genus. Most experimental subjects described as "*Sagunius* species" are referable to *S. fusicollis, S. nigricollis,* and *S. mystax.*

D. Prosimians

The names for members of this Suborder generally used in laboratories have long been stable: "*Galago crassicaudatus*" (greater or thick-tailed galago), "*G. senegalensis*" (lesser galago), and the less common "*Nycticebus coucang*" (slow loris) and "*Perodicticus potto*" (potto). Recently acquired biological information and new field data suggest a need for some readjustments in the classification (Groves, 1974). Since continuance of *G. crassicaudatus* (Figure 1.11) in the genus is in question, further use of "*Galago* species" is not advisable. Also, careless use of "Moholi bushbaby" for *G. senegalensis* should be avoided. "Moholi" is the subspecific designation for the small, southern members of this species; it is possible that this distinction may be advanced to the species level.

[11] Hill (1957) assigned this species to a separate genus, *Mico.*

FIG. 1.11 Adult *Galago crassicaudatus.*

IV. IDENTIFICATION

Knowing the correct names and how to use them in writing is not the same thing as knowing which monkeys they describe. Identification is an area in which laboratory scientists and taxonomists have yet to develop a mutually comfortable modus vivandi.

Classic taxonomy was based on description of external appearance and skeletal characteristics, attributes that could be determined from preserved specimens. The underlying assumption was, of course, that morphologic differences indicated different species. Modern taxonomy, however, sees the nonhuman primates as being much like the human in showing considerable variation in conformation and pelage within a species. Although biologically correct, the modern view does not simplify the problem of determining the identity of an experimental animal.

With limitation on the diagnostic value of morphology has come an increased emphasis on geographic origin as a clue to identity. Unfortunately, the laboratory scientist stands at the apex of the triangular maze inscribed when a laboratory buys from several importers, each of whom buys from several exporters, each of whom buys from several collectors, each of whom buys from several trappers. Often these trade routes cross zoologic and political boundaries. Even so, laboratory scientists probably have not been as stringent as they should be in demanding that importers name the port of export. It is doubtful that information transmitted from more remote points in the chain can be considered reliable.

Since taxonomy is unable to provide an infallible tool for identification, Thorington (1971) has suggested that an experimenter deposit a carcass representative of his subjects as a voucher specimen with the Smithsonian Institution. If questions later arise about the published identification, the specimen can be re-examined. This course certainly should be considered if results indicate strain differences or if the species is shown to be a particularly good model for some type of study.

Another suggestion sometimes made by taxonomists is that the Methods section of each paper should contain a paragraph describing the appearance of the animals and a photograph of a typical one. This suggestion shows some lack of insight into the constraints on publication of laboratory reports. To beg the question of whether persons not trained in taxonomy can write descriptions with taxonomic import, it is difficult to imagine the hard-pressed editors of biomedical and psychological journals devoting space and money to the paragraphs and illustrations for some 3000 articles a year. Perhaps the spirit, but not the letter, of this suggestion could be met by the author citing the reference on which he based his identification.

Despite the difficulties of identification, the attitude of some laboratory scientists that "taxonomy is for persons interested in animals and we're only interested in humans" is short-sighted. Overlooked is the fact that comparison is implicit in the use of an animal model. Taxonomy provides the only scientific basis for this comparison. Such parochialism is understandable, although not laudable, in scientists studying vital functions that vary within narrow limits over many genera; the attitude is incomprehensible, however, in biochemists and others studying metabolic and molecular attributes known to be sensitive to genetic variation.

A. Published Tools for Primate Identification

The basic taxonomic tool is the key, a series of multiple-choice statements with each choice yielding direction to another set of statements until the species is identified. In other words, the strategy of the taxonomic key is a forerunner of that used in the teaching machine. One difficulty with keys for identifying the laboratory monkey is that they are based on the characteristics of the mature animal, whereas the laboratory monkey is usually a juvenile. In several primate genera, the young of various species look very much alike. Also, although the species within a genus may differ in length and weight at a given age, size is not particularly helpful in identifying young monkeys from the wild whose age can only be guessed.

Another difficulty can develop in understanding the full implications of the vocabulary used in keys. Colors, for example, are closely defined. Even if a specialist in primate taxonomy is not available, a mammalian taxonomist may be willing to give assistance in learning the art of reading keys. Visits to a zoo and a natural history museum—which usually has many more specimens than are displayed—will often help.

1. The Order as a Whole

With an Order so diverse and so widely dispersed, it is not surprising that works attempting to cover all primates have not satisfied specialists in the various groups. Some of the problems associated with Elliot's "Review of the Primates" (1912) have been cited earlier, and it is now of historical interest rather than practical use.

Hill's monumental *Primates* (1953–66, 1970, 1974), of which eight volumes were published before his death, is also unreliable for full taxonomic identification. This work is a remarkable compendium of biological information, and perusal of the relevant sections will provide a useful sense of the animals. Because Hill leaned toward traditional taxonomy, however, his classification is excessively fractionated by modern standards.

Napier and Napier's *Handbook of living primates* (1967) provides a brief review of the general biology, some helpful pictures, and a list of species for each genus, but does not provide diagnostic information on the species. The list of common names and their taxonomic equivalents, mentioned earlier, is helpful in interpreting the intent of authors who have not given scientific names.

Chiarelli's *Taxonomic atlas of living primates* (1972) provides a taxonomic key which gives the species name (subspecies are not considered) and leads to a page providing a picture and the synonomy of the species. The index of synonyms is particularly helpful in interpreting the literature. Although not all of Chiarelli's taxonomic attributions are currently accepted, his work can easily be used in conjunction with a name list to arrive at a satisfactory identification and binomen.

A more conventional taxonomic work is section 3 of the identification manual of African mammals edited by Meester and Setzer (1971). For monkeys, there are some conflicts in nomenclature (and ranking of species) with that proposed by Thorington and Groves (1970). Section 3.2 covers African prosimians.

2. Apes

In recent years taxonomic interest in great apes has centered on fossil species. The general works cited above are as helpful as any for the living animals (*Gorilla, Pan, Pongo*). Hill's discussion (1969) of chimpanzees was published apart from his monographic series.

For the lesser apes (Hylobatinae), Groves' extensive discussion (1972) should be consulted.

3. Old World Monkeys

Kuhn's (1967) classification of genera and species presented at the First Congress of the International Primatological Society is a helpful overview of modern thinking about the Cercopithecidae, although it is a souce of nomenclature rather than of physical descriptions. Similarly, the classification provided by Thorington and Groves (1970), who followed Kuhn closely in many respects, is useful because it contains comments on those parts of the taxonomy needing further study, but it is not a source of descriptions. Persons working with the Celebes macaques and the lion-tailed and pig-tailed macaques should take special note of Fooden's monographs on those species (1969, 1975), which can serve as bases for identification.

4. New World Monkeys

It is to be hoped that Hershkovitz's (in press) forthcoming monograph will provide a badly needed tool for identification of New World monkeys. In the interim, his 1972 listing is helpful in dealing with the synonomy of the identifications given in the general works.

ACKNOWLEDGMENTS

This work was supported in part by grant RG-3774 from the National Institutes of Health and grant RR00166 from the Animal Resources Branch, Division of Research Resources, National Institutes of Health.

The illustrations were drawn by Phyllis J. Wood from animals living at the Regional Primate Research Center at the University of Washington, the Vivarium of the University of Washington School of Medicine, and the City of Seattle's Woodland Park Zoo.

REFERENCES

Audebert, J. B. *Histoire naturelle des singes et des makis* (Vol. 6). Paris: Desray, 1797.

Brumback, R. A. Two distinctive types of owl monkeys (*Aotus*). *Journal of Medical Primatology*, 1973, **2**, 284–289.

Brumback, R. A. A third species of the owl monkey (*Aotus*). *Journal of Heredity*, 1974, **65**, 321–323.

Brumback, R. A. Giemsa banding pattern of the karyotype of *Aotus griseimembra* Elliot 1912. A preliminary study. *Journal of Human Evolution*, 1975, **4**, 385–386.

Brumback, R. A. Taxonomy of the owl monkey (*Aotus*). *Laboratory Primate Newsletter*, 1976, **15**[1], 1–2.

Brumback, R. A., Staton, R. D., Benjamin, S. A., & Lang, C. M. The chromosomes of *Aotus trivirgatus* Humboldt 1812. *Folia Primatologica*, 1971, **15**, 264–273.

Buffon, G. L. L. *Histoire naturelle, générale et particulière, avec la description du cabinet du Roi* (Vol. 14). Paris: l'Imprimerie royale, 1766.

Buffon, G. L. L. *Histoire naturelle, générale et particulière* (Vol. 8). Paris: l'Imprimerie royale, 1789.

Chiarelli, A. B. *Taxonomic atlas of living primates.* London: Academic Press, 1972.

De Boer, L. E. M. Cytotaxonomy of the Platyrrhini (Primates). *Genen en Phaenen,* 1974, **17,** 1–115.

Elliot, D. G. A review of the primates. *Monograph Series, American Museum of Natural History,* 1912, No. 1, 3 vols.

Fiedler, W. Übersicht über das System der Primates. In H. Hofer, A. H. Schultz, & D. Starck (Eds.), *Primatologia: Handbuch der Primatenkunde* (Vol. 1). Basel: Karger, 1956.

Fooden, J. Rhesus and crab-eating macaques: Intergradation in Thailand. *Science,* 1964, **143,** 363–365.

Fooden, J. Identification of the stumptailed monkey, *Macaca speciosa* I. Geoffroy, 1826. *Folia Primatologica,* 1967, **5,** 153–164.

Fooden, J. *Taxonomy and evolution of the monkeys of Celebes (Primates: Cercopithecidae).* Basel: Karger, 1969. (Published simultaneously as *Bibliotheca primatologica,* No. 10.)

Fooden, J. Taxonomy and evolution of liontail and pigtail macaques (Primates: Cercopithecidae). *Fieldiana: Zoology,* 1975, **67,** 1–169.

Groves, C. P. Systematics and phylogeny of gibbons. In D. M. Rumbaugh (Ed.), *Gibbon and siamang* (Vol. 1). Basel: Karger, 1972.

Groves, C. P. Taxonomy and phylogeny of prosimians. In R. D. Martin, G. A. Doyle, & A. C. Walker (Eds.), *Prosimian biology.* London: Duckworth, 1974.

Hershkovitz, P. Notes on New World monkeys. *International Zoo Yearbook,* 1972, **12,** 3–12.

Hershkovitz, P. *Living New World monkeys (Platyrrhini) with an introduction to Primates.* Chicago: University of Chicago Press, in press.

Hill, W. C. O. *Primates: Comparative anatomy and taxonomy. I. Strepsirhini.* Edinburgh: Edinburgh University Press, 1953.

Hill, W. C. O. *Primates: Comparative anatomy and taxonomy. II. Haplorhini: Tarsioidea.* Edinburgh: Edinburgh University Press, 1955.

Hill, W. C. O. *Primates: Comparative anatomy and taxonomy. III. Pithecoidea: Platyrrhini (Families Hapalidae and Callimiconidae).* Edinburgh: Edinburgh University Press, 1957.

Hill, W. C. O. *Primates: Comparative anatomy and taxonomy. IV. Cebidae: Part A.* Edinburgh: Edinburgh University Press, 1960.

Hill, W. C. O. *Primates: Comparative anatomy and taxonomy. V. Cebidae: Part B.* Edinburgh: Edinburgh University Press, 1962.

Hill, W. C. O. *Primates: Comparative anatomy and taxonomy. VI. Catarrhini: Cercopithecoidea: Cercopithecinae.* Edinburgh: Edinburgh University Press, 1966.

Hill, W. C. O. The nomenclature, taxonomy and distribution of chimpanzees. In G. H. Bourne (Ed.), *The chimpanzee* (Vol. 1). Baltimore: University Park Press, 1969.

Hill, W. C. O. *Primates: Comparative anatomy and taxonomy. VIII. Cynopithecinae: Papio, Mandrillus, Theropithecus.* Edinburgh: Edinburgh University Press, 1970.

Hill, W. C. O. *Primates: Comparative anatomy and taxonomy. VII. Cynopithecinae: Cercocebus, Macaca, Cynopithecus.* Edinburgh: Edinburgh University Press, 1974.

Jones, T. C., Thorington, R. W., Hu, M. M., Adams, E., & Cooper, R. W. Karyotypes of squirrel monkeys (*Saimiri sciureus*) from different geographic regions. *American Journal of Physical Anthropology,* 1973, **38,** 269–277.

Kuhn, H.-J. Zur Systematik der Cercopithecidae. In D. Starck, R. Schneider, & H.-J. Kuhn (Eds.), *Neue Ergebnisse der Primatologie.* Stuttgart: Gustav Fischer, 1967.

Meester, J., & Setzer, H. W. (Eds.) *The mammals of Africa: An identification manual.* Washington, D.C.: Smithsonian Institution, 1971.

Miller, G. S., Jr. The groups and names of macaques. In C. H. Hartman & W. L. Straus, Jr. (Eds.), *The anatomy of the rhesus monkey* (Macaca mulatta). Baltimore: Williams & Wilkins, 1933. (Reprinted New York: Hafner, 1961.)

Napier, J. R., & Napier, P. H. *A handbook of living primates.* London: Academic Press, 1967.

Pennant, T. *Synopsis of quadrupeds.* Chester: J. Monk, 1771.

Struhsaker, T. T. Phylogenetic implications of some vocalizations of *Cercopithecus* monkeys. In J. R. Napier & P. H. Napier (Eds.), *Old World monkeys: Evolution, systematics and behavior.* New York: Academic Press, 1970.

Thorington, R. W., Jr. The identification of primates used in viral research. *Laboratory Animal Science,* 1971, **21,** 1074–1077.

Thorington, R. W., Jr., & Groves, C. P. An annotated classification of the Cercopithecoidea. In J. R. Napier & P. H. Napier (Eds.), *Old World monkeys: Evolution, systematics and behavior.* New York: Academic Press, 1970.

Tyson, E. *Orang-utang, sive Homo sylvestris: or, the anatomy of a pygmie compared with that of a monkey, an ape, and a man. To which is added, a philological essay concerning the pygmies, the cynocephali, the satyrs, and the sphinges of the ancients.* London: Thomas Bennet, 1699.

Zimmermann, E. A. W. von. *Geographische Geschichte des Menschen und der allgemein verbreiteten vierfüssigen Thiere, nebst einer heiber gehrigen zoologischen Weltcharte* (Vol. 2). Leipzig: Suder Weygandschen Buckhandburg, 1780.

2
Information Processing and Discrimination Learning Set

Douglas L. Medin

The Rockefeller University

I. INTRODUCTION

Because primate researchers cannot afford the luxury of using a new and "naive" group of subjects for each new experiment, it is not surprising that investigators of cognitive skills in primates have had a continuing interest in transfer of learning. One striking transfer phenomenon is learning set formation. In a learning set experiment, the subject is trained on a series of many different discriminations, each presented for only a few trials. The stimuli typically are pairs of objects that differ from each other in a variety of dimensions (e.g., color, form, size, texture). These objects usually are presented on the form board of a Wisconsin General Test Apparatus. For simultaneous object discriminations, the displacement of one object of each pair is always rewarded and the displacement of the other is consistently not rewarded (see Figure 2.1). All other cues, including positional cues, are irrelevant. After a few trials on one discrimination problem have been given, a new pair of objects is presented as a new discrimination problem. A special feature of learning set experiments is that the particular stimulus properties that are associated with reward on one problem (e.g., blue, large) are as likely to be associated with nonreward as with reward on a new problem. Indeed, performance on Trial 1 of each new problem stays at chance as long as the experiment is properly controlled.

On trials following the first, however, a remarkable change takes place in performance as a function of practice. Experimentally naive monkeys learn slowly and inefficiently, but after being trained on a few hundred problems, monkeys master new discrimination problems after a single trial. Harlow's (1949) classic data, shown in Figure 2.2, illustrate this point. By the 300th problem his rhesus monkeys (*Macaca mulatta*) were correct more than 90% of the time on Trial 2 of new problems.

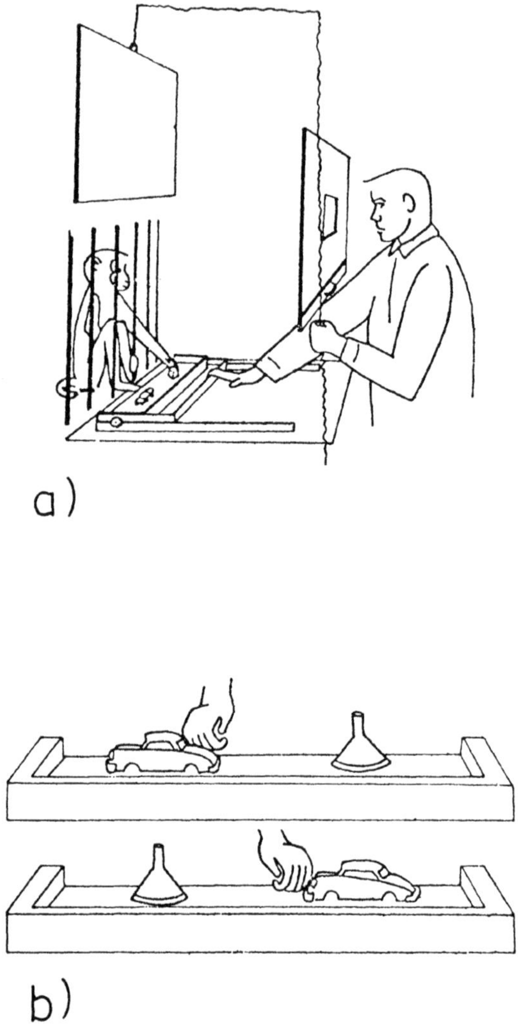

FIG. 2.1 (a) Components of the WGTA. The monkey reaches through the bars of a restraining cage to displace objects on a stimulus tray. It finds food in the foodwell beneath the object the tester has arbitrarily designated as correct. The tester views the monkey through a one-way window, withdraws the tray at the end of each trial, and lowers the opaque screen. (b) Simultaneous discrimination. The monkey must displace a particular object to obtain food. Position per se or pattern of position does not provide the solution. The car is correct in this example and continues to be as long as this pair of stimuli is used. On the next problem a completely new pair is introduced. [After Davis, 1974. Copyright 1974 by Academic Press, New York. Reproduced by permission.]

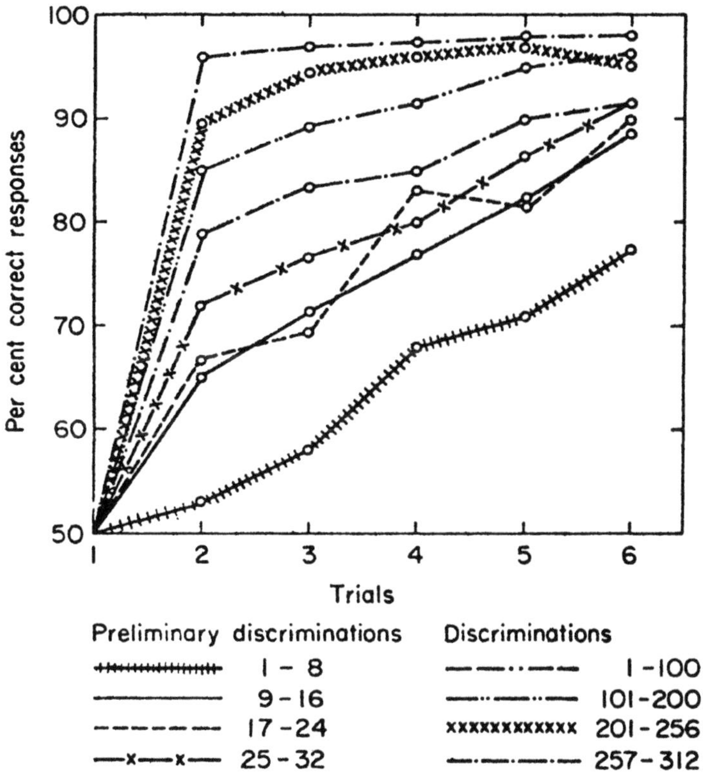

FIG. 2.2 Learning set curves showing performance as a function of trial and problem number. (From Harlow, 1949. Copyright 1949 by the American Psychological Association. Reproduced by permission.)

Apart from the natural interest in understanding the acquisition of learning skills, learning set formation traditionally has attracted a great deal of theoretical interest. An early hope was that learning set might bridge the gap between trial-and-error learning and insightful problem solution and thus settle the continuity-noncontinuity controversy. Naive monkeys learned discriminations in an incremental (trial and error) fashion while learning-set-experienced monkeys appeared to solve discriminations in an all-or-none (insightful) manner. Learning set data were also a means of providing consistency for those believing in a qualitative similarity between human and animal learning, since there was no longer any incompatibility between the apparently insightful nature of much of human learning and the trial-and-error behavior noted in animal learning by investigators from Thorndike on.

Far from providing a bridge between human and animal learning, however, primate research on learning set formation rapidly became isolated from mainstream research on animal learning. Several factors contributed to this isolation. First, the researchers concentrated on describing differences between initial and terminal stages of learning set formation and paid little attention to the transitions between such stages and the processes involved in within-problem learning. As a result, no common set of research problems existed to link primate learning set research with discrimination learning research using other animals.

Second, interaction between primate and nonprimate learning research has been undermined by the periodic conjecture that learning set formation in primates is qualitatively different from learning to learn in other animal species, the implication being that research with nonprimates could tell us nothing of consequence about primate learning. Even if we accept this dubious implication, the case for qualitative differences in learning is weak. Although large differences in the rate and asymptotic level of learning set formation often have been noted (e.g., Hodos, 1970), the basis for these differences is not at all clear. For example, Warren (1974) argues that one cannot tell to what extent such differences reflect differences in learning capacity as opposed to differences in sensory capacities or procedural variables. For example, dolphins are fairly slow to acquire a visual discrimination learning set (Herman, Beach, Pepper, & Stallings, 1969), but when given auditory discriminations they quickly reach a Trial 2 performance indistinguishable from that of monkeys (Herman & Arbeit, 1973). And the notoriously slow interproblem learning of rats (e.g., Wright, Kay, & Sime, 1963) is dramatically improved when rats are presented with odor discrimination problems (Slotnick & Katz, 1974). This is not to say that all differences in learning set performance arise from differences in sensory capacity, but rather that careful analyses of the sources of species differences in learning set formation are likely to be more productive and informative than the simple conclusion that qualitative or quantitative differences exist.

The segregation of learning set research from other issues in learning may be drawing to an end. Expanding research on selective attention in discrimination learning (e.g., Sutherland & Mackintosh, 1971) has led to the development of a series of transfer paradigms that lie between single-problem experiments and learning set studies. In addition, the last several years have witnessed an interest in memory processes in animals (e.g., Honig & James, 1971; Medin, Roberts, & Davis, 1976) and a focus on the informational rather than the hedonic properties of reward (e.g., Medin, 1972; Rescorla & Wagner, 1972). All of these factors suggest that an information-processing approach to the study of animal learning may facilitate our understanding of the processes operating during learning set formation by removing many of the artificial barriers to interaction between learning set research and the rest of animal research.

In this paper, I shall first review learning set research, attempting to focus on the information-processing skills operating during performance in this paradigm.

Then I shall examine specific learning set theories in relation to these data and in relation to each other. Finally, I will consider suggestions for improving the interaction between theory and data in learning set research. Other reviews of learning set research can be found in the papers of Reese (1964), Miles (1965), Medin (1972), and Bessemer and Stollnitz (1971).

II. INFORMATION PROCESSING IN LEARNING TO LEARN

What are the components of successful learning set performance? Without any pretense of producing an exhaustive list, I will suggest four important factors and then review some research related to these factors. First, subjects must come to appreciate the information value of a reward. In the days when theorists thought that reinforcement directly and automatically strengthened responses, this would not have been considered an important variable. Logically, however, there is no reason for a monkey to expect that because a raisin was under a particular stimulus object on Trial 1, there will be one under the same object on Trial 2. In fact, the monkey might expect that there would be no raisin under that stimulus on Trial 2, because it had already removed it on Trial 1.

A closely related factor involves selective coding. As one example, subjects must learn to associate the reward information with object rather than positional cues. This selection must happen on the first trial of new problems, since Trial 2 performance with experienced monkeys exceeds the theoretical maximum of 75% correct that would be possible if subjects were unable to tell if the Trial 1 reward was to be associated with the rewarded object or the position it occupied. The object cues must also be encoded in such a way that subjects can differentiate the correct and incorrect objects. It will not help to know the rewarded object is red if the incorrect object is also red.

Third, the subject must be able to remember the encoding of stimulus and reward information for at least the duration of the intertrial interval, which may range from seconds to minutes or to still longer intervals depending on the experiment. Several types of forgetting could occur: subjects might remember which object they chose but not whether or not it was correct; they might remember whether their response was correct but not which object they chose; or they might forget information necessary to differentiate the correct and incorrect object on the trial. They also might experience difficulty in remembering whether some attribute (e.g., yellow) is associated with reward on the current problem as opposed to on some preceding problem.

Finally, subjects must learn which of the habits and skills used in mastering one discrimination will be useful in solving other discrimination problems. A multitude of factors could produce positive or negative transfer on new problems, and a major task for researchers is to isolate and analyze these components.

The next section of this paper attempts to fill in this rough outline, based on the factors of reward function, selective coding, memory, and transfer in learning to learn.

A. Reinforcement as Information

There is abundant evidence that, apart from any strengthening function, rewards may serve as cues. The usual learning set procedure can be described as a task where the correct strategy consists of approaching rewarded objects (win-stay) and avoiding nonrewarded objects (lose-shift). One could also describe this task without the concept of strategies by proposing that rewards strengthen and nonrewards weaken response tendencies (i.e., by invoking the law of effect). These two interpretations can be distinguished by learning set procedures consisting of two-trial problems where the correct object on Trial 2 is the nonrewarded object from Trial 1 and the incorrect object on Trial 2 is the rewarded object from Trial 1. This task should be impossible if rewards automatically strengthen and nonrewards weaken response tendencies, because in this instance a win-shift, lose-stay strategy would be appropriate.

Experimenters have presented monkeys with problems whose solution involved only one of the four components of these strategies (namely, win-stay, win-shift, lose-stay, lose-shift) in a between-subjects design where only one of the four problem types was presented to a given group of monkeys. For example, if a group is trained on lose-stay, its Trial 1 choice will never be rewarded, but the correct object on Trial 2 will always be the object chosen on Trial 1. The results of a number of studies show that monkeys can master all four solution types (e.g., Brown & McDowell, 1963; Brown, McDowell, & Gaylord, 1965; McDowell & Brown, 1963a, 1963b, 1963c, 1965a, 1965b, 1965c, 1965d, 1965e; McDowell, Gaylord & Brown, 1965a, 1965b). Win-stay is by far the most difficult of the four solutions to learn, a very puzzling result from the point of view that rewards directly strengthen responses. That these findings are not wholly controlled by strong preferences for either novel or familiar stimuli is indicated by Behar's (1961) experiment using a larger number of trials per problem and showing that monkeys can perform well under an object-alternation learning set procedure (win-shift, lose-stay), where the correct object on one trial is incorrect on the next.

Monkeys also can use novelty and familiarity, independent of reward and nonreward, to master learning tasks. For instance, monkeys can solve two-trial learning set problems when the correct solution is to choose a newly-presented Trial 2 object and to avoid either the correct or incorrect Trial 1 object (Brown, Overall, & Blodgett, 1959). Likewise, they can learn to approach or avoid specific recurring stimuli from previous problems (Gentry, Overall, & Brown, 1958), even on Trial 1 of new problems (Riopelle, Chronholm, & Addison, 1962).

A series of studies by Riopelle and his colleagues demonstrated that a symbol (e.g., a marble) can be at least as effective as a reward on Trial 1 of problems (Riopelle, 1955; Riopelle & Francisco, 1955; Riopelle, Francisco, & Ades, 1954). In this procedure, six-trial problems were given with no food, food, or a marble on Trial 1 signaling whether the chosen or unchosen object was to be correct and rewarded with food on Trials 2 through 6. Groups trained on marble-stay actually performed somewhat better than animals trained on food-stay. Perhaps food was a less effective source of information than marbles because it distracted the animals' attention from the chosen object.

The same interpretation may apply to a study by Darby and Riopelle (1959) on observational learning in monkeys. Prior to the first trial on each of a series of problems, the monkeys witnessed another monkey execute a "demonstration" trial. Half of these demonstration trials were correct and rewarded and half were incorrect and nonrewarded. The observer was never rewarded on a demonstration trial. With practice, the observer's first test-trial performance rose from chance to 75% correct; moreover, performance was consistently better if the demonstration trial involved nonreward than if it involved reward.

Even extinction learning sets may be formed by monkeys. Behar (1973) trained monkeys on eight-trial discrimination problems with each problem followed by a series of extinction trials where neither object was rewarded. When 10 extinction trials followed each problem, monkeys eventually showed one-trial extinction on most of the problems.

All of these studies point toward the conclusion that reward and nonreward function primarily as sources of information that can be used in a variety of ways, depending on the particular experimental circumstances. Although one would not want to conclude that any arbitrary event can be used to direct a monkey's choice behavior, learning set formation in monkeys is not tightly constrained, if it is constrained at all by the law of effect (see Medin, 1972). Instead, learning is controlled more directly by whether or not an event is informative. A general discussion of this issue can be found in papers by Kamin (1969), Rescorla and Wagner (1972), and Wagner, Rudy, and Whitlow (1973); particular application to discrimination learning in primates is provided by Bartus and LeVere (1976).

B. Selective Coding

1. Relationship Between Within- and Between-Problem Learning

Procedural and stimulus variables that control within-problem learning indirectly control between-problem learning. Spatial separation of the relevant cues and the response has a powerful influence on discrimination learning in primates (for general reviews see Meyer, Treichler, and Meyer, 1965, and Stollnitz, 1965).

For example, Murphy and Miller (1955) trained monkeys on 672 three-trial problems and found that monkeys whose discriminations involved a 6-inch cue-response separation showed no sign of either within- or between-problem learning.

A corollary of the above conclusion is that monkeys should learn mainly about the object chosen. Lockhart, Parks, and Davenport (1963) directly tested this proposition using pigtailed monkeys (*Macaca nemestrina*). For one group of animals, the object not chosen on Trial 1 of problems was replaced with a new object for Trials 2 through 6 of six-trial problems, and for the other group, the displaced object was replaced for Trials 2 through 6. When the unchosen object was replaced, subjects averaged 85% correct on Trial 2; when the chosen object was replaced, subjects performed at a chance level, regardless of whether their initial response had been correct or incorrect. Analogous results were obtained by McDowell and Brown (1963a, 1965a).

Actually, learning is not completely restricted to the object chosen. Brown and Carr (1958) placed the objects to be used for the next problem 6 inches behind those being used on the current problem. Learning on new problems was better when the correct object had been paired with the correct object on the preceding problem than when the correct object had been behind the incorrect object on the preceding problem. Thus, the monkeys had learned something about the incidental cues.

Behar (1962) gave monkeys a series of problems where every few trials either the correct or the incorrect stimulus was replaced by a new correct or incorrect stimulus. On these shifts, monkeys preferred the old incorrect object to a new object if they had not chosen the incorrect object in the previous set of trials. The fact that the incorrect object had not been chosen previously indicates that it was not highly preferred, so something was learned about it during those preshift trials. However, whatever they were learning, it was obviously not that choices of the incorrect object would not be rewarded because the chosen object was being rewarded; if this were so the incorrect object should have decreased in attractiveness. A recent study suggests that the Trial 1 outcome may be associated with both the chosen and unchosen stimulus object, which would have the effect that unchosen negative stimuli would increase in attractiveness (Medin, 1977).

Cue salience is another factor determining the rate of learning set formation. Devine (1970) found that rhesus monkeys formed an object discrimination learning set faster than cebus monkeys when chromatic stimuli were used but that there were no differences in learning set formation when achromatic stimuli were used. Monkeys also form a learning set more easily when three-dimensional rather than two-dimensional stimuli are employed (Harlow & Warren, 1952).

A particularly striking example of cue salience effects arises from a study of oddity discrimination learning set by Draper (1965). For oddity problems, three stimuli are present on each trial, two like and one unlike, and the correct response is to choose the stimulus which is different from the other two. In Draper's experiment, rhesus monkeys were tested on 350 oddity problems that differed in color, form, size, or a combination of these. The results are shown in Figure 2.3 (redrawn from Draper's original 1965 figure). On problems where color differences were present learning to learn was observed and performance surpassed 90% correct. But when color differences were not present there was no significant improvement across blocks of practice, and performance was essentially at a chance level. It would have been interesting to have another group trained with color differences never present, to see if color was the only cue on which oddity learning could be based or whether the presence of color differences on many of the trials resulted in an actual inhibition of oddity learning on the basis of form and size differences (i.e., did color produce an overshadowing effect?).

The specific format in which object discriminations are presented may also affect learning set formation. Usually these problems are presented as simul-

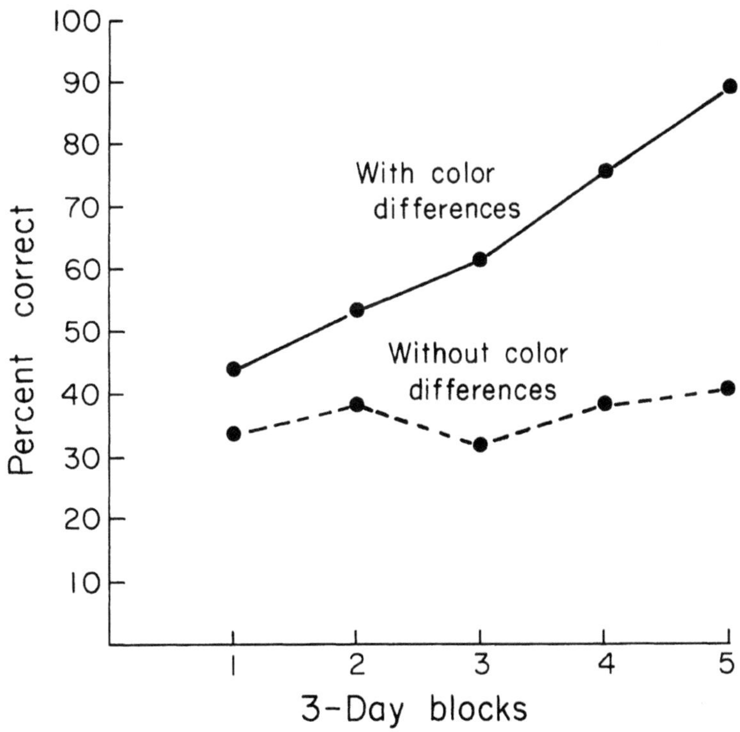

FIG. 2.3 Performance on oddity discriminations with color cues either present or absent as a function of stage of learning set training. (Redrawn from Draper, 1965.)

taneous discriminations and both objects appear on every trial. Figure 2.4 illustrates a successive discrimination paradigm which may also be used for object discriminations. Reward is always on the left when one pair of objects is presented and always on the right when the other pair of identical objects is presented. Medin and Davis (1968) gave stumptail monkeys (*Macaca arctoides*) 750 eight-trial successive discriminations and observed very slowly developing interproblem improvement. Successive discriminations are generally harder than simultaneous discriminations and possibly successive learning set formation was slowed down by the minimal intraproblem learning evident during the first several hundred problems.

Data that bear directly on the relationship between intraproblem and interproblem learning are scarce. Ideally, one would like to have a control group given some standard procedure and an experimental group given some other experience and then switched to the standard procedure. Then one could obtain direct evidence on whether the variable in question facilitates or impairs learning set formation. In one study meeting this criterion, Smith, King, and Newberry (1976) found that experimental subjects trained with reinforcers used directly as discriminanda learned discriminations markedly faster than control subjects; however, no statistically significant differences were evident when both groups then received the control task. More extensive use of this general design would add to our understanding of learning set formation. This recommendation calls for a between-subject design, which may be a drawback compared with the more sensitive within-subject design often preferred (with good reason) by investigators working with small numbers of subjects.

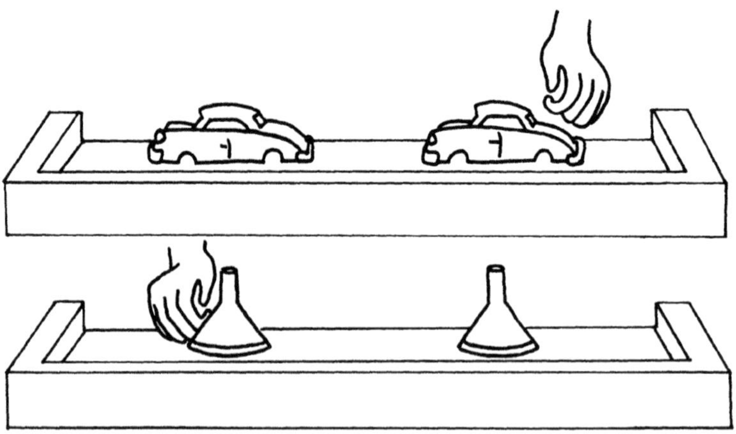

M.B.

FIG. 2.4 A successive discrimination problem. The right-hand position is correct when two cars are present; the left-hand when two funnels are shown. [After Davis, 1974. Copyright 1974 by Academic Press, New York. Reproduced by permission.]

2. *Coding Processes Evident Across Problems*

Some aspects of within-problem coding can best be seen by examining between-problem transfer. Evidence from many sectors of discrimination learning research shows that animals, including primates, attend selectively to different aspects of a learning situation and that this attentional process can be modified by experience (e.g., Sutherland and Mackintosh, 1971). Perhaps the best measure of selective learning is the comparison of intra- and extradimensional shifts. For an intradimensional shift the same dimension (e.g., form) is relevant during both the original problem and the shift problem, though the particular stimulus values are changed to prevent specific transfer. Extradimensional shifts also employ new stimuli, but the original learning problem and the shift problem involve different relevant dimensions (e.g., color relevant in original learning and form relevant for the shift problem). If animals learn to attend selectively to relevant dimensions and this attention transfers across problems, then intradimensional shifts should be easier to master than extradimensional shifts. Monkeys show this advantage for intradimensional shifts (e.g., Rothblatt & Wilson, 1968; Shepp & Schrier, 1969).

Schrier (1971, 1972) gave monkeys learning set training in which the same dimension (for one group, color, and for another group, form) was relevant for each problem. After animals had formed a learning set with that dimension relevant, they were given training on a series of learning set problems where a different dimension (e.g., form, if the animals had originally been trained on color-relevant problems) always was relevant. The monkeys showed excellent transfer, but the last problem in preshift learning was solved faster than the first problem of the extradimensional shifts (for other evidence, see Takemura, 1960). It seems clear, then, that monkeys can learn to selectively encode information about dimensional aspects of objects.

Selective coding also operates between object and position cues. If the correct object occupies the left side of the food-tray on Trial 1 of a problem, there is some ambiguity as to whether responses to the left or to the object itself are being reinforced. Errors made on the first trial on which the correct object shifts position are known as differential cue errors. These errors play an important role in Harlow's error factor theory, to be discussed later. For the moment we note that monkeys are able to associate the reward with object rather than positional cues because their Trial 2 performance eventually surpasses the theoretical maximum of 75% correct that could be achieved with nonselective coding.

A relative measure of differential cue errors is the percentage of errors on the trial when the correct object first shifts position divided by percentage errors on comparable nonshift trials. This ratio, known as the comparable-trial error-ratio, should equal 1 when no differential cue errors are occurring. In his original investigation, Harlow (1950) found that differential cue errors decreased across problems and the comparable-trial error-ratio approached 1. Davis, McDowell, and Thorson (1953) did not observe a decrease in this ratio, although the absolute number of differential cue errors clearly decreased with practice. It is hard to come to any conclusion concerning changes in this ratio, because it is rarely reported in the learning set literature.

Riopelle and Chinn (1961) demonstrated that monkeys can learn about object cues while responding to position. They gave learning set training where on Trial 1 of each problem the rewarded object was always on the right side, but varied from side to side in the usual manner on the remaining trials. By the end of the experiment their rhesus monkeys chose the correct position on 85% of initial trials and also selected the correct object on 85% of the second trials. This means that monkeys responded to the correct position on Trial 1, but that the reward outcome was associated with object rather than positional cues.

Although we have observed that selective coding is an important aspect of learning set formation, we do not know to what extent the improvement associated with learning "win-stay, lose-shift with respect to objects" depends on learning to attend to objects as opposed to either learning the general principle of win-stay, lose-shift or acquiring some other information about reward such as the level of reward to expect. Information bearing on this point could be gathered from a learning set experiment where normal training is given to one group of monkeys and object and positional discriminations are randomly intermixed for a second group. In the only study I know of where these two types of discriminations were intermixed, monkeys were able to shift rapidly among object discriminations, object discrimination reversals, positional discriminations, and position discrimination reversals (e.g., Zable & Harlow, 1946). This result, coupled with other evidence (e.g., Warren, 1966), suggests that acquiring information concerning reinforcement may play a substantial role in learning set development.

The exact nature of selective coding of stimuli, rewards, and their relationship will determine the extent to which this information is retained over time. We turn now to memory factors in learning to learn.

C. Memory

1. Normal Task Demands

At a minimum, animals must retain stimulus-reward information for the duration of the interval between trials in order to perform effectively on discrimination tasks. Studies which vary intertrial interval usually observe some decline in performance as the interval increases, but such losses are small (see Bessemer and Stollnitz, 1971, and Medin, 1972, for reviews). For example, Riopelle and Churukian (1958) reported about a 5% loss in performance as the intertrial interval increased from 10 to 60 seconds.

Normally a series of discriminations is presented to a monkey in such a way that all the trials of one problem are given before the next problem is introduced. Problems may also be presented in a concurrent discrimination format. In this procedure, presentations are given in a paired-associate fashion such that Trial 1 of each problem appears before Trial 2 of any problem is given. The concurrent procedure makes greater demands on memory because forgetting may arise either from the relatively long interpresentation intervals or from interference from other pairs in the list. As one would expect, consecutive stimulus presentation results in better performance than the concurrent procedure (Darby & Riopelle, 1955), and concurrent list performance decreases with increases in list length (e.g., Blomquist, Deets, & Harlow, 1973; King, 1971; King & Goodman, 1966). On the other hand, the concurrent procedure does not result in drastic memory losses; monkeys can form learning sets quite effectively under such a procedure (e.g., Blomquist et al., 1973; Leary, 1958). Figure 2.5, which summarizes the results of Leary's study, indicates that on nine-pair lists monkeys eventually reached a level of over 80% correct on Trial 2 of concurrently-presented problems.

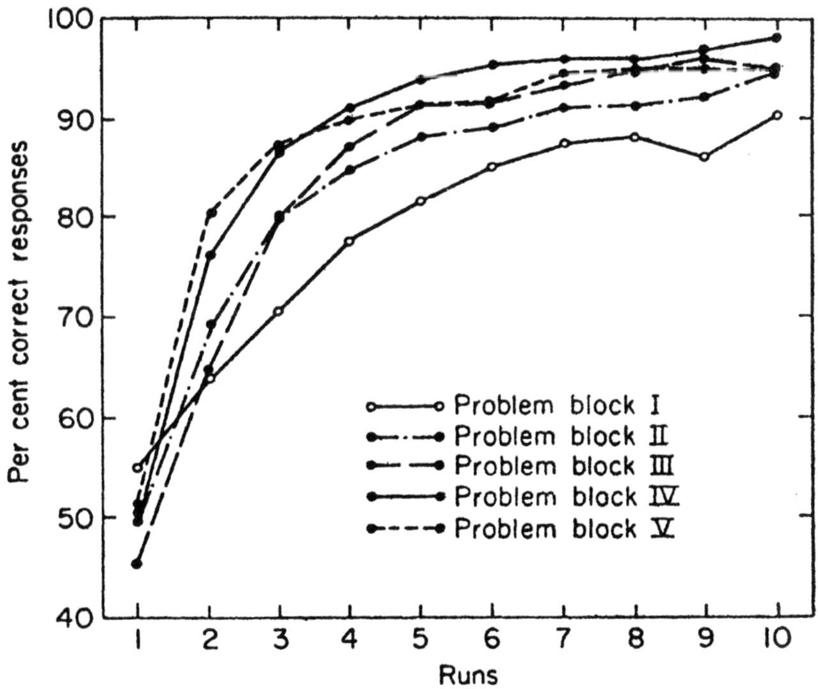

FIG. 2.5 Concurrent discrimination learning as a function of runs through lists of nine object-pairs. Each problem block includes five lists. [After Leary, 1958. Copyright 1958 by the American Psychological Association. Reproduced by permission.]

2. Long-term Memory and Transfer Suppression

Monkeys show reliable memory for discriminations for time periods measured in hours (e.g., Bessemer & Stollnitz, 1971 Riopelle & Moon, 1968), days (e.g., Zimmerman, 1969), and even months (e.g., Mason, Blazek, & Harlow, 1956; Strong, 1959). Such retention may represent a mixed blessing in a learning set experiment, because there is no possibility for consistent positive between-problem transfer based on memory for previous discriminations. Indeed, in order to perform optimally, monkeys must overcome transfer based on the earlier association of particular stimulus features with reward and nonreward.

Riopelle (1953) proposed that monkeys suppress transfer to the point where, eventually, responses to a particular problem do not transfer to succeeding problems. He tested this idea by giving monkeys six problems a day, with the sixth problem being a reversal of either the first or the fourth problem of that day. Monkeys initially made 80% errors on the first trial of reversal problems, but eventually reached 60% errors on Trial 1 of reversals with performance on Trials 2 through 6 not different from that on nonreversal problems.

These results do not unequivocally demonstrate that learning set formation is caused or accompanied by increased forgetting of specific object discriminations. Stollnitz and Schrier (1968) noted that the monkeys in Riopelle's study had largely formed their learning set *before* any transfer suppression was evident. Schrier and Stollnitz replicated Riopelle's procedure using learning-set-experienced monkeys and observed an average of only 17% correct on Trial 1 of reversals. Prior learning set training had not produced transfer suppression in these monkeys. In a later replication by Schrier (1969), one rhesus monkey eventually performed *above* chance on Trial 1 of the reversals, suggesting that the improvement in performance on Trial 1 of reversals represents learning to reverse when familiar stimuli reappear. In perhaps the most direct test of the transfer suppression hypothesis, Singh and Lewis (1974) trained different groups of monkeys to three different levels of performance before administering a reversal procedure. The decrease in performance associated with reversals did not interact with level of learning set performance, contrary to the transfer suppression hypothesis.

Connor and Meyer (1971) demonstrated that learning set training is associated with considerable proactive interference. They presented earlier problems a second time during a learning set experiment, with the reward contingencies remaining the same as for the original problems. Trial 1 retention performance declined across problem blocks, consistent with a transfer suppression hypothesis. However, in the Connor and Meyer experiment, two-week rest breaks were introduced between every three testing blocks. Although these breaks did not change Trial 2 performance on new problems, retention performance recovered to its original level over the breaks (and then again declined over consecutive training blocks). This study implies that "suppression" may simply result from proactive interference, and further, that this loss is not causally related to learning set formation. Incidentally, Kamil and Mauldin (1975), in a related study using bluejays, failed to observe memory recovery over a break.

Forgetting in learning set paradigms may be analogous to the forgetting associated with successive reversal learning paradigms. Gonzalez, Behrend, and Bitterman (1967) proposed that improvements in successive reversal learning in birds were partially caused by increased forgetting that would serve to decrease negative transfer. I want to add one word of caution here. Corresponding to the learning-performance distinction, one must always be aware of a memory-performance distinction, particularly in research with animals (for a full discussion, see Winograd, 1971). It is quite possible that animals retain information concerning which specific stimulus was associated with reward on an earlier occasion but may not act on the basis of this information. For example, the fact that a rat stops pressing a bar during an extinction procedure does not imply that the rat has forgotten that it was ever rewarded for pressing the bar. Likewise, examples of transfer suppression only imply that an earlier memory is not controlling performance, not that it does not exist.

3. *Changes in Retention Associated with Stage of Learning Set*

While Riopelle's transfer suppression hypothesis has not been supported, the question of whether memory performance changes over the course of learning set training is still of great theoretical interest. For example, Bessemer has proposed that naive monkeys either do not have or do not use their short-term memory to store stimulus outcome information to the degree that learning-set-experienced monkeys do. If this is true, experienced monkeys should show more rapid forgetting than naive monkeys over short retention intervals.

Unfortunately, assessing changes in forgetting rate is neither a simple nor a theoretically neutral proposition. In the next few paragraphs I will consider three possibilities, no one of which is entirely satisfactory.

First, one might use the procedures of signal detection theory to convert percentage correct scores into memory strength measures (d') and then see whether the rate of decrease in memory strength changes with stage of learning set. The chief disadvantage of this approach is that averaging over days within a practice block, over subjects, and over discriminations varying in difficulty introduces systematic biases in the estimation of memory strength. Nonparametric measures of memory strength (see Pastore and Scheirer, 1974) will circumvent some, but not all, of these difficulties. We shall not consider signal detection theory further in this paper because the qualitative results in regard to the forgetting rate correspond closely to those of a third measure, which we shall presently consider.

A second measure of the forgetting rate is simply the absolute retention loss. Although the idea of a forgetting *rate* implies a proportional or relative measure of retention, absolute retention loss has been, in practice, the most common measure of forgetting. Absolute measures are implicitly involved in analyses of variance on raw retention scores, where investigators assume that an interaction of retention intervals with blocks of practice gives evidence that the forgetting rate has changed.

My objection to this measure is not entirely theory-free, so let me offer some particular assumptions by way of arriving at a third measure of forgetting rate. Suppose that on a learning trial an association that will mediate correct responding at least over the shortest retention interval is developed with probability L, and that this association will be forgotten over a long retention interval with probability f. Further assume that an animal can produce a correct response by remembering the appropriate association or, if that is not available, by guessing. From these assumptions we can write the probability of a correct response after short and long retention intervals (P_S and P_L) as:

$$P_S = L + (1-L).50, \text{ and} \tag{1}$$

$$P_L = L(1-f) + [1-L(1-f)]\,.50 \tag{2}$$

The absolute measure of forgetting is P_S minus P_L which is equal to: $.50Lf$. Now imagine that the forgetting rate f stays constant while L increases (as learning set develops). The absolute difference between Equations 1 and 2 will increase and an interaction of forgetting rate with stage of practice will show up in our analysis of variance, even though we have explicitly held the forgetting rate constant.

Now consider relative measures. If Equation 2 is divided by Equation 1, as Balogh and Zimmermann (1971) did, the result is a complex fraction that still involves L in the equation. The problem is that we need to correct for guessing before dividing. But Equations 1 and 2 can be used to derive that

$$L = 2(P_S-.50), \text{ and that} \tag{3}$$

$$L(1-f) = 2(P_L-.50). \tag{4}$$

Now by dividing Equation 4 by Equation 3 we obtain just $(1-f)$, which is the measure of retention sought, a measure of forgetting rate that is not confounded with L.

I will now use this relative measure of retention to examine changes in forgetting with stage of learning set practice. Although this measure is specific to the assumptions I have sketched, an analysis in terms of signal detection theory would yield the same qualitative results.

a. Short retention intervals. Deets, Harlow, and Blomquist (1970) gave learning set training where Trial 2 was preceded by an intertrial interval of 5, 10, or 20 seconds. Effects of intertrial interval were evident only on the later practice blocks. Figure 2.6 shows for the different stages of practice, the percentage retained after the 20-second interval relative to that after the 5-second interval, when retention is measured in terms of Equations 3 and 4.

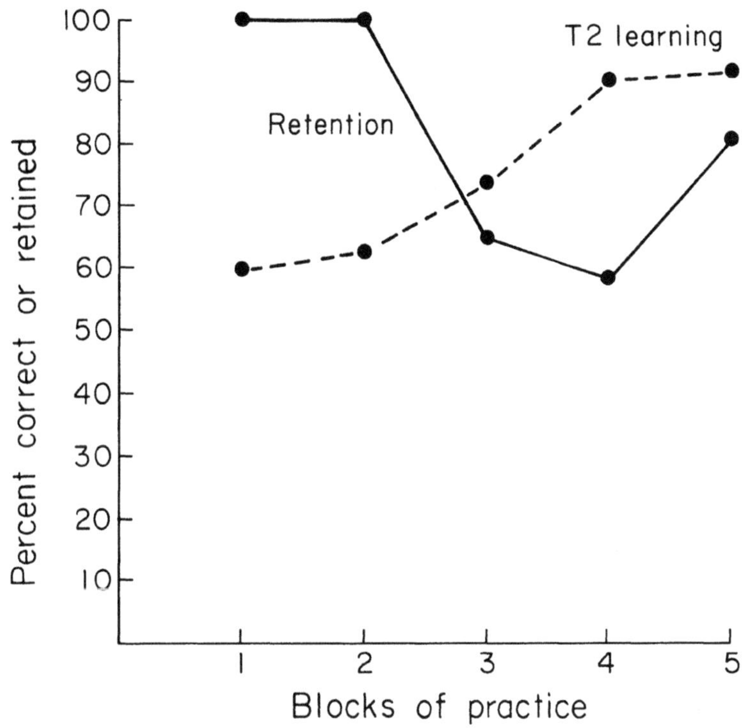

FIG. 2.6 Trial 2(T2) learning and short-term retention performance as a function of blocks of practice. (The Trial 2 data are from Deets, Harlow, and Blomquist, 1970, and the retention curve is based on the present reanalysis of their retention data.)

The figure indicates that retention initially deteriorated with practice but was better on the fifth block of practice than on either the third or fourth block.

b. Intermediate retention intervals. Blomquist, Deets, and Harlow (1973) conducted a learning set study using concurrent discrimination lists involving 2, 4, or 8 pairs. Using the list length 2 and list length 8 data to estimate forgetting, one finds that the percentage retained initially decreases over blocks of practice and then increases for the last few blocks of practice. A similar nonmonotonic change on a postcriterion retention test (of up to 5 minutes) was noted by Kamil and Mauldin (1975) in a study using bluejays.

c. Long retention intervals. Zimmermann (1969) tested both naive and learning-set-experienced monkeys on a series of six-trial discrimination problems that were repeated every 20 days. The retention results, again based on Equations 3 and 4, are shown in Figure 2.7, along with a Trial 2 index of learning. Naive monkeys (left panel) show a pattern of a decrease in retention

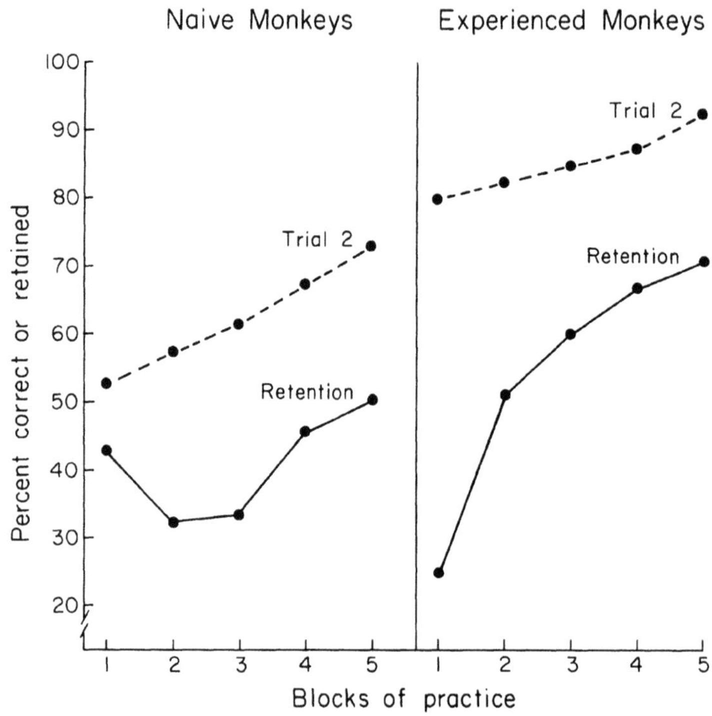

FIG. 2.7 Trial 2 learning and long-term retention performance in naive and experienced monkeys as a function of blocks of practice. (Redrawn from Zimmermann, 1969.)

followed by an increase; learning-set-experienced monkeys show only increases in retention with practice.

This nonmonotonic relationship between stage of practice and estimated forgetting rate appears for naive monkeys in studies involving retention intervals ranging between 20 seconds and 20 days. If we assume our measure corresponds to true rates of forgetting, then these results have some striking theoretical implications. One possibility is that the initial deterioration of retention scores reflects the development of proactive interference and that the later improvements reflect an increased tendency to attend to or encode cues that will support increased retention. That is, a learning-to-remember phenomenon may be hidden in the learning-to-learn literature.

A few more notes of caution should be added to attempts to interpret the observed interaction of forgetting rate with stage of learning set practice. Individual discrimination problems no doubt differ in difficulty, and performance at different points in learning set development may involve different mixtures of learned easy and learned difficult problems. For example, naive monkeys may readily learn easy problems but perform at chance on more difficult discriminations. If discriminations that are more difficult to learn are more difficult to remember, then some of the retention loss associated with practice may result from a different mixture of tests on learned easy and learned difficult discriminations (discriminations for which performance is at chance during learning will not affect measures of retention). Thus one might observe a change in forgetting rate with practice that is, in a sense, artifactual, because it would have arisen from item selection rather than from some mechanism such as proactive interference. The proactive interference observed in the previously mentioned Connor and Meyer (1971) experiment could not be explained in terms of such artifacts because the correlation between interference and stage of learning set was broken up by the interpolated rest intervals.

Another question needing an answer is whether stage of learning set or stage in learning a particular problem controls forgetting rates. King and Goodman (1966), studying the performance of squirrel monkeys (*Saimiri sciureus*) on concurrent discrimination problems, found with increased runs through the list that list size (1 versus 4 pairs) affected performance. The point at which list size effects appear may be governed by the monkey's stage in learning individual problems. In a later study, however, again using squirrel monkeys, King (1971) failed to observe any interaction of list size with degree of learning (trial number).

A conservative conclusion is that there are some intriguing results on changes in forgetting rate during learning set acquisition, but more experimentation is needed to clarify these results. We will reconsider the issue of changes in forgetting while discussing learning set theories.

D. Transfer to and from Learning Sets

Transfer tests are another way to study the coding and retention of information underlying learning set behavior.

1. Changes in Stimuli

Harlow and Warren (1952) gave monkeys extensive learning set practice with two-dimensional stimuli and then tested performance using three-dimensional discrimination problems. Monkeys showed only a slight drop in Trial 2 performance when the new stimulus population was introduced, indicating substantial positive transfer.

Schrier (1971, 1972) trained monkeys on a series of discriminations in which form (or color) was relevant and color (or form) was irrelevant. After subjects reached a high level of performance, further problems were given for which the relevant and irrelevant dimensions were reversed. Performance was significantly higher during shift learning than during original learning, and results from a control group showed that this excellent transfer could not be accounted for simply in terms of adaptation to testing. Takemura (1960) also reported positive transfer between color discrimination learning set and form discrimination learning set. Learning set skills may even survive changes in discrimination modality. Wilson and Wilson (1962) reported a small but reliable transfer between visual and tactual learning set (see chapter 3 by Ettlinger).

There is at least one report of a complete lack of transfer. Strong (1965) trained rhesus monkeys on oddity discriminations using a Wisconsin General Test Apparatus (WGTA) or two varieties of an automated primate testing apparatus (see Rohles, Belleville, and Grunzke, 1961). The WGTA testing involved three-dimensional stimuli, and two-dimensional stimuli were used in the automated test situations. After reaching a learning criterion on oddity discriminations, the monkeys were given the oddity problems in a new apparatus. The subjects learned as well with two-dimensional as with three-dimensional stimuli, but when they were shifted to a new apparatus their performance showed no evidence of positive transfer.

2. *Transfer to Discrimination Learning Set*

If one can identify the component skills necessary in learning set performance, then training on those component skills should show transfer to learning set. At least, instances of positive and negative transfer can provide sources of hypotheses concerning such component skills.

King (1966) reported that concept formation training (i.e., choose red, regardless of form) transferred to discrimination learning set better than training involving rewarded presentations of single objects. The very slow learning set development in both conditions suggests these treatments led to negative rather than positive transfer.

Rumbaugh, Sammons, Prim, and Phillips (1965) found that giving squirrel monkeys extensive pretraining with 500 different stimuli under a 50% reward schedule retarded learning set formation. A similar result was obtained by Davis (1956), who found that pretraining experience with inconsistent reward retarded oddity learning set in rhesus monkeys. Interposing a task where monkeys' performance does not rise much above chance may also disrupt discrimination learning set (Rumbauth & Prim, 1964; Warren & Sinha, 1959), but it would be hard to pin down such effects to the reward schedule itself.

Consistent reward associated with a single object does not speed up discrimination learning set, although there is some evidence that consistent reward associated with many different objects may facilitate learning set development (Rumbaugh et al., 1965). Familiarizing experience with discriminanda outside the test situation does not speed learning set development (Cross, Fletcher, & Harlow, 1963; Shell & Riopelle, 1958). A speculative summary is that, although neither extensive experience with consistent reward nor familiarity with a variety of objects shows transfer to learning set, the combination of these two factors facilitates learning set formation.

Extensive experience involving only a few discrimination problems does not result in a learning set being formed (e.g., Ricciardi & Treichler, 1970; Riopelle,

1953; Treichler, 1966). Riopelle and Moon (1968) provided some direct evidence that experiencing a variety of stimuli is important for the establishment of a learning set in monkeys. They gave groups of stumptail monkeys 10 six-trial problems each day for a series of days. For one group all 10 problems were new; for a second group 7 of the 10 problems were familiar (repeated) with the same objects designated as correct; and for a third group 7 of the 10 problems were familiar, but whether or not a previously correct object would again be rewarded was randomly determined. After this differential pretraining, all groups were given additional training on six-trial problems with new stimuli. In this transfer test, the group pretrained with new stimuli performed significantly better than either of the other groups, which had received less diverse stimuli.

On the other hand, when training on a small set of discriminations involves repeated reversal of the correct and incorrect stimuli, quite impressive transfer to object discrimination learning set has been obtained. For repeated reversals the optimal solution is to win-stay, lose-shift with respect to objects because no specific stimulus property is consistently rewarded. In fact, if repeated reversal and object discrimination learning set involve only learning win-stay, lose-shift for object cues, one might expect perfect transfer between these two problem types. Without reviewing the literature on transfer between repeated reversal learning and discrimination learning set in detail, there are few exceptions to the rule that there is substantial transfer, but that this transfer is well below what would be expected if repeated reversal training were equivalent to learning set training (Cross & Brown, 1965; Harlow, 1950, 1959; Komaki, 1974; Meyer, 1951; Ricciardi & Treichler, 1970; Riopelle & Kumaran, 1971; Schrier, 1966, 1974; Schusterman, 1962, 1964). Ricciardi and Treichler (1970) found that repeated reversals with a variety of discriminations transferred better to learning set than repeated reversals of a single discrimination, although the difference was not statistically reliable.

If learning win-stay, lose-shift for object cues underlies learning set, will practice on its components help? Behar and LeBedda (1974) used a novel procedure to train one group of monkeys on the win-stay component of a learning set strategy. For example, for win-stay subjects, the conditions for Trial 1 of a problem continued until an error was made (or until eight trials were completed). Experience with nonreward was given to the win-stay subjects by presenting them one-trial problems where neither choice was correct. Following this pretraining experience, subjects were given normal learning set training. The win-stay group was more likely than the lose-shift group to use a win-stay strategy and the lose-shift group was more likely than the win-stay group to use a lose-shift strategy on the normal learning set problems. There were no overall group differences in transfer performance. Although no appropriate comparison group was run, there was very little, if any, overall positive transfer. The subjects averaged only 60% correct over the first 100 problems of the learning set training.

Another question of theoretical interest is whether the win-stay, lose-shift experience is beneficial solely when it is associated with object cues. Here the picture is unclear. Warren (1966) reported that repeated reversals of a positional discrimination facilitated object discrimination learning set in monkeys, perhaps even as much as repeated reversals of a single object discrimination. More recently, however, Warren and Warren (1973) found no significant transfer between repeated reversals of a positional discrimination and repeated reversals of object discriminations. Clarity awaits further investigation.

III. LEARNING SET THEORIES

The preceding selective review indicates that in developing an account of learning set development, theories must address findings on selective coding, the informational aspects of reward, memory processes, and transfer of learning skills. I will now turn to a consideration of learning set theories, attempting to clarify their scope and to point out their strengths and weaknesses. Finally, I shall discuss how the theories generally seem to be working in advancing the analysis of learning to learn.

A. Reinforcement Theories

1. Spence's Theory

It may come as a surprise to many readers that Spence's (1936) original theory of discrimination learning predicts that learning to learn will occur. Spence conceived of discrimination learning as a cumulative process of building up the excitatory strength (or associative or habit strength) of the correct stimulus compound as compared with the competing excitatory strength of the incorrect stimulus compound. These strengths were assumed to be associated with the various stimulus components in a problem. Thus, if a monkey responds to a blue circle in the right position and is rewarded, the excitatory strengths of blue, circle, and right would all be incremented. Nonreward weakens the excitatory tendencies of the stimulus components of a compound by a negative process, known as inhibition.

The main factors in Spence's theory underlying improvement in the rate of learning object discriminations are: (1) the initial excitatory strengths associated with the two objects of a discrimination problem; (2) the difference in these initial strengths, which provides a basis for stimulus preferences; and (3) the difference in strengths of irrelevant cues, such as position, which must be overcome before a problem is solved. Initial strengths alter performance because Spence assumed that the effectiveness of a reward depends on the current excitatory strength of a component, with that effectiveness first increasing as excitatory strength increases to a high degree and then decreasing with further increases in excitatory strength. The change in strength produced by a nonreward increases linearly with increases in excitatory strength so that, overall, changes in excitatory strength are greatest when strengths are in the middle to high range. Differences in strength both for potentially relevant and for irrelevant cues serve to retard learning. A computer simulation of Spence's model by Medin (1974) using parameter values taken from the original Spence (1936) paper indicated that increases in the initial strengths of object cues are the main factor responsible for faster learning.

Reese (1964) provided a detailed analysis of a modified Hull-Spence theory in relation to learning set. The theory correctly predicts that early in learning set training a correct response reduces future errors more than an error, while later in training an error reduces future errors more than a success. The theory's other implications are that stimulus preferences must be overcome before efficient learning set performance can occur, and retention should be greater early in training than later.

There are, however, some problems with the theory. First of all, Spence's theory assumes that rewards have a direct and automatic strengthening function. Our review has indicated that the function of reinforcement is much more flexible than such an assumption implies, because, for example, monkeys are perfectly capable of learning problems involving win-shift or lose-stay solutions. A second problem is that stimulus preferences may not disappear as required by Spence's theory. Bessemer and Stollnitz (1971) describe clear evidence that stimulus preferences persist in learning-set-experienced animals and that these preferences are only temporarily suppressed during learning. The present analysis of memory processes during learning set formation suggests that retention does not show the predicted monotonic decline as the learning set develops. Finally, it has been suggested that Spence's theory cannot handle the observation that training on repeated reversals of a single discrimination shows strong positive transfer to learning set (e.g., Miles, 1965). I am not especially confident of this claim, because repeated reversal training would serve to reduce the difference in strengths of irrelevant cues and would also increase the initial strengths of object cues to an extent determined by the similarity of the single pair of stimuli to the set of stimuli used in the regular learning set procedure. Computer simulations of Spence's model would yield clearer predictions concerning the effects of repeated reversal training.

2. *A Feedback Theory*

According to a theory I advanced several years ago (Medin, 1972), a learning set develops because object cues come to have greater strength or feedback value than other cues. The theory assumes that rewards and nonrewards increase or decrease the expected feedback or anticipated reward value from the cue to which the animal responds. Choices are controlled by stimulus properties of cues (i.e., their saliance) and by expected feedback from previous rewards. The specific model assumed that a monkey responds to one of four cues: (a) one object, (b) the other object, (c) the left position, and (d) the right position. If the object cues are high enough in feedback value relative to other cues, virtually all choices will be controlled by object cues, and discriminations will be solved quickly.

The theory is different from Spence's theory in several respects. First of all, the feedback theory acknowledges the informational aspects of reward and denies that rewards and nonrewards work in an automatic manner. Second, the model draws a distinction between short- and long-term memory and allows for short-term loss of reward information. Third, the feedback theory assumes that individual cues control choices and subjects only learn about cues controlling responses, whereas Spence's theory assumes that choices are controlled by compounds and the subjects learn about each of the components comprising the chosen compound on a trial.

The two theories are similar in that they both assume that the mechanism controlling learning to learn is increased initial strength or feedback value for object cues. In a direct test of this idea (Medin, 1974), I trained pigtail monkeys on discrimination problems involving objects that had been previously paired with reward, previously paired with nonreward, or not used in any pretraining. Both theories predict that rewarded pretraining should facilitate learning; in addition, my theory predicts that nonrewarded pretraining should impair learning. Additional comparisons were included in the experiment to insure that the pretraining was effective. Latencies were recorded to see if discriminations comprised of objects previously paired with reward had shorter Trial 1 latencies than discriminations comprised of objects previously associated with nonreward. Also, following discrimination training, nondifferentially reinforced choice tests were given between objects pretrained with reward and objects pretrained with nonreward.

The latency and choice data indicated that the basic manipulation which was designed to produce differences in learning rate had been effective. Yet, in two separate experiments involving many observations, none of the predicted differences in learning rate were observed, although there was the usual interproblem improvement associated with learning set training. These results are inconsistent with both theories.

One possibility is that the strengths of the various cues in a problem are not independent. If the strength of, say, a position cue depends on its context (i.e., which particular objects cover the foodwell), then the pretraining experience would not place object cues at an advantage over position cues. In formalizing these assumptions concerning context, I have systematically explored predictions concerning the relative rates of learning various discrimination problems based on the assumption that, during learning, information concerning cues and the context in which they occur is stored together in memory, and the retrieval of information depends on the simultaneous activation of inputs from both a cue and its context (Medin, 1975). The context theory is quite successful in accounting for learning in a wide variety of discrimination learning paradigms, which leads me to question seriously the idea that cues are learned about in an independent manner. Consequently, I now think that if focusing attention on object cues underlies learning set formation, then some other mechanism must accomplish this selectivity. Some possibilities for such selectivity are considered below under the heading of attention theories (section III,C).

B. Hypothesis Theories

A major strength of hypothesis theories is that they treat reward as information. Strategies, in contrast to single responses, may incorporate Trial 1 outcomes as cues, and therefore a win-shift hypothesis is just as plausible as a win-stay hypothesis. Four versions of hypothesis theories, varying in explicitness, will be considered here.

1. Harlow's Error Factor Theory

Harlow (1949, 1959) proposed that response patterns of monkeys during learning set formation provide an informative supplement to proportion correct as a dependent variable. His uniprocess theory grew out of his analysis of these patterns or error factors. The correct response strategy is assumed to be immediately available but must compete with many inappropriate responses in the learning situation. According to Harlow's theory, learning set formation occurs when the monkey eliminates these error factors or "bad habits" and is left with the correct strategy (win-stay, lose-shift with respect to objects).

Although Harlow's theory was not developed in very much detail, it can still provide a general guide to research. Abordo and Rumbaugh (1965) trained squirrel monkeys on problems where the position of the correct and incorrect objects was switched on each trial following a correct response. This procedure was designed to reduce the error factor of position preference. When transferred to regular learning set procedures, these monkeys performed significantly better than a control group receiving only regular learning set procedures. Unfavorable to Harlow's theory are the findings reported by Bessemer and Stollnitz (1971) that stimulus preferences remain strong in learning-set-experienced monkeys.

2. Levine's Hypothesis Behavior Model

Levine's (1959, 1965) model includes both error-producing and reward-producing response patterns, hence the term hypothesis rather than error factor. He assumes that learning set occurs as a result of the strengthening of the correct hypothesis by 100% reinforcement and the gradual extinction of other hypotheses because of 50% reinforcement. These hypotheses are assumed to manifest themselves in the response patterns on a discrimination problem. The theory does not address within-problem learning and it is generally assumed that the same hypothesis is used throughout an individual discrimination. Levine gathered evidence for the theory by estimating the strengths of potential hypotheses (e.g., position alternation; win-stay, lose-shift with respect to objects) at a given stage of learning set training from a subset of the observed patterns and then using these estimates to predict the frequency of occurrence of the remaining response patterns. This enterprise has been moderately successful and in the last few years more efficient estimation procedures have been proposed which promise to further enhance the utility of this approach (Fisher, 1974; Thomson, 1972). In my opinion, Levine's technique has considerable heuristic value, regardless of the correctness or incorrectness of the underlying theory.

3. *Restle's Mathematical Model*

Restle (1958) was the first to propose hypothesis theory that directly addressed relationships between intraproblem and interproblem learning and detailed a mechanism for the acquisition of hypotheses. His explanation of learning set formation centers on an assumption of abstract cognition: "It is assumed that monkeys use an abstract understanding of the pattern of an LS experiment, transcending the 'stimulus-response' rule familiar in most theories of learning" (Restle, 1958, p. 77). The theory is an extension of Restle's (1955) theory of discrimination learning, which assumes that partially valid cues become adapted with respect to more valid cues present in an experimental situation (for some direct evidence see Wagner, Logan, Haberlandt, and Price, 1968). According to Restle, three classes of cues are available during learning set training: Type *a* cues, which are relevant and common to all problems; Type *b* cues, which are relevant within individual problems but which are not valid across problems; and Type *c* cues, which are not valid even within a problem. Learning set formation is seen to involve learning to use these abstract Type *a* cues and to ignore or adapt out invalid cues (Type *c*) and those valid within individual problems (Type *b* cues).

Restle cast his theory in explicit mathematical form and, with appropriate selection of parameter values, produced intraproblem and interproblem learning curves closely approximating real learning set data. If the parameters in the model are held constant, the theory predicts that giving a moderate number of trials per problem (twelve) will produce learning set formation in fewer total trials than giving just a few (three) trials per problem, a prediction inconsistent with the consensus that within a fairly broad range of trials per problem, learning set formation is a function of the total trials given (e.g., Levine, Levinson, & Harlow, 1959). One does not necessarily have to assume that parameter values will remain constant as the number of trials per problem is varied. The most glaring problem with the Restle theory is that it proposes that transfer suppression provides the basis for learning set formation. As already discussed, there is much evidence contrary to this idea.

4. *Bessemer's Theory*

We noted before that many response tendencies or error patterns seem to be suppressed only temporarily during learning. Bessemer proposed (Bessemer & Stollnitz, 1971) that sophisticated monkeys have developed and use relatively short-term information storage mechanisms that bridge the interval between information acquisitoion and its use, while naive monkeys either do not have or do not use these mechanisms (for a related view, see Meyer, 1971). He proposes that such mechanisms operate by "temporarily overriding other response tendencies and masking the slow-rate habit-formation mechanism of the naive monkey, which remains unmodified in the learning set experienced monkey" (Bessemer & Stollnitz, 1971, p. 54).

This theory focuses attention on the role of short-term memory in learning set performance. A major advantage of this approach is that it can address the question of where hypotheses come from. Bessemer points out that hypotheses may arise from learned associations of current response-outcome relations with prior trial events, which escapes the conceptual difficulty created by having to assume that all possible hypotheses preexist in the monkeys' minds. For example, if a monkey chooses object B and is rewarded and if the monkey remembers that it chose object A on the preceding trial and was rewarded, then it has the opportunity to learn or form the hypothesis, win-shift for object cues.

The chief new predictions arising from the Bessemer theory concern retention in relation to learning set. If the short-term storage decays in a matter of seconds, then learning set under a concurrent presentation procedure should be much more difficult than under a consecutive presentation procedure because the former method involves long intertrial intervals. Although there is not much favorable evidence on this point, Bessemer appears to be thinking in terms of short-term mechanisms lasting on the order of a few minutes. A clearer prediction is that learning-set-naive and learning-set-experienced monkeys should not differ on long-term retention tests inasmuch as the same slow-rate habit process should be controlling performance in either case. Our analysis of memory data, however, suggests that retention performance initially deteriorates and later improves as learning set training proceeds, regardless of whether retention is tested after seconds, minutes, or days.

5. *Summary*

Hypothesis theories, more than any other class of learning set theories, have clearly and directly stressed the cue or informational function of reward. This emphasis now receives wide attention throughout the animal learning literature (e.g., Mackintosh, 1974; Medin, 1976b; Rescorla, 1975). Aside from this one major issue, hypothesis theories have been characterized by a general lack of explicitness, particularly with respect to an analysis of intraproblem learning. It simply is not clear how to incorporate the accumulating findings on selective coding, memory, and transfer of learning set into these theories. To give one example, none of these theories addresses the finding that intradimensional shifts are learned faster than extradimensional shifts. On the other hand, these difficulties do not seem insurmountable. Bessemer has already proposed that hypotheses may arise from using a short-term storage mechanism to encode information concerning relationships between consecutive trial events, and a line of study relating properties of this short-term mechanism to the development of hypotheses could be quite fruitful. Capaldi (1971) has demonstrated the potential merits of such an approach in an analogous area of research. Overall, the main challenge to hypothesis theories is to show how the processes presumed to underlie learning set formation operate during the solution of individual problems and in other learning contexts.

C. Attention Theories

In its classic confrontations with continuity theory, noncontinuity theory seemed to have two main branches, one led by Krechevsky and emphasizing hypotheses, and the other led by Lashley and emphasizing selective attention. Hypothesis theories have always been popular in accounts of learning set formation, but attention theories have not received corresponding consideration. Attention theories have been concerned primarily with developing an account of within-problem learning and have used transfer tests mainly as a means of yielding evidence on processes assumed to operate during learning a discrimination. Perhaps the gaps in knowledge of the relationship between within-problem learning and learning set formation could be narrowed by efforts to apply attention theories to learning set formation.

The main idea underlying attention theories is that attention may be altered in such a way that relevant cues are more likely to be observed. To solve a discrimination, animals learn which dimension(s) to attend to and what values along that dimension to choose. Apart from this assumption, attention theories differ widely in detail and complexity (for a recent review, see Medin, 1976b). For example, one theory assumes that the effective similarity of two cues along a dimension is less when that dimension is attended to than when it is not, whereas other theories assume no generalization along observed dimensions and complete generalization for dimensions which are not observed. Attention theories can address most, if not all, of the phenomena that we reviewed in the section on selective coding and predict many between-problem transfer phenomena (such as the advantage of intra-dimensional over extradimensional shifts) that are outside the scope of hypothesis theories.

One apparent difficulty for attention theories is Schrier's (1971, 1972) finding that monkeys show excellent extradimensional transfer of learning set performance. Although such a result is awkward for some specific attention theories (e.g., Zeaman & House, 1963), these data can be used to develop theories in

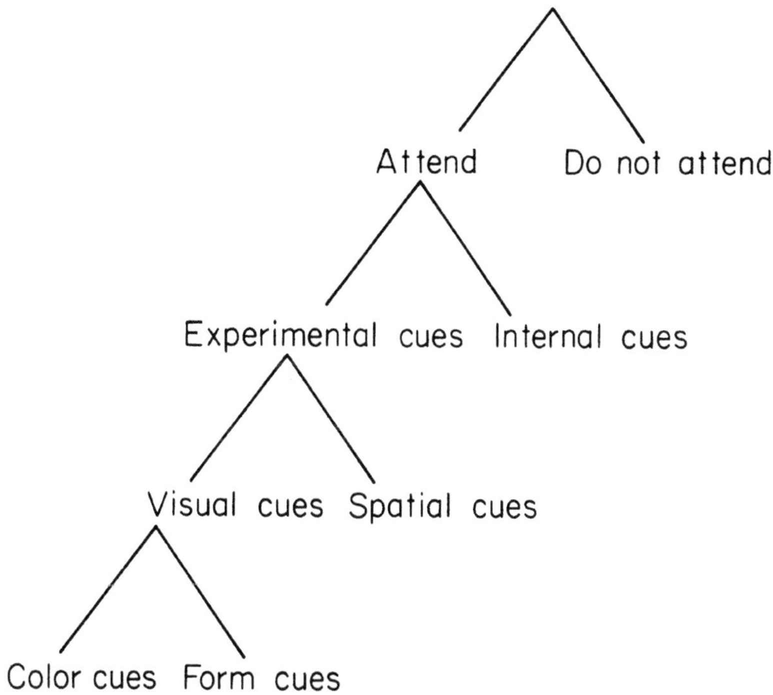

FIG. 2.8 A possible attentional hierarchy. It is assumed that when a lower level link is strengthened, associated higher level links will also be strengthened.

greater detail. For example, Sutherland and Andelman (1967) suggested that attention to dimensions may be arranged hierarchically. This possibility is represented in Figure 2.8. When a monkey solves a discrimination problem for which color is relevant, its tendency to attend to color should be increased and its tendency to attend to visual cues, experimental cues, or to attend at all also might be increased. From this one can generate such predictions as that extradimensional transfer from color discrimination learning set to form discrimination learning set should be greater than extradimensional transfer from position discrimination learning set[1] to form discrimination learning set. The only evidence I know that might bear on this point is that cross-modal transfer of

[1] A position discrimination learning set paradigm involves introducing new objects every few trials, and for each set of objects, always associating one of the positions with reward, regardless of the particular trial setting. Sometimes the introduction of new objects indicating (from the experimenter's view) a new problem is accompanied by a change (reversal) in the rewarded position and sometimes not.

learning set is much weaker than the transfer Schrier has observed. Incidentally, Thomas (1970) has claimed that the top level of the hierarchy, learning in general to attend to cues, controls much of animal learning and transfer.

Attention theories have had much less to say about memory processes, but this need not remain so (e.g., Fisher & Zeaman, 1973). Recently, I proposed a theory (Medin, 1976a) combining the context model for discrimination learning (Medin, 1975) with the Estes (1955a, 1955b) stimulus fluctuation model. This theory has the potential of accounting for improvements in memory in terms of learning to attend to cues that will support retention.

IV. RELATIONSHIP BETWEEN HYPOTHESIS THEORIES AND ATTENTION THEORIES

Attention theories have not addressed the issue of reward as information as directly as have hypothesis theories. But now may be the time to ask if hypothesis theories really are very different from attention theories. My answer is that they are not very different at all. Both imply selective learning and both imply an organism actively processing information. The specific mechanisms for changing attention in the Zeaman and House (1963) theory could be incorporated without much modification as a mechanism for changing hypotheses in, for example, the Levine model. Likewise, following the Bessemer and Stollnitz (1971) suggestion, one might incorporate into an attention model a mechanism for associating memory for stimulus-outcome sequences from a preceding trial with current trial events.

One major barrier to interaction between attention theories and hypothesis theories is that hypothesis theories treat learning to attend to relevant dimensions and learning how to interpret reward information as inseparable parts of a single process, hypothesis selection. Attention theories, however, raise the possibility that stimulus selection and interpreting outcome information may be at least partially independent. Suppose for one group of monkeys we randomly intermix position alternation problems with object alternation problems and for a second group randomly intermix position alternation problems with normal object discriminations. Levine's hypothesis theory predicts no group differences in the rate of learning position alternation problems because in either case the animals would be viewed as learning when to use the two hypotheses. If, however, the idea of reward alternation is learned somewhat independently of learning which dimension is relevant, position alternation problems should be solved more easily when mixed with object alternation problems.

As a means of gathering more direct evidence on the issue of independence, I gave a few of my colleagues problems involving mixtures of hypotheses. Although the number of subjects involved was small, position alternation problems mixed with object alternation problems were learned better than position alternation problems mixed with object-stay problems. Position alternation problems mixed with position-stay problems were easier than position alternation problems mixed with object-stay problems. In short, the human data support the idea of at least partial independence between interpreting reward information and learning to attend to the relevant dimension. Warren's (1966) finding of positive transfer by rhesus monkeys from repeated position reversals to object discrimination learning set supports this conclusion.

One might patch up hypothesis theories by proposing that when a hypothesis is rewarded, subjects increase their tendency to sample similar hypotheses. For example, if a position alternation hypothesis is rewarded, subjects might be more likely to sample other hypotheses involving position (e.g., position-stay) and other hypotheses involving reward alternation (e.g., object alternation). Note, however, that this modification in hypothesis theories is exactly the step needed to remove the barrier between hypothesis theories and attention theories. With this barrier removed, the cumulative evidence on selective attention during within-problem learning can be used to construct a generation of hybrid models concerned with the relationship between learning to attend to relevant dimensions and learning to interpret outcome information.

The above considerations lead me to think that a useful strategy would be to gloss over the differences between attention theories and hypothesis theories for a while as a means of bringing information concerning processes operating during within-problem learning to bear on theoretical accounts of learning set formation. For now the main question seems to be not which particular theory is most nearly correct but rather which theories can be extended to address the flood of new data concerning the cognitive skills of animals. I believe that an information-processing view of learning set formation most clearly indicates a rationale for ending the segregation of learning set research from the main body of research on learning and memory in animals and a means of developing more cogent theoretical accounts of the processes by which animals learn how to learn.

ACKNOWLEDGMENTS

This research was supported by United States Public Health Service Grants MH 25134 and MH 16100. Cathy Lee, Donald Robbins, Mark Altom, and Donald Meyer read earlier drafts of this paper and provided helpful suggestions.

REFERENCES

Abordo, E. J., & Rumbaugh, D. M. Response contingent learning set training in the squirrel monkey. *Psychological Reports,* 1965, **16,** 797–802.

Balogh, B. A., & Zimmermann, R. R. Short-term retention of object discriminations in experienced and naive rhesus monkeys. *Perceptual and Motor Skills,* 1971, **33,** 543–549.

Bartus, R. T., & LeVere, T. Storage and utilization of information within a discrimination trial. In D. L. Medin, W. A. Roberts, & R. T. Davis (Eds.), *Processes of animal memory.* Hillsdale, New Jersey: Lawrence Earlbaum Associates, 1976.

Behar, I. Analysis of object-alternation learning in rhesus monkeys. *Journal of Comparative and Physiological Psychology,* 1961, **54,** 539–542.

Behar, I. Evaluation of the significance of the positive and negative cue in discrimination learning. *Journal of Comparative and Physiological Psychology,* 1962, **55,** 502–504.

Behar, I. Formation of extinction sets in monkeys. *Bulletin of the Psychonomic Society,* 1973, **2,** 367–369.

Behar, I., & LeBedda, J. M. Effects of differential pretraining on learning set formation in rhesus monkeys. *Journal of Comparative and Physiological Psychology,* 1974, **87,** 227–283.

Bessemer, D. W., & Stollnitz, F. Retention of discrimination and an analysis of learning set. In A. M. Schrier & F. Stollnitz (Eds.), *Behavior of nonhuman primates* (Vol. 4). New York: Academic Press, 1971.

Blomquist, A. J., Deets, A. C., & Harlow, H. F. Effects of list length and first-trial reward upon concurrent discrimination performance. *Learning and Motivation,* 1973, **4,** 28–39.

Brown, W. L., & Carr, R. M. The learning of incidental cues by rhesus monkeys. *Journal of Comparative and Physiological Psychology,* 1958, **51,** 459–460.

Brown, W. L., & McDowell, A. A. Response shift learning set in monkeys. *Journal of Comparative and Physiological Psychology,* 1963, **56,** 335–336.

Brown, W. L., McDowell, A. A., & Gaylord, H. A. Two-trial learning set formations by baboons and by stump-tailed macaques. *Journal of Comparative and Physiological Psychology,* 1965, **60,** 288–289.

Brown, W. L., Overall, J. E., & Blodgett, H. C. Novelty learning sets in rhesus monkeys. *Journal of Comparative and Physiological Psychology,* 1959, **52,** 330–332.

Capaldi, E. J. Memory and learning: A sequential viewpoint. In W. K. Honig and P. H. R. James (Eds.), *Animal memory.* New York: Academic Press, 1971.

Connor, J. B., & Meyer, D. R. Assessment of the role of transfer suppression in learning set formation in monkeys. *Journal of Comparative and Physiological Psychology,* 1971, **75,** 141–145.

Cross, H. A., & Brown, L. T. Discrimination reversal learning in squirrel monkeys as a function of number of acquisition trials and pre-reversal experience. *Journal of Comparative and Physiological Psychology,* 1965, 54, 429–431.

Cross, H. A., Fletcher, H. J., & Harlow, H. F. Effects of prior experience with test stimuli on learning set performance of monkeys. *Journal of Comparative and Physiological Psychology,* 1963, **56,** 204–207.

Darby, C. L., & Riopelle, A. J. Differential proglem sequences and the formation of learning sets. *Journal of Psychology,* 1955, **39,** 105–108.

Darby, C. L., & Riopelle, A. J. Observational learning in the rhesus monkey. *Journal of Comparative and Physiological Psychology,* 1959, **52,** 94–98.

Davis, R. T. Problem-solving behavior of monkeys as a function of work variables. *Journal of Comparative and Physiological Psychology,* 1956, **49,** 499–506.

Davis, R. T. Monkeys as perceivers. In L. A. Rosenblum (Ed.), *Primate behavior: Developments in field and laboratory research* (Vol. 3). New York: Academic Press, 1974.

Davis, R. T., McDowell, A. A., & Thorson, N. Four-trial object-quality discrimination learning by monkeys. *Proceedings of the South Dakota Academy of Science,* 1953, **32,** 132–142.

Deets, A. C., Harlow, H. F., & Blomquist, A. J. Effects of intertrial interval and trial 1 reward during acquisition of an object-discrimination learning set in monkeys. *Journal of Comparative and Physiological Psychology,* 1970, **73,** 501–505.

Devine, J. V. Stimulus attributes and training procedures in learning set formation in monkeys. *Journal of Comparative and Physiological Psychology,* 1970, **73,** 62–67.

Draper, W. A. Cue dominance in oddity discriminations by rhesus monkeys. *Journal of Comparative and Physiological Psychology,* 1965, **60,** 140–141.

Estes, W. K. Statistical theory of distributional phenomena in learning. *Psychological Review,* 1955, **62,** 369–377. (a)

Estes, W. K. Statistical theory of spontaneous recovery and regression. *Psychological Review,* 1955, **62,** 145–154. (b)

Fisher, M. A. Estimating hypothesis strengths. *Behavior Research Methods and Instrumentation,* 1974, **6,** 309–311.

Fisher, M. A., & Zeaman, D. An attention-retention theory of retardate discrimination learning. In N. R. Ellis (Ed.), *International review of research in mental retardation* (Vol. 6). New York: Academic Press, 1973.

Gentry, G. V., Overall, J. E., & Brown, W. L. Discrimination after pretraining on component stimuli. *Journal of Comparative and Physiological Psychology,* 1958, **51,** 464–466.

Gonzalez, R. C., Behrend, E. R., & Bitterman, M. E. Reversal learning and forgetting in bird and fish. *Science,* 1967, **158,** 519–521.

Harlow, H. F. The formation of learning sets. *Psychological Review,* 1949, **56,** 51–65.

Harlow, H. F. Analysis of discrimination learning by monkeys. *Journal of Experimental Psychology,* 1950, **40,** 26–39.

Harlow, H. F. Learning set and error factor theory. In S. Koch (Ed.), *Psychology: A study of a science* (Vol. 2). New York: McGraw-Hill, 1959.

Harlow, H. F., & Warren, J. M. Formation and transfer of discrimination learning sets. *Journal of Comparative and Physiological Psychology,* 1952, **45,** 482–489.

Herman, L. M., & Arbeit, W. R. Stimulus control and auditory discrimination learning sets in the bottlenose dolphin. *Journal of the Experimental Analysis of Behavior,* 1973, **19,** 379–394.

Herman, L. M., Beach, F. A. III, Pepper, R. L., & Stallings, R. B. Learning set formation in the bottlenose dolphin. *Psychonomic Science,* 1969, **14,** 98–99.

Hodos, W. Evolutionary interpretation of neural and behavioral studies of living vertebrates. In F. O. Schmidt (Ed.), *The neurosciences: Second study program.* New York: Rockefeller University Press, 1970.

Honig, W. K., & James, P. H. R. *Animal memory.* New York: Academic Press, 1971.

Kamil, A. C., & Mauldin, J. E. Intra-problem retention during learning set acquisition in bluejays (Cyanocitta cristata). *Animal Learning and Behavior,* 1975, *3,* 125–130.

Kamin, L. J. Predictability, surprise, attention, and conditioning. In R. M. Church & B. A. Campbell (Eds.), *Punishment and aversive behavior.* New York: Appleton-Century-Crofts, 1969.

King, J. E. Transfer relationships between learning set and concept formation in rhesus monkeys. *Journal of Comparative and Physiological Psychology,* 1966, **61,** 416–420.

King, J. E. Determinants of serial discrimination learning by squirrel monkeys. *Learning and Motivation,* 1971, **2,** 246–254.

King, J. E., & Goodman, R. Successive and concurrent discrimination by rock squirrels and squirrel monkeys. *Perceptual and Motor Skills,* 1966, **23,** 703–710.

Komaki, J. The influence of overtraining and successive reversal training on strategic behavior of Japanese monkeys. *Japanese Psychological Research,* 1974, **16,** 149–156.

Leary, R. W. Analysis of serial-discrimination learning by monkeys. *Journal of Comparative and Physiological Psychology,* 1958, **51,** 82–86.

Levine, M. A model of hypothesis behavior in discrimination learning set. *Psychological Review,* 1959, **66,** 353–366.

Levine, M. Hypothesis behavior. In A. M. Schrier, H. F. Harlow, & F. Stollnitz (Eds.), *Behavior of nonhuman primates: Modern research trends.* (Vol. 1). New York: Academic Press, 1965.

Levine, M., Levinson, B., & Harlow, H. F. Trials per problem as a variable in the acquisition of discrimination learning set. *Journal of Comparative and Physiological Psychology,* 1959, **52,** 396–398.

Lockhart, J. M., Parks, T. E., & Davenport, J. W. Information acquired in one trial by learning set experienced monkeys. *Journal of Comparative and Physiological Psychology,* 1963, **56,** 1035–1037.

Mackintosh, N. J. *The psychology of animal learning.* New York: Academic Press, 1974.

Mason, W. A., Blazek, N. C., & Harlow, H. F. Learning capacities of the infant rhesus monkey. *Journal of Comparative and Physiological Psychology,* 1956, **49,** 449–453.

McDowell, A. A., & Brown, W. L. Learning mechanism in response perseveration learning sets. *Journal of Comparative and Physiological Psychology,* 1963, **56,** 1032–1034. (a)

McDowell, A. A., & Brown, W. L. The learning mechanism in response shift learning set. *Journal of Comparative and Physiological Psychology,* 1963, **56,** 572–574. (b)

McDowell, A. A., & Brown, W. L. Sex and radiation as factors in peripheral cue discrimination learning. *Journal of Genetic Psychology,* 1963, **102,** 261–265. (c)

McDowell, A. A., & Brown, W. L. Further evidence for excitatory properties of nonrewarded cues. *Journal of Genetic Psychology,* 1965, **106,** 137–140. (a)

McDowell, A. A., & Brown, W. L. Learning mechanisms in response shift learning set to nonrewarded cues. *Journal of Genetic Psychology,* 1965, **106,** 173–176. (b)

McDowell, A. A., & Brown, W. L. Perseveration learning set formation to nonrewarded cues by normal and previously irradiated rhesus monkeys. *Journal of Genetic Psychology,* 1965, **107,** 309–311. (c)

McDowell, A. A., & Brown, W. L. Response perseveration under constant stimulus-position conditions by normal and previously irradiated female rhesus monkeys. *Journal of Genetic Psychology,* 1965, **106,** 81–84. (d)

McDowell, A. A., & Brown, W. L. Response shift learning set formation by normal and previously irradiated female rhesus monkeys. *Journal of Genetic Psychology,* 1965, **72,** 339–342. (e)

McDowell, A. A., Gaylord, H. A., & Brown, W. L. Learning set formation by naive rhesus monkeys. *Journal of Genetic Psychology,* 1965, **106,** 253–257. (a)

McDowell, A. A., Gaylord, H. A., & Brown, W. L. Perseveration learning set formation by monkeys with previous discrimination training. *Journal of Genetic Psychology,* 1965, **106,** 345–347. (b)

Medin, D. L. Role of reinforcement in discrimination learning set in monkeys. *Psychological Bulletin,* 1972, **77,** 305–318.

Medin, D. L. Reward pretraining and discrimination learning set. *Animal Learning and Behavior,* 1974, **2,** 305–308.

Medin, D. L. A theory of context in discrimination learning. In G. H. Bower (Ed.), *The psychology of learning and motivation.* (Vol. 9). New York: Academic Press, 1975.

Medin, D. L. Animal models and memory models. In D. L. Medin, W. A. Roberts, & R. T. Davis (Eds.), *Processes of animal memory.* Hillsdale, New Jersey: Lawrence Erlbaum Associates, 1976. (a)

Medin, D. L. Theories of discrimination learning and learning set. In W. K. Estes (Ed.), *Handbook of learning and cognitive processes* (Vol. 3). Hillsdale, New Jersey: Lawrence Erlbaum Associates, 1976. (b)

Medin, D. L. Status of unchosen objects in discrimination learning by monkeys. *Bulletin of the Psychonomic Society,* 1977, **9,** 118–120.

Medin, D. L., & Davis, R. T. Formation of a successive (sign-differentiated-position) learning set in stumptail monkeys. *Perceptual and Motor Skills,* 1968, **27,** 835–838.

Medin, D. L., Roberts, W. A., & Davis, R. T. *Processes of animal memory.* Hillsdale, New Jersey: Lawrence Erlbaum Associates, 1976.

Meyer, D. R. Intraproblem-interproblem relationships in learning by monkeys. *Journal of Comparative and Physiological Psychology,* 1951, **44,** 162–167.

Meyer, D. R. The habits and concepts of monkeys. In L. E. Jarrard (Ed.), *Cognitive processes of nonhuman primates.* New York: Academic Press, 1971.

Meyer, D. R., Treichler, F. R., & Meyer, P. M. Discrete-trial training techniques and stimulus variables. In A. M. Schrier, H. F. Harlow, & F. Stollnitz (Eds.), *Behavior of nonhuman primates: Modern research trends* (Vol. 1). New York: Academic Press, 1965.

Miles, R. C. Discrimination-learning sets. In A. M. Schrier, H. F. Harlow, & F. Stollnitz (Eds.), *Behavior of nonhuman primates: Modern research trends* (Vol. 1). New York: Academic Press, 1965.

Murphy, J. V., & Miller, R. E. The effect of spatial contiguity of cue and reward in the object quality learning of rhesus monkeys. *Journal of Comparative and Physiological Psychology,* 1955, **48,** 221–224.

Pastore, R. E., & Scheirer, C. J. Signal detection theory: Considerations for general application. *Psychological Bulletin,* 1974, **81,** 945–958.

Reese, H. W. Discrimination learning set in rhesus monkeys. *Psychological Bulletin,* 1964, **61,** 321–340.

Rescorla, R. A. Pavlovian excitatory and inhibitory conditioning. In W. K. Estes (Ed.), *Handbook of learning and cognitive processes.* (Vol. 2). Hillsdale, N. J.: Lawrence Erlbaum Associates, 1975.

Rescorla, R. A., & Wagner, A. R. A theory of Pavlovian conditioning: Variations in the effectiveness of reinforcement and nonreinforcement. In A. H. Black & W. F. Prokasy (Eds.), *Classical conditioning II.* New York: Appleton-Century-Crofts, 1972.

Restle, F. A theory of discrimination learning. *Psychological Review,* 1955, **62,** 11–19.

Restle, F. Toward a quantitative description of learning set data. *Psychological Review,* 1958, **65,** 77–91.

Ricciardi, A. M., & Treichler, F. R. Prior training influences transfer to learning set by squirrel monkeys. *Journal of Comparative and Physiological Psychology,* 1970, **73,** 314–319.

Riopelle, A. J. Transfer suppression and learning sets. *Journal of Comparative and Physiological Psychology,* 1953, **46,** 108–114.

Riopelle, A. J. Learning sets from minimum stimuli. *Journal of Experimental Psychology,* 1955, **49,** 28–32.

Riopelle, A. J., & Chinn, R. McC. Position habits and discrimination learning by monkeys. *Journal of Comparative and Physiological Psychology,* 1961, **54,** 178–180.

Riopelle, A. J., Chronholm, J. N., & Addison, R. G. Stimulus familiarity and multiple discrimination learning. *Journal of Comparative and Physiological Psychology,* 1962, **55,** 274–278.

Riopelle, A. J., & Churukian, G. A. The effect of varying the intertrial interval in discrimination learning by normal and brain-operated monkeys. *Journal of Comparative and Physiological Psychology,* 1958, **51,** 119–125.

Riopelle, A. J., & Francisco, E. W. Discrimination learning performance under different first-trial procedures. *Journal of Comparative and Physiological Psychology,* 1955, **48,** 143–145.

Riopelle, A. J., Francisco, E. W., & Ades, H. E. Differential first-trial procedures and discrimination learning performance. *Journal of Comparative and Physiological Psychology,* 1954, **47,** 293–297.
Riopelle, A. J., & Kumaran, M. B. Learning of repeated and nonrepeated discrimination-reversal problems by patas monkeys. *Journal of Comparative and Physiological Psychology,* 1971, **74,** 185–191.
Riopelle, A. J., & Moon, W. H. Problem diversity and familiarity in multiple discrimination learning by monkeys. *Animal Behavior,* 1968, **16,** 74–78.
Rohles, R. H., Belleville, R. E., & Grunzke, M. E. Measurement of the higher intellectual functioning in the chimpanzee. *Aerospace Medicine,* 1961, **32,** 121–125.
Rothblat, L. A., & Wilson, W. A. Intradimensional and extradimensional shifts in the monkey within and across sensory modalities. *Journal of Comparative and Physiological Psychology,* 1968, **66,** 549–553.
Rumbaugh, D. M., & Prim, M. M. Temporary interference of insolvable discrimination reversal training upon learning set in the squirrel monkey. *Journal of Comparative and Physiological Psychology,* 1964, **57,** 302–304.
Rumbaugh, D. M., Sammons, M. E., Prim, M. M., & Phillips, S. Learning set in squirrel monkeys as affected by pretraining with differentially rewarded single objects. *Perceptual and Motor Skills,* 1965, **21,** 63–70.
Schrier, A. M. Transfer by macaque monkeys between learning set and repeated reversal tasks. *Perceptual and Motor Skills,* 1966, **23,** 787–792.
Schrier, A. M. Learning set without transfer suppression: A replication and extension. *Psychonomic Science,* 1969, **16,** 263–265.
Schrier, A. M. Extradimensional transfer of learning set formation in stumptailed monkeys. *Learning and Motivation,* 1971, **2,** 173–181.
Schrier, A. M. Learning set formation and transfer in rhesus and talapoin monkeys. *Folia Primatologica,* 1972, **17,** 389–396.
Schrier, A. M. Transfer between the repeated reversal and learning set tasks: A reexamination. *Journal of Comparative and Physiological Psychology,* 1974, **87,** 1004–1010.
Schusterman, R. J. Transfer effects of successive discrimination reversal training in chimpanzees. *Science,* 1962, **137,** 422–423.
Schusterman, R. J. Successive discrimination reversal training and multiple discrimination training in one–trial learning by chimpanzees. *Journal of Comparative and Physiological Psychology,* 1964, **58,** 153–156.
Shell, W. F., & Riopelle, A. J. Progressive discrimination learning in platyrrhine monkeys. *Journal of Comparative and Physiological Psychology,* 1958, **51,** 467–470.
Shepp, B. E., & Schrier, A. M. Consecutive intradimensional and extradimensional shifts in monkeys. *Journal of Comparative and Physiological Psychology,* 1969, **67,** 199–203.
Singh, S. D., & Lewis, J. K. An evaluation of transfer suppression phenomenon at different stages of learning-set formation. *Primates,* 1974, **15,** 205–208.
Slotnick, B. M., & Katz, H. Olfactory learning-set performance in rats. *Science,* 1974, **185,** 796–798.
Smith, H. J., King, J. E., & Newberry, P. Facilitation of discrimination learning set in squirrel monkeys by colored food stimuli. *Bulletin of the Psychonomic Society,* 1976, **7,** 5–8.
Spence, K. W. The nature of discrimination learning in animals. *Psychological Review,* 1936, **43,** 421–449.
Stollnitz, F. Spatial variables, observing responses, and discrimination learning sets. *Psychological Review,* 1965, **72,** 247–261.
Stollnitz, F., & Schrier, A. M. Learning set without transfer suppression. *Journal of Comparative and Physiological Psychology,* 1968, **66,** 780–783.

Strong, P. N., Jr. Memory for object discriminations in the rhesus monkey. *Journal of Comparative and Physiological Psychology,* 1959, **52,** 333–335.

Strong, P. N., Jr. Learning and transfer of oddity as a function of apparatus and trials per problem. *Psychonomic Science,* 1965, **3,** 19–20.

Sutherland, N. S., & Andelman, L. Learning with one and two cues. *Psychonomic Science,* 1967, **15,** 253–254.

Sutherland, N. S., & Mackintosh, N. J. *Mechanisms of animal discrimination learning.* New York: Academic Press, 1971.

Takemura, K. [Inter-categorical transfer of discrimination learning sets in monkeys.] *Annual Animal Psychology,* 1960 **10,** 55–63.

Thomas, D. R. Stimulus selection, attention, and related matters. In J. H. Reynierse (Ed.), *Current issues in animal learning.* Lincoln, Nebraska: University of Nebraska Press, 1970.

Thomson, W. J. Least squares application of Levine's hypothesis model to missing reward sequence situations. *Psychological Bulletin,* 1972, **77,** 356–360.

Treichler, F. R. Transfer effects in monkey discrimination learning after extensive two–problem training. *Psychonomic Science,* 1966, **5,** 201–202.

Wagner, A. R., Logan, F. A., Haberlandt, K., & Price, T. Stimulus selection in animal discrimination learning. *Journal of Experimental Psychology,* 1968, **76,** 171–180.

Wagner, A. R., Rudy, J. W., & Whitlow, J. W. Rehearsal in animal conditioning. *Journal of Experimental Psychology Monographs,* 1973, **97,** 407–426.

Warren, J. M. Reversal learning and the formation of learning sets by cats and rhesus monkeys. *Journal of Comparative and Physiological Psychology,* 1966, **61,** 421.

Warren, J. M. Possibly unique characteristics of learning by primates. *Journal of Human Evolution,* 1974, **3,** 445–454.

Warren, J. M., & Sinha, M. M. Interaction, between learning sets in monkeys. *Journal of Genetic Psychology,* 1959, **95,** 19–25.

Warren, J. M., & Warren, H. B. Pretraining and discrimination reversal learning by rhesus monkeys. *Animal Learning and Behavior,* 1973, **1,** 52–56.

Wilson, M., & Wilson, W. A. Intersensory facilitation of learning sets in normal and brain-operated monkeys. *Journal of Comparative and Physiological Psychology,* 1962, **55,** 931–934.

Winograd, E. Some issues relating animal memory to human memory. In W. K. Honig & P. H. R. James (Eds.), *Animal memory.* New York: Academic Press, 1971.

Wright, P. L., Kay, H., & Sime, M. E. The establishment of learning sets in rats. *Journal of Comparative and Physiological Psychology,* 1963, **56,** 200–203.

Zable, M., & Harlow, H. F. The performance of rhesus monkeys on series of object-quality and positional discriminations and discrimination reversals. *Journal of Comparative Psychology,* 1946, **39,** 13–23.

Zeaman, D., & House, B. J. The role of attention in retardate discrimination learning. In N. R. Ellis (Ed.), *Handbook of mental deficiency.* New York: McGraw-Hill, 1963.

Zimmermann, R. R. Effects of age, experience and malnourishment on object retention in learning set. *Perceptual and Motor Skills,* 1969, **28,** 867–876.

3

Interactions Between Sensory Modalities in Nonhuman Primates

George Ettlinger

The Institute of Psychiatry, London

I. INTRODUCTION

In the past 20 years there have been a rapidly increasing number of experiments on the equivalence of sensory inflow from different sense-modalities. The earliest work was on man (Cannon, 1955; Gaydos, 1956; Jastrow, 1886; Kelvin & Mulik, 1958; Krauthamer, 1959), generally in the area now termed cross-modal matching or recognition. Excluding studies of single animals (Klüver, 1936; Lögler, 1959) and nonspecific training effects in fish (Schiller, 1933) and rats (Wylie, 1919), which might not have been genuinely cross-modal (Ettlinger, 1960), the two earliest investigations on animals reported conflicting findings. Stepien and Cordeau (1960) described dramatic cross-modal equivalence between complex auditory and visual training in vervet monkeys (*Cercopithecus aethiops*). However, Ettlinger (1960) and Burton and Ettlinger (1960) found no evidence of cross-modal equivalence between vision and touch or vision and audition in their rhesus monkeys (*Macaca mulatta*) that were trained to make simple discriminations.

Since 1960 there has been notable progress in two directions. Theoretically, distinctions between different kinds of cross-modal performance have come to be recognized as important—and thereby apparent discrepancies between observations of different kinds have been resolved. Empirically, the design of experiments has been much improved, novel methods have been devised, and a large body of observations on a wide range of species has accumulated. Nevertheless, unsolved problems remain at almost every level, as is evident from the recent reviews on aspects of cross-modal performance by Bryant (1974), Ettlinger (1973), Freides (1974), and von Wright (1970). The aim of the present review is to reconsider cross-modal equivalence, both theoretically, in order to define the issues and clarify the possible outcomes of experiments, and empirically, in order to evaluate the actual outcomes and present an up-to-date description of cross-modal equivalence. Emphasis will fall on work with nonhuman primates, although reference will be made to observations on man and on nonprimate mammals where appropriate.

II. THEORETICAL CONSIDERATIONS

A. Classes of Sensory Interaction

1. Kinds of Performance Not Further Considered

Certain kinds of cross-modal performance will not be further considered in this review. First, stimuli presented in one sense-modality could influence the psychophysical thresholds determined by presenting stimuli in another sense-modality. In this situation, within-modality thresholds would be altered by concurrent or virtually concurrent stimulation in another sense-modality. Second, stimuli in one sense-modality could be psychophysically equated, by scaling, with stimuli in another sense-modality, but by reference to some physically independent rather than essential, communal quality. Thus visual and olfactory stimuli might be scaled for equal "brightness." Third, stimuli in one sense-modality could constitute instructions to the subject as to how to respond in a task presented in a different sense-modality. In such "cross-modal conditional responding" a red light could indicate that response to the larger tactile object is correct, and a green light that response to the smaller tactile object is correct. Fourth, stimulus onset could be the signal for a response, and the sense-modality of the stimuli could subsequently be altered. Thus a sound could substitute for a light as a signal. (For the purposes of this review, situations involving the onset of single stimuli in one sense-modality–e.g., "respond to the tone but not to the absence of a tone"–and those involving differential stimulation within one sense-modality–e.g., "respond to a particular tone but respond differently to another tone"–will be treated as distinct, although the evidence to justify this distinction is not compelling.) Fifth, words belonging to a natural language could be presented to mediate performance in separate sense-modalities. None of these situations will be considered in this review of sensory interactions.

2. Bi-modal Performance

Stimuli can be experienced concurrently in more than one sense-modality: this concurrence is what distinguishes bi-modal from cross-modal performance. For example, an object can be both palpated and seen, or a temporal sequence can be both heard and seen. The inflow can subsequently be restricted to each sense-modality separately and an evaluation made whether learning occurred in both sense-modalities. Thus an experimenter can train a subject to discriminate between temporal sequences or patterns which are concurrently heard and seen, and can then present the same patterns in each sense-modality individually and require the previous discrimination. Alternatively, bi-modal matching can be evaluated (see below for details of such an experiment). A positive outcome (i.e., good performance in both sense-modalities) would not imply cross-modal equivalence, which might or might not be observed in separate experiments. However, a negative outcome on bi-modal tasks (i.e., deficient performance in one sense-modality) would confirm negative findings in work on cross-modal equivalence. This is so because a negative bi-modal transfer experiment would indicate uni-modal learning, despite bi-modal opportunities, and also deficient cross-modal equivalence. A negative bi-modal matching experiment would indicate uni-modal perception, despite bi-modal opportunities, and also deficient cross-modal equivalence. For even if the subject were to perceive or learn uni-modally when given bi-modal opportunities, the outcome should nonetheless have been positive if cross-modal equivalence were operative. Therefore a negative outcome would suggest that cross-modal equivalence is not operative. A negative outcome with bi-modal matching would be more important than with bi-modal transfer since uni-modal learning could occur despite bi-modal perception, but bi-modal learning is unlikely to occur with uni-modal perception.

3. Cross-modal Matching, Comparisons, and Recognition

These three terms have often been used interchangeably to describe one and the same kind of cross-modal equivalence. However, some workers have applied the terms to three kinds of situation differing in procedural detail. According to this distinction, cross-modal matching involves one of a set of stimuli being presented in one sense-modality and the total set, including the sample, in another sense-modality. The presentations in the two sense-modalities can be concurrent or virtually concurrent. The subject can be required to identify the stimulus in the total set that is identical to the sample. The stimuli within the total set can differ qualitatively (e.g., different objects) in cross-modal matching. The term cross-modal comparisons, however, is sometimes restricted to situations in which all stimuli can be ordered along a single dimension (e.g., size) so that they differ only quantitatively. The subject can still be required to identify the stimulus in the total set that is quantitatively the same as the sample in another sense-modality. In cross-modal recognition, the stimuli can be the same as in cross-modal matching, but either the interval between presentation of the sample and of the set can be prolonged (so that cross-modal recognition = successive cross-modal matching or delayed cross-modal matching) or the set can be changed from trial to trial.

Essentially the distinctions between cross-modal matching, cross-modal comparisons, and cross-modal recognition are procedural, and although different processes may be involved in each performance, this possibility has not been tested. Indeed, cross-modal matching, cross-modal comparisons, and cross-modal recognition could all be subsumed under the term "cross-modal perception" when sample and set are presented concurrently, and under "cross-modal recognition" when an interval is enforced between the presentation of the sample and of the set. However, again there would be no strong evidence that cross-modal perception and recognition were separate processes. Nor has it yet been shown that the processes of cross-modal matching, cross-modal comparisons, and cross-modal recognition differ according to the two modalities that are tested, although to the experimenter "identities" can exist between visual and tactile stimuli whereas only "analogies" can exist between visual and auditory or visual and olfactory stimuli. This distinction between identity and analogy is valid because visual and tactile stimuli have a common source whereas visual and auditory stimuli rarely correspond in normal experience.

4. *Cross-modal Transfer*

Because in studies of man it is easier to assess cross-modal matching than cross-modal transfer, whereas the converse is true for nonhuman animals, there was some confusion in the early literature. There are accepted procedural differences between the two kinds of experiment: explicit instructions or opportunities to detect cross-modal equivalence in the matching but not in the transfer experiment; no necessary change of performance *within* one sense-modality in matching instead of the expectation of such an intramodal *change* of performance in the transfer experiment; concurrent or virtually concurrent presentations in two sense-modalities in matching, but long intervals of minutes or days between presentations in different sense-modalities in transfer. A more important basis for distinguishing between cross-modal matching and cross-modal transfer is logical: good cross-modal transfer presupposes good cross-modal matching but good cross-modal matching does not presuppose good cross-modal transfer. Thus a clear demonstration of cross-modal transfer would imply the ability to match across sense-modalities, but good cross-modal matching could co-exist with poor or absent cross-modal transfer.

Since in cross-modal transfer it is essentially a *change* of performance within one sense-modality that could become manifest in another sense-modality, there can be as many different kinds of cross-modal transfer experiment as there are changes of performance within one sense-modality. There could be, for example, cross-modal transfer of specific discrimination learning; of learning-set formation; of within-modal conditional learning; of habituation, or of many other kinds of performance. In general, whenever the subject's performance has changed in one sense-modality, this change should be evident if cross-modal transfer is operative when the subject is placed in a similar situation in another sense-modality.

B. The Nature of Cross-modal Equivalence

In considering the kinds of organization likely to underlie cross-modal equivalence three main distinctions appear important: first, whether the organization is structurally determined or acquired; second, whether the modality of sensory inflow is or is not relevant; and third, whether or not the equivalence is achieved by the appreciation of actual similarity. In the light of empirical findings only four of the possible combinations of these variables appear to be probable.

1. Structurally Determined, Sense-modality Irrelevant

The position of an object in space is generally irrelevant to its recognition. Analogously, the organization of a mammalian brain could be such that inflow from each sense-modality leads to a single process of perception and recognition in which the sense-modality of the inflow is totally disregarded. (Although disregarded, the modality of inflow may, or may not, be discriminable as with location in space.)

2. Structurally Determined, Sense-modality Relevant

Alternatively, inflow from different sense-modalities might again lead to a single process of perception and recognition as a consequence of brain organization, but the sense-modality of the inflow might be treated as relevant. Although the object or stimulus is perceived or recognized as one and the same through different sense-modalities, the subject could normally distinguish and would normally register the sense-modality of the inflow.

3. Acquired, with True Equivalence

Due to brain organization, perception and recognition might take place separately (i.e., in different brain regions) for each sense-modality. Nevertheless, such individual modality-specific processes might come to be mapped one against the other so that, as a result of experience, perception or recognition in one sense-modality comes to evoke some truly equivalent process in another (relevant) sense-modality. Cross-modal equivalence might be achieved as a result of experience either (a) once and for all during early life so that, subsequently, unfamiliar inflow could be directly mapped in other sense-modalities by a system established in early life; or (b) there and then for each new inflow, so that cross-modal mapping of unfamiliar inflow is never accomplished without further learning.

4. Acquired, Conditionally

If brain organization entails separate perception and recognition for each sense-modality, then "accurate" cross-modal mapping (based on physical similarities) from one sense-modality to another might never be accomplished, irrespective of experience. Instead, stimuli in different sense-modalities might come to be associated merely as a consequence of temporal coincidence and relevance but irrespective of true similarity (as object-names bear no similarity to the objects).

Theoretically, it remains possible that cross-modal equivalence is organized differently in different species. (Certain possibilities, e.g., the role of language as cross-modal mediator, have purposely been excluded from consideration). It also remains possible that within one species cross-modal equivalence is organized differently for (a) different combinations of sense-modalities and/or (b) for different types of behavior.

C. Acceptable Standards of Evidence for Cross-modal Equivalence

1. *Cross-modal Matching*

a. "True"- and "false"- matching. As long ago as 1949 Lashley found it necessary to distinguish between what are now called "true"-matching and "false"-matching, although he was investigating within-modal and not cross-modal performance. In true-matching, the subject would perceive the equivalence of two stimuli possessing the same physical properties; in false-matching, the subject would have learned that an arbitrary correspondence exists between any two stimuli, irrespective of their physical properties. The human subject can readily distinguish these varieties of performance. In true-matching, the stimuli are described as similar in appearance, i.e., as sharing certain physical properties; in false-matching, stimulus A_1 is known to correspond to stimulus X_2, and B_1 to Y_2, in some lawful manner that is unrelated to their appearance. With animal subjects, however, the experimenter must determine the basis for the "match," if performance is to be termed "matching." For it is generally accepted that mammals can false-match across modalities by conditional learning: "if A_1 is presented in one sense-modality then choice of X_2 in another sense-modality is rewarded; if B_1 is shown in the former sense-modality, then Y_2 is correct in the latter." The identical strategy could also underlie apparent cross-modal matching of physically similar stimuli (i.e., "if A_1 is shown in one sense-modality, then A_2 is correct in another sense-modality; if B_1, then B_2 is correct," based not upon perception of similarity but on conditional learning).

Although the distinctions between true-matching and false-matching are well understood, it can be difficult in practice to differentiate the two performances. Three ways of distinguishing between these two kinds of performance are used. First, if good cross-modal performance is based on true-matching, then performance is likely to be maintained when new sets of stimuli that are physically similar in the two sense-modalities are introduced (whereas, if based on false-matching, it is likely initially to fall to chance until the new correspondence has been learned). However, the animal might have previously learned a special conditional strategy based on, for example, size: "If A_1 is larger than the middle of the range of previous stimuli in this sense-modality, then the larger of X_2 and Y_2 in the second sense-modality is correct; if A_1 is smaller, then the smaller of X_2 and Y_2 is correct" (Milner, 1971). Wilson (1972) has shown that such learning normally occurs within one modality. Then, provided the new stimuli differed appreciably in the relevant dimension, for example, size, a high level of cross-modal performance could be maintained even initially after the introduction of new sets of stimuli although performance would be based on conditional learning instead of true-matching. Second, if good cross-modal performance is based on true-matching, then performance is likely to fall to chance when new sets of physically unrelated stimuli, i.e., "false-object controls," are introduced in different sense-modalities. (If based on ordinary conditional false-matching, performance with new sets of physically unrelated stimuli is not in general likely to be inferior to performance with sets of physically similar stimuli.) However, in practice animals trained to true-match cannot be subjected to many "false-object controls" without risk of their performance deteriorating, because such control trials should be insoluble under a true-matching strategy. Third, if good cross-modal performance is based on true-matching, then performance is not likely to deteriorate when both samples in the first sense-modality and choice-objects in the second modality are displaced from the midpoint toward the same end of any dimension (e.g., size, texture), except possibly to a minimal extent as a consequence of the lesser discriminability of the two samples and two objects. In other words, the match chosen for a given sample should be independent of the set of samples or set of choice-objects. (If performance is based on Milner's conditional strategy, then it should fall to chance, provided the stimuli were displaced along the dimension relevant to the strategy.)[1]

b. Accuracy of the match. If A_1 and B_1 are stimuli in one sense-modality and A_2 and B_2 are equivalent stimuli in another sense-modality, it might seem that true-matching can be inferred if A_2 is reliably chosen when A_1 is the sample, and B_2 is chosen when B_1 is the sample. However, as already discussed

[1] Another procedure would be that devised by I. S. Russell (personal communication, 1975) in which three or more comparison objects are presented. The additional comparison objects (for which there are no samples) can vary in certain dimensions or features to determine whether the animal selects these features in preference to those possessed by the comparison objects (and samples). Yet another control procedure for the same kind of conditional strategy requires that sets of stimuli vary along only one dimension (e.g., size) and that the sets in the two sense-modalities are not identical but are displaced along the dimension relative to each other. Thus A_1 and D_1 might be offered in one modality and C_2 and F_2 in another; or C_1 and E_1 in one, B_2 and D_2 in the other, where A through F are stimuli varying in size or texture. With true-matching, performance should deteriorate (but not fall to chance, because of stimulus generalization). With false-matching, as proposed by Milner (1971), performance should be maintained, provided the stimuli were displaced along the dimension relevant to the strategy and fall one to each side of the midpoint of the dimension, even if all previous experience was with identical pairs of samples and objects.

in the previous section, this inference might not be valid even when the procedures described in that section have in general indicated true-matching instead of false-matching. Uncertainty persists if the outcome of any "control" procedure is ambiguous. Thus, for example, performance might not fall to chance with "false-object controls." The animal would then be responding to some equivalence between the samples and the nonequivalent "false-objects." This can happen because "false-object controls" cannot be made to differ from the samples in every respect; indeed, they can legitimately be chosen at random. (To meet this problem a control group could be trained to "non-match," i.e., select the nonequivalent object, so that nonequivalences in false-object controls could control performance.) The animal would, however, also be disregarding one or more nonequivalences between the samples and the nonequivalent "false-objects." If, say, performance differed significantly from chance when new "false-objects" were introduced that were nonequivalent with the samples in shape but were equivalent in size, the animal would be responding to the equivalence in size but to some extent neglecting the nonequivalence in shape. Perhaps it could likewise have been utilizing size but neglecting shape when required to match A_1 with A_2 and B_1 with B_2, i.e., in the absence of "false-object controls." This performance would have to be regarded as a very limited form of matching, particularly if the same single dimension is used on many probldms and the animal cannot use any other dimension although cues are available.

This argument leads to the conclusion that the current concept of cross-modal matching should be refined. For some authors, cross-modal matching seems to have been sufficiently established when responding to equivalences in at least one dimension, e.g. size, has been demonstrated. There are two main objections to this view. First, matching is generally (and properly) regarded as a process in which objects or stimuli, not single dimensions, are treated as equivalent. If an important dimension such as shape has been shown to be neglected, the process is at best only a partial match and should be termed "dimensional matching" or, more strictly, "dimensional-value matching" instead of "stimulus matching." (This line of argument does not imply that dimensional matching is without interest or cannot be distinguished from stimulus matching: rather that the positive outcome of a cross-modal experiment could, in principle, be of different kinds.) Second, we have seen in the previous section that a conditional strategy could be based on discrimination along a single dimension: "If A_1 is larger than the middle of the range of previous stimuli in this sense-modality, then choice of the larger of X_2 and Y_2 is correct; if A_1 is smaller, then the smaller of X_2 and Y_2 is correct." As the occurrence of cross-modal conditional learning is beyond dispute, the onus would seem to fall on the investigator to demonstrate by further control procedures that he has a new finding, namely true cross-modal "dimensional matching" instead of mere conditional performance.

The general problem of the evidence for cross-modal matching has been illustrated by a particular example, but others might have been chosen. Irrespective of which control findings are ambiguous, there are two conclusions: (a) "dimensional matching", i.e., a possible version of cross-modal equivalence in which the animal attends to only one dimension and thus could disregard major nonequivalences in one (or more) dimensions, should not be confused with "stimulus matching," i.e., cross-modal equivalence based on several or all dimensions, which is likely to have relevance to natural objects; and (b) the onus to show that any new cross-modal performance is not a consequence of conditional learning should rest with the investigator, because yet another instance of what is already known to occur is of little interest.

2. *Cross-modal Transfer*

a. Bridging stimuli. If the animal has learned to distinguish A_1 and B_1 in one sense-modality and is then offered equivalent stimuli A_2 and B_2 in another sense-modality, immediate or early good performance with A_2 and B_2 would seem to indicate cross-modal transfer. However, in practice stimuli are not easily confined rigorously to one sense-modality. Thus, if two rates of interruption of a light are to be discriminated and the onsets of the light flashing are accompanied by sounds, these sounds could act as a bridge (i.e., common element) between visual and auditory performance. Or, visual discrimination between objects may involve tactile experience if, for example, the hands displace the objects as part of the response. Then "transfer" to or from touch could be bridged by the bi-modal "visual" experience. Fortunately, the role of such bridging stimuli can often be readily evaluated: the light flashes can be occluded and, if sounds are emitted by the switching circuits, performance may remain above chance even without light stimuli; or, exclusively visual performance can be ensured by encasing objects in transparent covers or by requiring the animal to respond by pushing a handle or other constant feature instead of touching the object itself. In all cases the investigator should demonstrate, instead of assume, that bridging stimuli are not responsible for so-called transfer.

b. Specific and nonspecific transfer. Irrespective of the actual tasks involved, performance at discrimination learning tends to improve over weeks and months of training. This improvement is due to nonspecific factors such as increasing familiarity with the experimenter, test apparatus, test procedures, and so forth. Since transfer tests are sequential, performance in the sense-modality in which cross-modal transfer is assessed will follow after performance in the sense-modality of original learning, and will thereby benefit from nonspecific transfer effects. These have generally been taken into account when dealing with transfer of an individual discrimination. A control group will have been trained on the same number of tasks, albeit with a different training history, and comparisons are made at equal stages in the training histories of the experimental and control groups. However, a different procedure has generally been used in studies of cross-modal transfer of learning sets. One group, $V_1 T_2$, is trained first in vision and then in touch; the other, $T_1 V_2$, in the opposite order. Any superiority of performance at stage V_2 in comparison with V_1 is then attributed to "transfer of learning set" acquired at stage T_1, even though the V_2 but not V_1 group also has the benefit of non-specific prior experience at stage T_1; and likewise any superiority at T_2 relative to T_1 is attributed to cross-modal transfer of a set originating at stage V_1. However, cross-modal transfer can be inferred only if the experimental design includes an additional control group, or better two groups, C_vT_2 and C_tV_2, where C_v and C_t are visual and tactile control tasks from which no relevant set can be transferred to T_2 and V_2 (e.g. C = go-left, go-right). These two control groups permit an evaluation to be made of the magnitude of certain kinds of non-specific transfer. This should then be taken into account when interpreting comparisons between V_2 and V_1 and between T_2 and T_1.

III. EXPERIMENTAL OBSERVATIONS

A. Bi-modal Studies

1. *Bi-modal Matching.*

The writer knows of no investigations of this kind with animals, but the design is not complex. For instance, a sample object which is visible but cannot be palpated, has to be matched to comparison objects which are visible and available for palpation; then, the samples and objects have to be matched, the former only visible, the latter only available to touch. Alternatively, a sample object which is both visible and palpated has to be matched to objects which can only be palpated; then, both the samples and objects have to be matched exclusively by vision (or touch). Formally, either (a) A_1 and B_1 are samples in one sense-modality to be matched with A_{1+2} and B_{1+2} which are the same stimuli but presented in two sense-modalities—subsequently A_1 and B_1 have to be matched with A_2 and B_2, or A_2 and B_2 have to be matched with A_1 and B_1; or (b) A_{1+2} and B_{1+2} are samples presented in two sense-modalities, to be matched with A_1 and B_1—then A_2 and B_2 have to be matched with A_1 and B_1, or A_1 and B_1 have to be matched with A_2 and B_2. From the point of view of cross-modal equivalence the only important outcome would be clear deterioration in performance when bi-modal matching was changed to cross-modal matching. Deterioration would imply that the animal had neglected one sense-modality of the bi-modal stimuli in the initial matching, and that no compensation for such neglect had taken place through a process of cross-modal equivalence.

2. *Bi-modal Transfer*

In an early investigation of this kind by Ettlinger (1961), three groups of rhesus monkeys were trained on the same tactile task after either irrelevant visual training (Group I, N=8), or after bi-modal (i.e., visual and tactile) experience with the stimuli to be used in the tactile task (Group II, N=6; Group III, N=7). Groups I and II were treated identically during tactile training. Group III, however, received alternate visual and tactile trials at this stage, but the visual trials were discounted from the tactile learning scores. Group II's performance was found to be significantly superior to that of Group I, but no other differences attained significance. Combined visual and tactile experience can, therefore, promote accelerated tactile learning, but this effect seems to be small. In earlier work by Ettlinger (1960), four rhesus monkeys were trained first by touch and then with the same stimuli by vision and touch combined. Only one animal made immediate good use of its prior tactile experience when confronted with bi-modal stimuli. However, there was no control group in that study and bi-modal training was discontinued before learning to criterion was achieved.

No other explicit investigation of bi-modal transfer in primates is known to the author. However, this kind of transfer has represented a possible confounding factor in certain studies of cross-modal transfer (see the earlier discussion of bridging stimuli in Section II,C,2,a). For example, in the investigation of Ettlinger and Blakemore (1969) and in a recent study by Jarvis and Ettlinger (a) (in press), both of which are more fully described in the section on cross-modal studies, the monkeys received prolonger training on visual problems. These problems consisted of pairs of stimuli or objects presented in the light. The animals displaced an object, and thereby gained tactile experience of it, to make a response. Subsequent tactile assessment in the dark could not be considered independent of this bi-modal experience. In the experiment of Ettlinger and Blakemore (1969), in which the animals were also permitted on most, but not all, tactile problems to see the objects after choice in the dark, bi-modal effects appeared to be weak. In the more extensive investigation of Jarvis and Ettlinger they likewise appeared not to be of great importance. On a single trial in the dark following acquisition in the light, three out of four monkeys reached 80% correct performance or better. However, when touch was prevented in the light by interposing a translucent screen, performance in the dark initially declined somewhat, but then recovered almost to earlier levels. It appears that the previously good performance may have been mediated at least in part bimodally, but other explanations of the initial decline in performance with use of screens cannot be excluded. Rumbaugh and Gill (1976) have reported the "cross-modal" performance of a chimpanzee (*Pan*) in their study of the acquisition of linguistic competence. The animal had extensive opportunity to see and handle the objects before testing, in most instances. It was immediately correct on 80–92% of "cross-modal" trials when required to answer "same" or "no same" to pairs of stimulus objects of which one was presented tactually and the other visually. However, performance fell to 57% correct on 30 trials when totally unfamiliar objects were presented, i.e., when no opportunity for bi-modal learning was made available before testing. In another series the chimpanzee performed better with named (88%) than with unnamed (63%) familiar food objects.

A different kind of investigation has been undertaken by Jane, Masterton, and

Diamond (1965) with cats. After a preliminary study with compound auditory and visual stimuli which required an accurate spatial response, the cats were trained with new compound stimuli in a two-choice box. A pilot study had shown that auditory stimuli were "prepotent" over visual stimuli, so in the main experiment a soft tone was combined with an intense flashing light. The cats learned to respond to the combined stimulus to avoid electric shock (no food reward was given). Subsequently, when only the tone or the light was presented, three of four unoperated cats responded to the tone (on 1, 6, 6, and 9 of 10 trials), but none responded well to the light (on 1, 1, 1, and 3 of 10 trials). Training did not continue to criterion. In subsequent work by D. N. Elliott and L. Haber (unpublished but quoted by Wegener, 1976) these findings were not obtained, however.

Tree-shrews (*Tupaia*) were found by B. Masterton and J. P. Ward to behave like the cats of Jane *et al.* (1965) when trained to avoid electric shock, i.e., they avoided shock most effectively to the sound alone after earlier training on compound visual and auditory stimuli (Ward, personal communication, 1975). In more recent work by Ward and M. Moss (personal communication, 1975), tree-shrews responded more effectively to visual as opposed to auditory stimuli, but in a situation which initially required approach to one of six compound visual and auditory stimulus sources arranged in a semicircle for food reward. It is not known whether the spatial distribution of the stimuli, the change in response from avoidance to approach, or the motivation (food instead of shock) is critical for the different outcome.

In summary, too few experiments have been undertaken to permit a meaningful evaluation of bi-modal effects.

B. Cross-modal Studies

1. *Cross-modal Matching*

As previously mentioned, matching is readily achieved by verbal mediation, but not in nonhuman primates. This probably explains why so few cross-modal matching experiments are to be found in the animal literature and why work on cross-modal transfer preceded that on cross-modal matching. The earliest published reference to cross-modal matching in animals is contained in a brief review by Wilson (1965). Unfortunately, no details of his procedure or findings are available.

Subsequently, Ettlinger and Blakemore (1967) described in detail their attempts to demonstrate cross-modal matching in six rhesus monkeys. In their first experiment, an experimental group (N=3) was required to match one of two visual objects A_V and B_V to a tactile sample which could be either A_T or B_T. The control group (N=3) had X_T and Y_T as tactile samples and the same visual objects A_V and B_V as the experimental group. No animal learned to match proficiently within 1500 trials, and there was no difference between the groups. It appeared from a further control procedure that the poor performance might have been due to failure to attend to the tactile samples. In their second experiment, the same six animals were reallocated to experimental and control groups, three to each. The monkeys in the experimental group were required to match one of two new tactile objects A_T and B_T to one of the new visual samples A_V or B_V. Only two animals, one in each group, met the criterion of 90 correct responses in 100 consecutive trials (90/100), although two others, one experimental and one control, performed better than chance. The writers concluded that they had failed to demonstrate cross-modal matching unequivocally with their procedures, and this conclusion seems inescapable from their observations.

A more careful investigation was that of Milner (1973). The main supposition was that cross-modal matching might more readily become evident if monkeys were "instructed" by prior training in uni-modal matching. Therefore seven rhesus monkeys were trained to match on up to 10 visual tasks with shape and/or size relevant and were then assessed for true-matching performance on one visual task with only color relevant (or were trained on seven visual color true-matching tasks and then assessed for true-matching on one visual shape/size task). Three control monkeys were trained on five visual false-matching tasks with shape/size relevant and then assessed for false-matching on a color task. The learning scores on the initial two tasks of the first dimension were similar for all groups, but from the third task onward the scores of the seven true-matching monkeys were superior to those of the three false-matching animals. Only the seven true-matching animals were rapidly proficient at matching in the second visual dimension, irrespective of whether they transferred from shape/size to color or from color to shape/size. Milner was therefore able to conclude that his seven true-matching monkeys had learned to match within vision. Since matching was rapidly proficient even in an unfamiliar (visual) dimension it could be expected to become evident also in the cross-modal condition.

In the next part of Milner's investigation, four of the seven true-matching monkeys and one false-matching animal were assessed for matching by touch alone, but prior visual matching seemed not to improve tactile matching. However, relatively few animals were tested for tactile matching, and these for only a limited number of trials.

Lastly, there were two attempts to demonstrate cross-modal matching. The original seven true-matching monkeys were allocated to two groups, one true-true group (N=4) trained on true cross-modal matching tasks and one true-false group trained on false cross-modal matching tasks; and two of the original false-matching animals formed a false-false group, which was trained on false cross-modal matching tasks. These nine animals were all trained to match tactile objects to visual samples. Two of the true-true animals failed to reach the required standard of performance on the first of five cross-modal matching tasks and were eliminated; one other true-true monkey and one false-false animal failed to meet this standard on any of the first four of the cross-modal matching tasks and were eliminated; no convincing differences occurred, either on the early or subsequent cross-modal matching tasks, between the one remaining true-true animal and the four on false cross-modal matching tasks. Three monkeys were then trained on 12 10-trial true cross-modal matching tasks followed by 12 10-trial false cross-modal matching tasks, in which the same sample was presented on all 10 trials of each problem. Performance did not differ with condition (true or false cross-modal matching).

Under three conditions (within vision, within touch, and cross-modal) of Milner's study, learning of true-matching was not more rapid than learning of false-matching on initial tasks. Even when cross-dimensional transfer indicated that visual true-matching had been achieved, the true-matching and false-matching animals differed only after the second task. This finding accords with a suggestion by Drewe, Ettlinger, Milner, and Passingham (1970) that monkeys may initially solve matching problems on a conditional basis; and it may explain why Jackson and Pegram (1970) did not find cross-dimensional transfer within vision since they trained their rhesus monkeys on only one matching task before testing for transfer. Visual true-matching seems not to have facilitated subsequent tactile true-matching, but the tactile training was not prolonged. Nonetheless, since one monkey attained a criterion of 45/50 in 130 trials of tactile matching and two others rapidly performed better than chance, monkeys are apparently able to match by touch. Milner and Bryant (1970) have correctly argued that cross-modal matching presupposes adequate visual and tactile matching, so that defective cross-modal matching could be due to defective tactile matching. The comparable performance of animals trained on true and false cross-modal matching tasks may indeed, therefore, reflect a genuine cross-modal incapacity under the conditions of Milner's experiment.

At the very least Milner has shown that visual true-matching does not "instruct" the animal how to match in touch or cross-modally; that in certain situations monkeys may have to proceed to visual true-matching through a transitional stage of conditional learning; and that tactile matching is unlikely to be the limiting factor in cross-modal matching. Moreover, he gave two important warnings: "First, . . . monkeys could successfully adopt a conditional strategy which was generalized at the level of stimulus dimensions. For example, trials where the wider of two samples was presented might be conditionally associated with the wider of the two choice objects and the narrower sample trials with the selection of the narrower choice object" (Milner, 1973, p. 283). In the present terminology, "dimensional matching" can be conditionally based. "Second, . . . stimulus generalization from one task to the next (of both samples and choice objects) . . . would tend to result in positive transfer between successive true-matching tasks" (Milner, 1973, p. 283), but not reliably between successive false-matching tasks. Put differently, progressively better performance by true-matching animals could result from similarities between tasks instead of from improved matching on the later tasks each independently of the other; but false-matching animals cannot benefit from any such similarities.

Two groups of workers have reported findings seemingly at variance with those of Ettlinger and Blakemore and of Milner, but not necessarily so because quite different training procedures were used. Davenport, Rogers, and Russell, in a series of papers (Davenport & Rogers, 1970, 1971; Davenport, Rogers, & Russell, 1973, 1975), have presented evidence that chimpanzees and orangutans can perform cross-modal matching tasks; and Cowey and Weiskrantz (1975) have successfully devised a new method of assessing cross-modal recognition in monkeys. In addition, the recent positive findings by Jarvis and Ettlinger a & b (in press) with monkeys and with chimpanzees indicate that cross-modal recognition and some degree of cross-modal matching can be attained by both species.

Davenport et al. have used similar training for all their investigations but have widely varied the stimulus materials, introduced delay, and assessed cross-modal matching of tactile objects to visual samples and in the opposite direction. As in earlier work, they used an apparatus with a single central sample and two outer comparison objects presented to the ape in the alternate modality. The important novel feature (in addition to the use of apes instead of monkeys) was the method of training. The animals were initially trained on a long series of cross-modal matching problem. The same 20 problems were rotated for a block of 500 trials so that successive problems differed but reoccurred after 20 problems in the earliest report (Davenport & Rogers, 1970); four trials were given on each of 10 problems (making 40 trials) in the later report (Davenport et al., 1973). In each case, new combinations of the same 20 objects were then formed for further blocks of 500 or 40 trials. After initial training the apes (two chimpanzees and one orangutan in the earliest, five chimpanzees in the later report) were assessed for cross-modal matching with 40 or 60 "critical test problems" in which the stimuli were unfamiliar but otherwise appropriate to those used in training. Performance on these critical one-trial test problems varied between animals and stimuli but (with the exception of one chimpanzee which performed close to chance) generally fell within the range of 72–82% correct. This performance range was achieved even when in two studies (Davenport & Rogers, 1971; Davenport et al., 1975) matching was between objects in one sense-modality and photographs or other representations in another modality. (Surprisingly, performance by the same group of subjects with photographs, reported in 1971, was superior to performance with objects, reported in 1970.) The authors concluded that apes can achieve bi-directional cross-modal matching.

These highly important findings are not, however, entirely unequivocal, as comprehensive controls for the possibility that performance was conditional are not reported. Certainly the "critical" problems can, as claimed, exclude rapid intraproblem learning, whether of true-matching or of false-matching; but they do not exclude conditional learning of the kind discussed above in our section on theory (Section II,C,1,a). On critical problems with objects, cross-modal matching proficiency averaged only 77% correct overall, although after about 750 trials of preliminary training at cross-modal matching, performance was stated by Davenport and Rogers (1970) to be maintained by all subjects at better than 90% correct even with recombinations of (familiar) objects. The reasons given by Davenport et al. (1973) for the relatively poor performance on cross-modal matching tasks do not relate to the difference in performance during training and critical problems. Also, any limitation in the selection of stimuli suitable for tactile palpation cannot account for the difference in performance on training and critical problems. If no comparable decrement of performance on critical problems were to be found for within-modality matching by apes (and such a decrement need not be anticipated for either true within- or true across-modality matching), either cross-modal matching would appear to be less than optimally efficient for some reason, or the change to novel stimuli might have required a change in a conditional strategy (e.g., from ordinary conditional learning to Milner's strategy).

If, however, cross-modal matching is regarded as established in apes, it remains unclear whether the important differences are between species (positive findings with apes, negative with monkeys) or between training procedures (positive findings with many single-trial problems, negative with the few cross-modal matching tasks trained to criterion). The answer will be obtained by training monkeys on many single-trial problems, and apes on a few cross-modal matching tasks to criterion. In a newly published reference for which only a few details are available, Davenport (1976) failed to obtain cross-modal performance with monkeys apparently under conditions which had proved successful with apes. This might suggest a difference between species. However, other recent work fails to support such a difference.

The point of origin for a recent important approach to the problem of cross-modal equivalence by Cowey and Weiskrantz (1975) is their view that monkeys may "... never grasp the principle that the discriminanda in the two modalities are identical. One reason why this is likely is that the discriminanda used (usually objects) are not rewarding or aversive in their own right but are simply learned cues to obtaining food ..." (p. 117). Instead of objects they used shapes made of edible substances which were rendered palatable or unsavory. Cross-modal equivalence was evaluated between tactile samples and visual objects in two experiments with the same six rhesus monkeys. Only the second experiment is described here as it was essentially a replication of the first with improved procedure and similar outcome.

The animals were individually presented with 20 objects in total darkness. Ten were all of the same shape and edible; the other 10 were all of another shape and unpalatable (containing sand and quinine). The animal was allowed time to sample all 20 shapes by touch (and to eat the edible ones). Then one of each of the two shapes that had just been presented in the dark was exposed for selection in the light. These two trials (one with 20 shapes in the dark, the other with two in the light) completed one day's test. Three new pairs of shapes were used on three succeeding days to total four trials in the light for each of six animals. The palatable shapes were selected on 19 of 24 visual trials, four times by two monkeys, three times by three and twice by one.

The procedure used by Cowey and Weiskrantz bears some resemblance both to the earlier matching studies, in that soon after experience in the first sense-modality there is a single trial with two objects in the second sense-modality, and to the earlier transfer studies, in that 10 sets of one pair of shapes are presented in the first sense-modality and the monkey learns which shape is correct by tasting. Cowey and Weiskrantz use the term cross-modal matching but this writer prefers the designation cross-modal recognition because the animal identifies which of the two shapes in the first sense-modality is the "sample" by a process of learning. This distinction between cross-modal matching and cross-modal recognition may yet prove to be more than semantic if future work were to indicate that they are separate processes (see below in this section). Most important is the finding by Cowey and Weiskrantz that cross-modal recognition can be immediate, without improvement between successive pairs of shapes. This investigation has been replicated by Elliott (1977) with only minor modifications of method. He found that the edible shape was chosen in the light on 30 out of 39 trials by eight monkeys (four rhesus monkeys and four Cebus monkeys, *Cebus apella*), and on 23 out of 29 trials by three chimpanzees.

A modification of the procedure by Cowey and Weiskrantz (1975) was subsequently described by Weiskrantz and Cowey (1975). Only a single pair of shapes was presented on 12 days to the six monkeys of their previous report. On six days, 10 examples of one shape were edible, 10 examples of the second shape were inedible, and all 20 shapes were as before presented in the dark; on another six days (randomly interspersed), examples of the second shape were edible and of the first shape were inedible. The edible shape was chosen on 55 of 72 single visual trials (12 trials for each of six monkeys), and there was stated to be no evidence of a trend toward improved performance. In a second (control) experiment the same animals were required either (a) to match A_T edible to A_V edible or equally often B_T edible to B_V edible (true-matching), or (b) to match A_T edible to X_V edible or equally often B_T edible to Y_V edible (false-matching). All four shapes were familiar. The order of true-matching and false-matching was balanced. Twenty-six responses in 36 trials of true-matching were correct, but only 12 of 36 trials of false-matching (despite reward tending to counteract any strategy resulting in below-chance performance). In a third experiment, the procedure of the first was followed exactly but a highly discriminable pair of shapes was used, of which one shape was new. The edible shape was selected on 63 of 72 visual trials.

At first sight the findings of Weiskrantz and Cowey (1975) seem to extend the earlier observations of Cowey and Weiskrantz (1975). Nonetheless, the clearly below-chance performance with "false-object controls" in the second experiment indicates that the animals were disregarding nonequivalences between tactile shapes and nonequivalent visual shapes. It seems unlikely that they would do this only in a control task. Probably they were responding to equivalences between nonequivalent objects (i.e., recognizing dimensional values instead of stimuli).

In unpublished work E. Norris and G. Ettlinger have attempted to modify the basic procedure of Cowey and Weiskrantz (1975): their 8 monkeys were pretrained to non-match to sample with a series of objects given only in the light; then single edible shapes were presented in the dark, followed by visual choice trials in which the new shape was edible, the previous sample was inedible; and 5 such problems (i.e., 5 different pairs of shapes) were given each day. Preliminary findings indicate that performance does not then attain the same level as with the original procedure of Cowey & Weiskrantz (1975).

Jarvis and Ettlinger (a) (in press) set out to devise a different cross-modal recognition procedure, based on that successfully used for cross-modal matching with apes by Davenport and Rogers (1970). Discrimination learning in the first sense-modality was to take place on many problems, and on each was to be brief; evaluation of cross-modal recognition in the second sense-modality was to be confined to a single trial so as to prevent learning *within* that sense-modality. The rationale was that cross-modal recognition might become evident with single trials in the second sense-modality if (a) the monkey learned that it could solve these trials *only* by reference to prior experience in the first sense-modality, and (b) these trials formed an appreciable proportion of all trials so that correct response was worthwhile. The four rhesus monkeys and three chimpanzees in the experiment learned a total of 480 problems, 240 in the light interleaved with 240 in the dark, composed by random pairings of 220 junk-objects. Training in the first sense-modality was to an adjusted criterion, lasting for as many trials as were necessary to demonstrate statistically a consistent choice of the positive object. Thus 20 to 60 trials in all might be needed if the problem were found to be "difficult," but only six if "easy." Most problems were "easy" after about 100 problems in each sense-modality and there was good evidence of rapid intraproblem learning in both first sense-modalities. Performance in the second sense-modality was eventually at about 70% correct and significantly better than chance for three of the four monkeys and all chimpanzees, even in the condition touch to vision in which bi-modal experience could not help. It remained above chance for two of the four monkeys and two of the three chimpanzees on 20 further tactile to visual problems (interleaved with 20 visual to tactile problems) when only unfamiliar objects were presented on all 40 problems. Performance on visual to tactile problems was even better, although at this stage some bi-modal effects may have occurred (see section II,A,2). Subsequent control procedures which excluded this possibility indicated good cross-modal recognition in this direction also by two monkeys and three chimpanzees. Performance by the monkeys on "false-object controls" was at chance, as it was also on controls described in section II,C,1,a for the conditional strategy of Milner (1971). These controls were not undertaken with the chimpanzees. Certain aspects of the findings with monkeys and with one chimpanzee are shown in Figure 3.1.

Jarvis and Ettlinger (b) (in press) reported an attempt to progressively modify their training procedure to make it more like the procedure of cross-modal

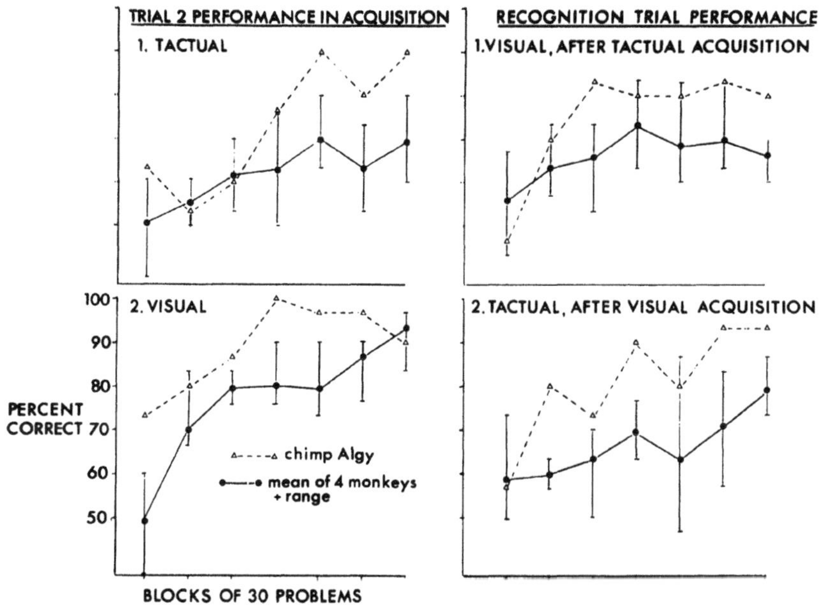

FIG. 3.1 Performance range of four monkeys and performance of one of three chimpanzees—the one most advanced in training—on acquisition of problem solving and on cross-modal recognition. Performance on tactual recognition trials could have been mediated by bi-modal learning in the light for the problems presented in this figure. Later in training, however, suitable control procedures were undertaken. For visual recognition trials no bi-modal mediation was possible for any animal on the last two blocks of training: previously light had been allowed after choice in the dark. (From early observations later extended in Jarvis and Ettlinger (a) in press.)

matching. Using a method termed "titration" the number of training trials in the first sense-modality was gradually reduced from 6 to 1 (or, if this gradual method failed, the number of trials in the first modality was eventually reduced to 1 abruptly). In the direction light to dark performance was significantly better than chance (range 62%-80%) for all 3 chimpanzees and 2 monkeys; but in the direction dark to light only one chimpanzee was significently better than chance (78%) whereas the remaining 2 chimpanzees and 2 monkeys ranged from 49% correct to 59% correct over the 100 problems. When animals were given a further 100 problems randomly intermixing 1- and 2-trial training procedures, one additional chimpanzee attained performance significantly better than chance in the direction dark to light.

At the time of writing, it remains uncertain whether the positive findings of Cowey and Weiskrantz (1975) and of Jarvis and Ettlinger (a) (in press) with monkeys are interrelated due to formal similarities between the two procedures. For example, in both studies the monkeys rapidly *learned* in the first sense-modality which stimulus was to be the "sample," and in both studies there was only one trial per problem in the second sense-modality. If such similarities were to prove critically important for a positive outcome, then future work could indicate a functional separation between what has here been termed cross-modal matching and cross-modal recognition. However, it must be recalled that in the work of Cowey and Weiskrantz cross-modal recognition was immediately apparent, whereas it developed slowly with training in the experiment of Jarvis and Ettlinger. If these two studies are ultimately shown to be unrelated, then presumably different factors are responsible for the positive outcome of each. For example, the shapes were edible in the former, and this could be critical; the prolonged and successful tactile training might have facilitated cross-modal equivalence in the latter.

In summary, with monkeys, classical matching-to-sample procedures failed to give evidence of cross-modal matching. Nonetheless, such procedures have so far been applied in only two investigations and they should be tried again with modifications. In contrast, cross-modal recognition appears to be possible for the monkey at a level varying from about 70–90% correct. Still different procedures have been used to assess cross-modal matching in apes, with positive outcomes of about 70–85% proficiency.

2. *Cross-modal Transfer*

This kind of cross-modal equivalence, being easy to evaluate in nonhuman primates, has been the subject of many investigations. In the great majority of studies, when adequate control procedures were undertaken, cross-modal transfer was not observed. Not all investigations of cross-modal transfer can be described in this review. The intention rather is to refer to those reports that made some procedural or conceptual advance. For clarity of presentation cross-modal transfer of specific and of general learning will be considered separately, although the current evidence no longer supports a functional distinction along these lines.

a. Cross-modal transfer of specific learning: vision and touch. In the earliest study of specific cross-modal transfer by Ettlinger (1960), the design was capable of revealing any substantial transfer between vision and touch. However, the procedure was not especially sensitive to lesser degrees of cross-modal transfer, being able to reveal only positive transfer effects; and only four monkeys were observed. Therefore Ettlinger's negative findings needed extension.

Wilson and Shaffer (1963) assessed the performance of six monkeys in two experiments. In the first, there were 11 cross-modal transfer tasks with three-dimensional objects, but significant transfer was not observed. In the second, there was a single task designed to ensure that the monkey "felt" the same part of the stimulus that it "saw." One measure of initial cross-modal transfer was significant, although not on subsequent replication with eight other monkeys which lacked the cross-modal experience of the original group (Ettlinger, 1967). In the light of subsequent work (see below), this outcome can be viewed as the first of several instances of weak and, especially, transient cross-modal effects. However, the real importance of Wilson and Shaffer's report lies not in their findings but in the novel procedure devised for their second experiment. To obtain a sensitive indication of cross-modal transfer, half of the animals were trained on the *reverse* of the original discrimination after changing sense-modality. Therefore, as a consequence of merely minimal cross-modal transfer, the group of monkeys that were reversed and the group that were not reversed should have performed in the second sense-modality respectively below and above chance, increasing the probability of a significant effect.

Blakeslee and Gunter (1966) failed in their second experiment to obtain specific cross-modal transfer between vision and touch in cebus monkeys (*Cebus albifrons* and *C. griseus*) with a design like that of Ettlinger (1960). Moffett and Ettlinger (1966) trained rhesus monkeys to select a different one of a pair of objects in the light and in the dark. Such "opposite responding" to a single pair of objects in two sense-modalities was acquired independently in each sense-modality, and the opposite habits could concurrently become manifest without mutual interference. Moffett and Ettlinger (1967) showed, analogously, that opposite responding to position (i.e., to the left and to the right) in the light and in the dark was readily acquired by rhesus monkeys and was not conditionally based. Ettlinger and Blakemore (1969) extended Wilson and Shaffer's (1963) first experiment, and sought to establish a "cross-modal transfer set" between vision and touch in rhesus monkeys by multiple alternations between visual and tactile training with 11 pairs of objects. Little if any evidence for the formation of such a transfer set was obtained even though animals received between 3500 and 5150 trials of training overall. Milner (1970) examined the possibility that cross-modal transfer between vision and touch was not manifested in earlier work because of the changes in the lighting conditions which accompanied changes in sense-modality. His rhesus monkeys transferred significantly between tasks requiring the discrimination of two self-luminous shapes in the dark and of the same two shapes in the light; but there was no significant cross-modal transfer between a visual (self-luminous) size task in the dark and the same task given tactually in the dark. Therefore change in illumination does not prevent cross-modal transfer.

In contrast to these many failures to demonstrate cross-modal transfer between vision and touch in monkeys (apart from the one measure reported to be significant by Wilson and Shaffer, 1963), there are two recent reports of partial success. Frampton, Milner, and Ettlinger (1973) assessed cross-modal transfer between vision and touch and found a significant effect on initial performance (i.e., the first 10 trials in the new sense-modality) but not on learning scores (i.e., trials to criterion). The chief difference between this experiment and all previous work on cross-modal transfer is that Frampton et al. trained their four rhesus monkeys to make successive instead of simultaneous discriminations. However, without replication it cannot be confidently asserted that this training variable is critical. Jarvis and Ettlinger (1975) obtained much more substantial cross-modal transfer between vision and touch, with overall savings in the second sense-modality averaging 72%. Their four rhesus monkeys were trained to alternate between the left and right food-wells and were not taught to make a discrimination between stimuli, in contrast to all previous studies except that of Moffett and Ettlinger (1967). Jarvis and Ettlinger had predicted a positive outcome because the same area of cortex (the frontal cortex) is known to be involved in spatial alternation whether in the light or in the dark, whereas different areas of cortex in the temporal and parietal lobes are involved respectively in visual and tactile discriminations. A. D. Milner (personal communication, 1975) has suggested that cross-modal transfer may be found for all tasks mediated by frontal cortex, including successive discriminations as used by Frampton et al. (1973), spatial alternation as used by Jarvis and Ettlinger (1975), and also discrimination reversals, which have so far not been given in studies of specific cross-modal transfer.

Specific cross-modal transfer in apes has so far been assessed only by Ettlinger and Jarvis (1976). Their three chimpanzees (*Pan troglodytes verus*) showed no clear indication of cross-modal transfer between vision and touch with stimulus pairs differing in shape, size, roughness, or orientation. The training procedure was closely modeled on earlier work with monkeys, except that the apes were trained to a lower criterion of 45/50 (although in one task training was to 160/200). Subsequently (Ettlinger, unpublished), two of these three chimpanzees were again assessed for cross-mocal transfer, but after reaching a high level of proficiency at cross-modal recognition as described by Jarvis & Ettlinger (a) & (b) (in press). In these subsequent transfer tests, cross-modal performance was generally still not evident.

b. Cross-modal transfer of specific learning: vision and audition. Burton and Ettlinger (1960) failed to observe cross-modal transfer of a frequency discrimination presented successively from vision to audition in rhesus monkeys. Wegener (1965) similarly failed to detect cross-modal transfer of an intensity discrimination, also presented successively, from vision to audition in rhesus monkeys. However, on reanalysis there was evidence of a small positive effect in the first 10 trials of the second sense-modality (cf. Frampton et al., 1973). Wilson and Zieler (1976) improved the earlier training procedures. In their first experiment on cross-modal transfer of intensity discriminations, the level of intensity *during* trials (high or low) was achieved by altering an intermediate level present always *between* trials. In another experiment they assessed cross-modal transfer by auditory and visual generalisation subsequent to auditory go, no-go training. Their squirrel monkeys (*Saimiri sciureus*) showed no cross-modal transfer even on initial trials in the first experiment. In the second, the findings were ambiguous.

This overall failure to observe cross-modal transfer is contraindicated by one report of positive findings in rhesus monkeys, and many such findings in non-simians. E. H. Yeterian and W. A. Wilson were quoted by Ettlinger (1973, p. 60) to have observed considerable initial cross-modal transfer between vision and audition in rhesus monkeys with go, no-go training involving electric shock for errors instead of the food reward for correct responses which was given in the other investigations. This experiment was intended to replicate the earlier work of Ward, Yehle, and Doerflein (1970) with bushbabies (*Galago senegalensis*). These animals learned to discriminate between frequencies of 3 and 18 Hz in a "shuttle box," in which the animal is expected to move from one end to the other in response to the positive but not the negative stimulus. Although the authors in their original report assessed cross-modal transfer only for early performance in the second sense-modality, they subsequently showed (Ward, Silver, & Frank, 1976) cross-modal transfer to persist in bushbabies during retraining to criterion. Other species have also shown cross-modal transfer: the tree-shrew (*Tupaia glis*) from visual to auditory frequencies with electric shock for errors (but again no food reward for correct responses) made on a go, no-go task, but interestingly *not* from audition to vision (J. P. Ward, S. Adams, & R. Taylor, personal communication, 1975); the cat between auditory and visual intermittent stimuli with either food reward or electric shock as punishment on a go-left, go-right task (John & Kleinman, 1975); the rat between visual and auditory intensities with food reward for correct depression of a lever, but only in early performance in the second sense-modality (Over & Mackintosh, 1969); and the mouse from auditory to visual pulsed stimuli with electric shock for errors on an avoidance task, but not from auditory to visual steady stimuli (Oliverio & Bovet, 1969). The electrophysiological findings of John and Kleinman (1975) suggest that low rates of intermittence of visual and auditory stimuli may be organized across sense-modalities in an atypical manner.

It is far from certain from this evidence whether there exist genuine differences in specific cross-modal transfer between species (e.g., prosimians like *Galago* may be capable of cross-modal transfer whereas simians like *Macaca* may not) or whether the training procedures adopted with non-simians have differed in any important way, and if so which factors are critical. The evidence that go, no-go training promotes cross-modal transfer is not consistent, nor yet do early measures in the second sense-modality always indicate cross-modal transfer; finally, Over and Mackintosh (1969) observed cross-modal transfer without the use of electric shock for errors. Our knowledge of cross-modal transfer in apes remains minimal.

c. Cross-modal transfer of general learning: vision and touch. In a series of studies M. Wilson (e.g., Wilson, 1964, 1966; Wilson & Wilson, 1962) has found that improvement at learning discrimination tasks (i.e., learning-set formation) transfers consistently, but not to a large extent, between vision and touch. Her rhesus monkeys were first trained to solve 30 to 144 discrimination problems by vision or by touch. Their performance generally improved during this training even though nothing specific about one problem could be transferred to succeeding ones. When assessed in the second sense-modality, performance was overall a little better than in the first. However, Milner and Ettlinger (1970) introduced an additional control procedure to detect any nonspecific effects which might produce savings from the first to the second sense-modality, e.g., emotional adaptation, learning to ignore extraneous stimuli, etc. They found that in their rhesus monkeys such nonspecific effects seem to be of the same magnitude as the apparent cross-modal transfer effects (for serial reversal learning set) so that the latter can be explained by the former.

The first experiment of Blakeslee and Gunter (1966) followed the general procedure of Wilson, but with cebus monkeys (*Cebus albifrons*) and more extensive training in the first sense-modality (450 six-trial problems followed by 60 problems trained to a criterion of 20/25). Performance on 150 six-trial problems in the second sense-modality did not significantly benefit from prior training in the first sense-modality. However, one of their seven monkeys did seem to show good cross-modal transfer. This animal ultimately performed at a level of 74% correct on trials 2–6 in the original (visual) sense-modality, and 79% correct on trials 2–6 of the (tactile) transfer problems.

Ettlinger and Blakemore (1966) trained rhesus monkeys to make a tactile conditional discrimination, e.g., select the narrower cylinder if both were tall, the wider if both were short. With such conditional training the animal does not learn a single specific stimulus-reward association since on some trials it selects the thin rod, on others the fat rod depending on their height. The same objects were then presented in the light and later once more in the dark with the reward conditions reversed for half of the eight monkeys on each change on sense-modality. There were no clear indications of cross-modal transfer.

In an elegant experiment, Rothblat and Wilson (1968) trained eight rhesus monkeys on a series of about 20 reversals of a complex tactile task. Half the animals could solve the tactile task by reference to the differences in shape in each of two stimulus pairs (i.e., shape was "relevant" but differences in size were "irrelevant"); for the remainder size was relevant (and shape irrelevant). On changing the sense-modality, for half the animals the previously relevant dimension remained relevant with two new stimulus pairs (so-called intradimensional shift); for the rest, the dimension relevant to the visual problems was the dimension that had been irrelevant in touch (so-called extradimensional shift). These two groups performed indistinguishably on the visual problems (learning followed by two reversals) although on control procedures *within* touch, performance was clearly superior with intradimensional shifts.

Reference has already been made elsewhere in this review to Milner's (1973) failure to detect transfer from vision to touch of matching performance in rhesus monkeys, although matching transferred across dimensions within vision. However, no control condition was used, so the conclusion remains uncertain.

d. Cross-modal transfer of general learning: vision and audition. Stepien and Cordeau (1960) trained seven Green monkeys (*Cercopithecus aethiops sabaeus*) to perform a difficult auditory task: if two click frequencies, in the range of 5 to 20 Hz and separated by 5 seconds, were the same, food could be obtained by opening a door; but if the two frequencies were different, the door was not to be touched (an error being followed by mild electric shock). All animals required in excess of 1500 trials to learn this task. Nonetheless, all except one showed good performance within a single test session in which 25 auditory trials were followed by 25 analogous visual trials. This apparent cross-modal transfer could have been a reflection of bi-modal learning in four animals, since they were trained to criterion with the auditory and visual stimuli presented together on each trial before being assessed on exclusively visual trials. However, the immediate cross-modal transfer from audition to vision in two of the other three monkeys was unexpected. Controls for the specificity of the effect were not reported. Unfortunately, this experiment has not been replicated in the intervening 17 years.

An important but unpublished experiment by J. G. Wegener was quoted by Ettlinger (1973, p. 55) as having possibly obtained cross-modal transfer from vision to audition in rhesus monkeys. In this complex task, if green-green-green but not red-red-red signified "go" in the first stage, then in the next stage green-red-green but not red-green-red signified "go"; analogously, if a tone of 1200 Hz but not of 800 Hz (in either case presented as a triplet) signified "go," then 1200-800-1200 Hz but not 800-1200-800 Hz signified "go" at the next stage. Errors were punished with electric shock. A group of three monkeys trained on the two auditory tasks after the two visual tasks showed a small cross-modal transfer effect, but another three monkeys trained in the opposite order gave negative transfer.

An experiment by R. Fouts, W. Chown and L. Goodin quoted by Fouts (1974, p. 479) might be considered relevant. A chimpanzee was trained to respond to 10 vocal English object-names to a criterion. The words then became exemplars for signs in Ameslan, the American Sign Language (see chapter 4 by Rumbaugh). Lastly, the animal was tested with the actual objects and was found to use the Ameslan signs correctly. In formal terms, a (visual) object was linked with an (auditory) word; the (auditory) word was linked with a (visual) sign; the sign was then found to signify the object. This interesting experiment is, however, not comparable to the studies of cross-modal transfer: first, because there was explicit associative learning across and within modalities, and second, because the word and the sign bear no physical resemblance to the object.

At first sight the work on general cross-modal transfer between vision and touch is almost uniformly negative for monkeys, but there is a suggestion of occasional positive effects between vision and audition.

In summary, although the majority of experiments on cross-modal transfer in monkeys have been negative, there are a few with a positive outcome. At present it must remain doubtful that the critical feature for a positive outcome is merely the training procedure (e.g., go, no-go training, a "frontal" task, or electric shock for errors), the sense-modality (e.g., auditory instead of tactile training, with vision as the alternate sense-modality), or the measure of performance in the second sense-modality (e.g., early trials).[2] However, there are clear differences between animals of the same species on certain cross-modal transfer tasks, and major differences between species have been claimed (although so far in only five studies have two species been compared under precisely comparable conditions). (These additional studies are all since 1976–Davenport, 1976; Elliott, 1977; Jarvis & Ettlinger, 1977a, 1977b.) Apes have not been adequately assessed. It may turn out that different training variables are critical for different species.

C. Lesion Studies

1. *Cross-modal Matching*

Sahgal, Petrides, and Iversen (1975) have sought to identify the brain structures concerned with cross-modal matching in the monkey. Using the method of Cowey and Weiskrantz (1975), they have investigated the effects of foveal prestriate lesions (N=3), posterior infero-temporal removals (N=2), and anterior infero-temporal ablations (N=2) in rhesus monkeys and baboons (*Papio papio*). The animals with posterior removals performed at chance on 20 problems requiring cross-modal recognition of shape, whereas those with anterior removals performed as well as did unoperated control animals, at 73–75% correct. Performance on four visual shape discrimination tasks, with each task presented for 10 trials on one day with reward for a correct response, did not subsequently distinguish the groups. To the extent that the visual abilities of the lesioned

[2] The occasional finding (e.g., Frampton et al., 1973) of positive cross-modal transfer exclusively on early trials in the second sense-modality might seem to be explained as follows. Generally, the more remote in time the outcome of a particular trial, the less the influence it will have on the outcome of the current trial. At first, performance in the second sense-modality is greatly influenced by the very recent outcomes in the former modality, giving correct performance. Then after a few trials the effect of the outcomes in the former sense-modality is rapidly attenuated, and due to the imperfection of the transfer process across modalities, the outcomes in the former modality have lost control over performance before the outcomes in the new sense-modality–treated separately by the brain–have gained control. This model implies separate neural systems for associative learning and memory in each sense-modality (but does not exclude a common multi-modal system if the learning is strongly motivated). It also implies that each uni-modal learning system has weak cross-modal effects, provided reinforcement in that modality has taken place recently. At variance with such a model are the findings of Ettlinger and Blakemore (1969) and Moffett and Ettlinger (1966, 1967), where visual and tactile trials were interleaved but cross-modal performance failed to improve.

animals can be regarded as unimpaired, the authors have shown that two cortical removals along the boundary between temporal and occipital cortex can each abolish cross-modal recognition of this kind. Using the same procedures, Petrides and Iversen (1976) reported that bilateral ablations of cortex in the banks of the arcuate sulcus (i.e., limited frontal removals) significantly impaired cross-modal recognition (N=4), whereas removals from the banks of the principal sulcus did not (N=4).

2. *Cross-modal Transfer*

In the course of a comprehensive analysis of the behavioral effects of bilateral striate cortical removals, N. K. Humphrey (personal communication, 1975, and cited in Weiskrantz & Cowey, 1970) observed that destriate monkeys which had been trained to reach out and grasp small visually-presented objects showed immediate transfer to reaching to an "auditory object" (a small sound source presented in the dark). Not only did the transfer take place spontaneously, but at least at first, the monkeys appeared genuinely not to notice the difference between auditory and visual stimuli: it took over 1000 trials to establish even a low level of discrimination between a flashing light source and a clicking sound source driven at the same frequency. Humphrey suggested that destriate monkeys tend to treat localised sensory stimuli, visual or auditory, simply as equivalent *amodal* "events." If this is so, the equivalence must be regarded as an "emergent" consequence of the brain lesion.

Ward, Silver, and Frank (1976) evaluated cross-modal transfer of a frequency discrimination in two bushbabies (*Galago senegalensis*) with bilateral removals of medial temporal cortex and in two others with removals of parietal, lateral occipital, and posterior temporal cortex. These four animals transferred as proficiently as four intact bushbabies.

Yeterian, Waters, and Wilson (1976) have observed the effects of bilateral cortical removals in rats on cross-modal transfer of an intensity discrimination from vision to audition. The rats with cortical lesions did not show the early but transient cross-modal transfer which, in replication of the findings of Over and Mackintosh (1969), took place in the control animals on the first day in the second sense-modality. However, the lesioned rats were significantly slower than the controls also at learning the visual and auditory intensity tasks. The poor initial performance by the lesioned group in the second sense-modality may, therefore, reflect either impaired learning in the first sense-modality, or impaired performance (e.g., partial deafness) in the second sense-modality, or a genuine cross-modal defect. Preliminary results indicate that rats with lesions of the superior colliculi, studied under similar training conditions, show no transfer (M. A. Goodale, A. D. Milner and N. G. Foreman, personal communication, 1975).

In summary, the dearth of work on lesion effects is surely a function of the difficulty of obtaining clear cross-modal equivalence in intact animals. However, the procedures introduced by Over and Mackintosh (1969) for rats, Ward, Yehle, and Doerflein (1970) for prosimians, and by Cowey and Weiskrantz (1975) and

Jarvis and Ettlinger (a) & (b) (in press) for monkeys give rise to the expectation of an increasing volume of work. At this time it appears that cross-modal equivalence may be subcortically organized in prosimians but not in intact monkeys under all conditions of assessment.

D. The Generality of Cross-modal Performance

Elliott (1977) assessed 3 chimpanzees with the procedure of Cowey & Weiskrantz (1975) while these same animals were also being trained on another cross-modal task (Jarvis & Ettlinger, (a), in press). Their performance at cross-modal recognition of objects did not improve noticeably as a consequence of the intercurrent assessment with edible and inedible shapes. Subsequent to all of the cross-modal training reported by Jarvis & Ettlinger (a & b) (in the press) G. Ettlinger (unpublished) evaluated the performance of two of the chimpanzees (Algy and Blue) on 5 tests of cross-modal transfer, with the method of Moffett and Ettlinger (1966). Evidence for cross-modal transfer was obtained on 2 of the 10 possible occasions it could have become evident. These observations are to be extended to monkeys. Meanwhile, taken in conjunction with the difficulties reported by Jarvis & Ettlinger (b) (in press) in maintaining good cross-modal performance after a progressive reduction of the number of training trials to one per problem, it seems that cross-modal performance is fragile: it lacks generality, in that alterations of procedure that seem unimportant can nonetheless lead to dramatic deterioration of performance.

IV. OVERVIEW AND CONCLUSIONS

No reference has been made in this review to investigations of cross-modal equivalence in man. And yet during the 20 years since the work of Cannon (1955) and of Gaydos (1956) there has been a rapid expansion of research in this area. Indeed, the publications on cross-modal equivalence in man considerably outnumber those on cross-modal equivalence in nonhuman animals. Nevertheless, despite the high quality and even elegance of much of this work, the nature of cross-modal equivalence in man is not yet understood.

It is often argued (e.g., Millar, 1975) that Burton and Ettlinger's (1960) proposal that language serves as a cross-modal bridge has been shown to be incorrect. The reason given is that infants and apes possess cross-modal equivalence but not language (Bryant, Jones, Claxton, & Perkins, 1972; Davenport & Rogers, 1970). Certainly the strong form of this "language hypothesis" is wrong in that some kinds of cross-modal equivalence do occur in preverbal infants, in nonhuman primates, and even in nonprimate mammals such as the mouse. But only seldom has such cross-modal equivalence exceeded 70–80% correct; often it has been found to be transient (becoming evident only for a few trials), or unidirectional (occurring from one sense-modality to another but not conversely), or dependent on special procedures (such as go, no-go, or use of electric shock as punishment for errors); and in other respects also it is far less robust than in adult man.

One possible resolution of the many inconsistent findings is to suppose, as foreshadowed by Milner (1971) and Ettlinger (1973), that cross-modal equivalence is not a unitary process. Then cross-modal equivalence may be achieved at three different levels: (1) Language may be essential for the most effective forms of cross-modal equivalence in man, but its precise role may be variable, depending on the requirements for cross-modal equivalence in each particular context. Overall, even this kind of cross-modal equivalence is less accurate than intramodal equivalence. (2) Cross-modal equivalence may also be achieved perceptually, without recourse to any language process, but at a further cost in the accuracy of the equivalence under certain conditions. (3) Cross-modal equivalence may be achieved by wide stimulus generalization, possibly at a subcortical level, as part of a process which fails to take the sense-modality of the sensory inflow into account.

No further consideration will here be given to the suggested process of language-based cross-modal equivalence, since, at the present time, at least, it is surely exclusive to man and to specially trained apes. That this is not the only process available to man is demonstrated by work on preverbal infants (Bryant et al., 1972) and on one adult, studied after commissure section (Gazzaniga, Bogen, & Sperry, 1965), who could recognize cross-modally with the nonverbal right hemisphere.

The proposed perceptually-based process for cross-modal equivalence appears to have severe limitations, at least in nonhuman animals. Although this cross-modal equivalence system may be structurally determined, only those features of the world that possess strong motivational significance for the organism (e.g., sound-emitting objects [Bryant et al., 1972], food objects [Cowey & Weiskrantz, 1975], and stimuli associated with electric shock [Yeterian & Wilson, and Wegener, both cited in Ettlinger, 1973]) may be able to gain access to it without prolonged further learning. Such limitations may be related to the nature of sensory processing by the brain, each modality of sensory inflow being processed separately.[3] If the features of the world have no special motivational significance, then access to the proposed cross-modal equivalence system may be gained only as a result of prolonged training (Davenport & Rogers, 1970; Jarvis & Ettlinger, (a) & (b) (in press) described in section III,B,1). This argument implies that a structurally determined system with severe limitations on the kind of inflow it handles may be rendered more accessible to new kinds of inflow by

[3] This argument entails that association learning is generally mediated by modality-specific systems which have little reciprocal interchange, but that under circumstances of high motivation a multi-modal learning system (perhaps not neocortical) is activated.

a process of learning. To borrow some of Bryant's (1974) terminology, an additional class of entries into the "cross-modal dictionary," which schematically is in operation from birth, can be made as a result of learning, and such learning progressively facilitates successive entries of the new class. With either unlearned or learned operation of the "dictionary," requirements for what we have called cross-modal matching or cross-modal recognition may be more readily met than those of cross-modal transfer. If, however, a kind of behavior (such as go, no-go [Frampton et al., 1973], or spatial alternation [Jarvis & Ettlinger, 1975]) that is organized by a single cortical region, irrespective of the sense-modality of the inflow, makes demands on the cross-modal equivalence system, it may be dealt with more directly than the other examples already mentioned (but even then with some loss of cross-modal efficiency).

Finally, the proposed primitive and subcortical amodal system underlying a process of cross-modal equivalence which is more akin to stimulus generalization than to perceptual equivalence, may exist in non-simian species such as bushbabies (*Galago*), tree-shrews (*Tupaia*), rats, and mice. It may, perhaps, also be manifested by monkeys and apes if the perceptual cross-modal dictionary or an access route to it has been damaged by brain lesions. This primitive system may be more readily accessible to the behavior we have called cross-modal transfer than to cross-modal matching. But if it is actually found to give rise to wide stimulus generalization with total neglect of sense-modality, then any such apparent cross-modal equivalence would be quite distinct from the genuine cross-modal equivalence already discussed above.

In conclusion, it is obvious that any attempts to systematize the discrepant observations on cross-modal equivalence contained in this review are premature. This implies that the outline scheme just proposed will probably be shown to be inadequate or incorrect. That will not matter if the scheme leads to more refined experiments. In particular, there is a need for experiments with more than a single species. In such experiments, training procedures should be systematically varied but held equivalent for the different species. Thus, for example, apes and monkeys should be trained (1) with those procedures known to give positive cross-modal equivalence effects with apes, in order to ascertain whether monkeys will also show positive effects, and also (2) with those procedures known to give negative cross-modal equivalence effects with monkeys, in order to ascertain whether apes will also show negative effects. Only in this way can we be certain that there are real as opposed to likely differences between species. J. P. Ward, S. Adams and R. Taylor (personal communication, 1975; see section III,B,2,b) have pioneered by demonstrating that cross-modal equivalence is differently organized in *Galago* and *Tupaia.* Davenport (1976) has reached a similar conclusion for apes and monkeys, but this is not supported by the findings of Elliott (1977) or of Jarvis & Ettlinger (a) & (b) in press. Therefore, it remains possible that important differences in cross-modal capacity will yet be established between species. If in addition it were then found that the rules for the use of the cross-modal dictionary also varied between species, a happy consumption of the present indigestible crop of cross-modal findings could be achieved.

ACKNOWLEDGMENTS

I am grateful to various colleagues for permission to quote their unpublished findings; to them and to others for critical comments on an early version of this review; and to Mrs. V. Allan for patiently and accurately typing and retyping the manuscript.

REFERENCES

Blakeslee, P., & Gunter, R. Cross-modal transfer of discrimination learning in Cebus monkeys. *Behaviour,* 1966, **26,** 76–90.

Bryant, P. E. *Perception and understanding in young children.* London: Methuen & Co., 1974.

Bryant, P. E., Jones, P., Claxton, C. C., & Perkins, G. M. Recognition of shapes across modalities by infants. *Nature,* 1972, **240,** 303–304.

Burton, D., & Ettlinger, G. Cross-modal transfer of training in monkeys. *Nature,* 1960, **186,** 1071–1072.

Cannon, R. C. *A systematic investigation of sensory discrimination in human brain damage.* Unpublished Ph.D. thesis, University of Colorado, 1955.

Cowey, A., & Weiskrantz, L. Demonstration of cross-modal matching in rhesus monkeys, Macaca mulatta. *Neuropsychologia,* 1975, **13,** 117–120.

Davenport, R. K., & Rogers, C. M. Intermodal equivalence of stimuli in apes. *Science,* 1970, **168,** 279–280.

Davenport, R. K. Cross-modal perception in apes. In S. R. Harnard, H. D. Steklis & J. Lancaster, Eds., *Origins and Evolution of Language and Speech,* Annals of the New York Academy of Science, **280,** 1976.

Davenport, R. K., & Rogers, C. M. Perception of photographs by apes. *Behaviour,* 1971, **39,** 318–320.

Davenport, R. K., Rogers, C. M., & Russell, I. S. Cross-modal perception in apes. *Neuropsychologia,* 1973, **11,** 21–28.

Davenport, R. K., Rogers, C. M., & Russell, I. S. Cross-modal perception in apes: Altered visual cues and delay. *Neuropsychologia,* 1975, **13,** 229–335.

Drewe, E. A., Ettlinger, G., Milner, A. D., & Passingham, R. E. A comparative review of the results of neuropsychological research on man and monkey. *Cortex,* 1970, **6,** 129–163.

Elliott, R. C. Cross-modal recognition in three primates. *Neuropsychologia,* 1977, **15,** 183–186.

Ettlinger, G. Cross-modal transfer of training in monkeys. *Behaviour,* 1960, **16,** 56–65.

Ettlinger, G. Learning in two sense-modalities. *Nature,* 1961, **191,** 308.

Ettlinger, G. Analysis of cross-modal effects and their relationship to language. In F. L. Darley & C. H. Millikan (Eds.), *Brain mechanisms underlying speech and language.* New York: Grune & Stratton, 1967.

Ettlinger, G. The transfer of information between sense-modalities: A neuropsychological review. In H. P. Zippel (Ed.), *Memory and transfer of information.* New York: Plenum, 1973.

Ettlinger, G., & Blakemore, C. B. Cross-modal transfer of conditional discrimination training in monkeys. *Nature,* 1966, **210,** 117–118.

Ettlinger, G., & Blakemore, C. B. Cross-modal matching in the monkey. *Neuropsychologia,* 1967, **5,** 147–154.

Ettlinger, G., & Blakemore, C. B. Cross-modal transfer set in the monkey. *Neuropsychologia,* 1969, **7,** 41–47.

Ettlinger, G., & Jarvis, M. J. Cross-modal transfer in the chimpanzee. *Nature,* 1976, **259,** 44–45.

Fouts, R. S. Language: Origins, definitions and chimpanzees. *Journal of Human Evolution,* 1974, **3,** 475–482.

Frampton, G. G., Milner, A. D., & Ettlinger, G. Cross-modal transfer between vision and touch of go, no-go discrimination learning in the monkey. *Neuropsychologia,* 1973, **11,** 231–233.

Freides, D. Human information processing and sensory modality: Cross-modal functions, information complexity, memory, and deficit. *Psychological Bulletin,* 1974, **81,** 284–310.

Gaydos, H. F. Intersensory transfer in the discrimination of form. *American Journal of Psychology,* 1956, **69,** 107–110.

Gazzaniga, M. S., Bogen, J. E., & Sperry, R. W. Observations on visual perception after disconnexion of the cerebral hemispheres in man. *Brain,* 1965, **88,** 221–236.

Jackson, W. J., & Pegram, G. V. Comparison of intra- vs. extradimensional transfer of matching by rhesus monkeys. *Psychological Science,* 1970, **19,** 162–163.

Jane, J. A., Masterton, R. B., & Diamond, I. T. The function of the tectum for attention to auditory stimuli in the cat. *Journal of Comparative Neurology,* 1965, **125,** 165–192.

Jarvis, M. J., & Ettlinger, G. Transfer of spatial alternation between responding in the light and in the dark. *Neuropsychologia,* 1975, **13,** 115–116.

Jarvis, M. J., & Ettlinger, G. Cross-modal recognition in chimpanzees and monkeys. *Neuropsychologia,* in press. (a)

Jarvis, M. J. & Ettlinger, G. Cross-modal performance in monkeys and apes: is there a substantial difference? In Chapter 7, Vol. I "Primate Behaviour" of "Recent Advances in Primatology" (D. J. Chivers, Ed.) Academic Press, in press. (b)

Jastrow, J. The perception of space by disparate senses. *Mind,* 1886, **11,** 539–554.

John, E. R., & Kleinman, D. "Stimulus generalization" between differentiated visual, auditory and central stimuli. *Journal of Neurophysiology,* 1975, **88,** 1015–1034.

Kelvin, R. P., & Mulik, A. Discrimination of length by sight and touch. *Quarterly Journal of Experimental Psychology,* 1958, **10,** 187–192.

Klüver, H. An analysis of the effects of the removal of the occipital lobes in monkeys. *Journal of Psychology,* 1936, **2,** 49–61.

Krauthamer, G., *An experimental study of form perception across sensory modalities.* Unpublished Ph.D. thesis, New York University College of Medicine, 1959.

Lashley, K. S. Persistent problems in the evolution of mind. *Quarterly Revue of Biology,* 1949, **24,** 28–42.

Lögler, P. Versuche zur Frage des "Zahl"-Vermögens an einem Graupapagei und Vergleichversuche an Menschen. *Zeitschrift für Tierpsychologie,* 1959, **16,** 179–217.

Millar, S. Effects of input conditions on intramodal and crossmodal visual and kinesthetic matches by children. *Journal of Experimental Child Psychology,* 1975, **19,** 63–78.

Milner, A. D. Cross-modal transfer between touch and vision without change of illumination. *Neuropsychologia,* 1970, **8,** 501–503.

Milner, A. D. *Cross-modal transfer and matching in primates.* Unpublished Ph.D. thesis, London University, 1971.

Milner, A. D. Matching within and between sense modalities in the monkey (Macaca mulatta). *Journal of Comparative and Physiological Psychology,* 1973, **83,** 278–284.

Milner, A. D., & Bryant, P. E. Cross-modal matching by young children. *Journal of Comparative and Physiological Psychology,* 1970, **71,** 453–458.

Milner, A. D., & Ettlinger, G. Cross-modal transfer of serial reversal learning in the monkey. *Neuropsychologia,* 1970, **8,** 251–258.

Moffett, A., & Ettlinger, G. Opposite responding in two sense-modalities. *Science,* 1966, **153,** 205–206.

Moffett, A., & Ettlinger, G. Opposite responding to position in the light and dark. *Neuropsychologia,* 1967, **5,** 59–62.

Oliverio, A., & Bovet, D. Transfer of avoidance responding between visual and auditive stimuli presented in different temporal patterns. *Communications in Behavioral Biology A.,* 1969, **3,** 61–68.

Over, R., & Mackintosh, N. J. Cross-modal transfer of intensity discrimination by rats. *Nature,* 1969, **224,** 918–919.

Petrides, M., & Iversen, S. D. Cross-modal matching and the primate frontal cortex. *Science,* 1976, **192,** 1023–1024.

Rothblat, L. A., & Wilson, W. A. Intradimensional and extradimensional shifts in the monkey within and across sensory modalities. *Journal of Comparative and Physiological Psychology,* 1968, **66,** 549–553.

Rumbaugh, D. M., & Gill, T. V. Language and the acquisition of language-type skills by a chimpanzee (Pan). In K. Salzinger (Ed.), *Annals of the New York Academy of Science,* 1976, **270,** 90–123.

Sahgal, A., Petrides, M., & Iversen, S. D. Cross-modal matching in the monkey after discrete temporal lobe lesions. *Nature,* 1975, **257,** 672–674.

Schiller, P. von. Intersensorielle Transposition bei Fischen. *Zeitschrift für die Vergleichende Physiologie,* 1933, **19,** 304–309.

Stepien, L. S., & Cordeau, J. P. Memory in monkeys for compound stimuli. *American Journal of Psychology,* 1960, **73,** 388–395.

Ward, J. P., Adams, S., & Taylor, R. *Comparison of cross-modal transfer in the tree shrew (Tupaia glis) and the Bushbaby (Galago senegalensis).* Unpublished manuscript, 1975. Available from Dr. J. P. Ward, Dept. Psychology, Memphis State University, Memphis, Ten. 38152.

Ward, J. P., Silver, B. V., & Frank, J. Preservation of cross-modal transfer of a rate discrimination in the bushbaby (Galago senegalensis) with lesions of posterior neocortex. *Journal of Comparative and Physiological Psychology,* 1976, **90,** 520–527.

Ward, J. P., Yehle, A. L., & Doerflein, R. S. Cross-modal transfer of a specific discrimination in the bushbaby (Galago senegalensis). *Journal of Comparative and Physiological Psychology,* 1970, **73,** 74–77.

Wegener, J. G. Cross-modal transfer in monkeys. *Journal of Comparative and Physiological Psychology,* 1965, **59,** 450–452.

Wegener, J. G. Some variables in auditory pattern discrimination learning. *Neuropsychologia,* 1976, **14,** 149–159.

Weiskrantz, L., & Cowey, A. Filling in the scotoma: A study of residual vision after striate cortex lesions in monkeys. In *Progress in Physiological Psychology* (Vol. 3). New York: Academic Press, 1970.

Weiskrantz, L., & Cowey, A. Cross-modal matching in the rhesus monkey using a single pair of stimuli. *Neuropsychologia,* 1975, **13,** 257–261.

Wilson, M. Further analysis of intersensory facilitation of learning set in monkeys. *Perceptual and Motor Skills,* 1964, **18,** 917–920.

Wilson, M. Strategies and cross-modal transfer in monkeys. *Psychonomic Science,* 1966, **4,** 321–322.

Wilson, M. Assimilation and contrast effects in visual discrimination by rhesus monkeys. *Journal of Experimental Psychology,* 1972, **93,** 279–282.

Wilson, M., & Wilson, W. A. Intersensory facilitation of learning sets in normal and brain-operated monkeys. *Journal of Comparative and Physiological Psychology,* 1962, **55,** 931–934.

Wilson, W. A. Intersensory transfer in normal and brain-operated monkeys. *Neuropsychologia,* 1965, **3,** 363–370.

Wilson, W. A., & Shaffer, O. C. Intermodality transfer of specific discriminations in the monkey. *Nature,* 1963, **197,** 107.

Wilson, W. A., & Zieler, S. Some tests of intermodality transfer of intensity in squirrel monkeys. *Neuropsychologia,* 1976, **14,** 237–241.

Wright, J. M. von. Cross-modal transfer and sensory equivalence–A review. *Scandinavian Journal of Psychology,* 1970, **11,** 21–30.

Wylie, H. H. An experimental study of transfer of response in the white rat. *Behavior Monographs,* 1919, **16**(3, Serial No. 16).

Yeterian, E. H., Waters, R. S., & Wilson, W. A. Posterior cortical lesions and specific cross-modal transfer in rats. *Physiological Psychology,* 1976, **4,** 281–284.

4
Language Behavior of Apes

Duane M. Rumbaugh

Georgia State University
and
The Yerkes Regional Primate Center
of Emory University

I. INTRODUCTION

Man's interest in the origins of human attributes has probably been strong from the time his intelligence first allowed him to reflect upon the nature of things and the relationships between events in his environment. Increasingly, sheer conjecture on the topic has been supplanted by biological and archaeological findings, by formal theory, and by the intrusion of research programs into the study of human attributes and skills once held to be unique, immutable, and/or god-given.

The surge of research interest in the nature of language and the requisites of language acquisition is a case in point. Because only man manifests language with a productive syntax by which novel messages are formulated and publicly transmitted, it is understandable that until now language has been regarded as uniquely human. Language *is* uniquely human in that man and man alone develops this skill with apparent spontaneity and with high probability; however, the results of the last decade's research with chimpanzees that have developed language-type skills have raised a new question: Are the *requisites* to linguistic competence also uniquely human?

The purpose of this chapter is to consider evidence emanating from the various chimpanzee language projects along with selected theoretical perspectives and other related research in an attempt to formulate at least a tentative answer to this question. Since language is viewed here as only one of the behaviors which can enhance the probability of successful adaptation to challenge from the environment, a general statement regarding behavior is in order.

A. Behavior and Access to Language Origins

It is through behavior that animal cells, either singly or in concert, effect an interface with the environment. To the degree that the interfacing sustains the life and reproduction of those cells, adaptation is said to have occurred. Single-celled animals or even the single cells of multicellular organisms can and do manifest behavior, for all cells have the general characteristic of being "irritable" or responsive to some type of environmental stimulation, whether external or internal. Clearly, single cells have fewer options for adaptative behavior than *systems* of cells, which can respond in a coordinated manner. Systems of cells are able to adapt through various tactics to a greater variety of environmental challenges and to more difficult ones than are single cells. In general, the more complex the cell systems, the greater is the array of behavioral options available for possible adaptation. Man has greatly increased his behavioral options for adaptation to seemingly limitless challenges and niches through the evolution of language. In all probability, the evolution of language has been contingent upon brain evolution and the behavioral plasticity which this evolution provides through open genetic programs (Mayr, 1974; Dingwall, 1975).

Although this perspective is not new, it should be kept in focus while considering the requisites to language. Although it is possible that genetic alterations or mutations unique to *Homo erectus,* to one or more of his descendants, and/or to *H. sapiens* may have provided totally for man's language skills, it is more probable that language evolved gradually (Toulmin, 1971) and that comparative research will yield traces of language origins. Since our immediate precursors have long been extinct, their capabilities for language can only be assessed inferentially through studies of their artifacts (e.g., Marshack, 1976) and through their fossil remains. Regrettably, behavior does not fossilize.

As far as direct empirical research on the origins of language is concerned, behavioral studies with extant animal forms offer the only possibility for systematic study. Since apes and monkeys are more closely related to man than are other animal forms, it is reasonable that such research should focus on them, although they are not, of course, the precursors of modern man. Man does share common evolutionary roots with both apes and monkeys, the root common to apes being the more recent one, but since the time of the radiations which gave rise to monkeys, apes, and men as we now know them, all the varieties of primates have been novelly shaped through selective environmental forces. That fact notwithstanding, it remains possible that apes and monkeys (not necessarily to the exclusion of nonprimate forms) may have carried forward through their own evolution the behavioral processes and potentials which provided for the evolution of the linguistic competence in modern man. In short, comparative behavioral studies may reveal that the requisites to linguistic competence are not unique to *H. sapiens.*

B. Language in Comparative Perspective

The pivotal question is: What is linguistic competence, i.e., language? It is easy to define language in such a way as to preclude comparative research. If language is defined in terms of *human speech,* none other than *H. sapiens* can possibly have linguistic competence: no other form is human and even if it could speak, its language would not be human speech. Speech is so salient a characteristic of human language that speech and language have understandably come to be synonyms. Speech is surely the most efficient medium of human language, but to relegate all other linguistic-relevant media such as writing and reading to a secondary or derived status probably hinders efforts to define the psychological substrates of linguistic competence and performance. Dingwall, for example has concluded that apart from speech there are no aspects of language that are unique to man (1975, p. 45).

Rumbaugh and Gill (1976) have suggested a comparative perspective regarding language. They see it as having private (covert) and public (overt) dimensions and as being only one of many forms of animal communication—one set apart from others by its infinite openness, to use Hockett's (1960) term. It may or may not be the case that some feral animal form will be found to exhibit openness in its communication, being able to produce and to employ new signals (lexical units) in new combinations (syntax) with other signals to generate and transmit novel messages. Remote as that possibility seems at present, it may still occur in the foreseeable future. That possibility notwithstanding, the comparative language projects of the past decade support the conclusion that chimpanzee subjects benefit rather readily from training in skills which allow for public exchanges of linguistic-type (open) communication. Perhaps they do so because they are naturally equipped with the processes and/or potential for developing the *private* dimensions of language which include symbolizing, the ability to relate different concepts to each other, and the ability to synthesize information and skills for application to novel problems (Mason, 1976; Premack, 1975). Given the instigation by man and language systems contrived by man which circumvent their inability to speak, they seem able to acquire at least the rudiments of public linguistic skills. The chimpanzee's capacity for such skills is due, possibly, to a brain which bears close similarity to man's (Hill, 1972; Jerison, 1973; Radinsky, 1975; Shantha & Manocha, 1969) and to a relatively advanced form of intelligence which is basically, though not exclusively, hominian (e.g., Menzel, 1973, 1974; Menzel & Johnson, 1976).

This writer's comparative view of the evolution of the primate brain and attendant abilities for learning, intelligence, and language is as follows: The higher-order psychological abilities of nonhuman primates are a function of the degree to which their brains are hominian. To the degree that they have such brains they appear to have sensory, perceptual, and learning processes and intelligence similar to man's (see King & Fobes, 1974; Menzel & Halperin, 1975; Parker, 1974; Warren, 1974; Young & Farrer, 1971, for representative evidence). To the degree that these parameters are collectively requisite to the covert structures and functions of expressive (public) language, the possibility exists that the psychological foundations of language can be identified. Language in this view is a *behavioral* domain and not just an attribute of man; other animals, notably the chimpanzee, are capable of behaviors which may form a continuum with human language (Dingwall, 1975; Rumbaugh & Gill, 1976).

C. Primate Intelligence and Learning

Despite the initial interest of comparative psychologists in "animal intelligence" several decades ago, the use of intelligence as a concept came increasingly to be reserved for use in reference to man until very recent years; however, with the development of a more adequate comparative perspective regarding brain development and brain function, it is now reasonable to use the term with certain restrictions in reference to nonhuman primates. If man's intelligence is primarily a function of his advanced brain development, then other nonhuman primates, to the degree that their brains approximate man's, might likewise possess dimensions of intelligence which are requisites to "language." Restrictions in the use of the term intelligence include the following: (1) It is unreasonable to expect nonhuman primate forms to manifest all dimensions of human intelligence. By the same token, it is unreasonable to expect man's intelligence to manifest all dimensions of nonhuman primate intelligence. (2) Major dimensions of intelligence for the various primate forms, including man, have quite possibly been selectively shaped by ecological factors, and this shaping may have occurred through unique interactions of selective pressures across millions of years with the various radiations of primate forms. By implication, wide variation in the dimensions of intelligence can be expected when the diverse primate forms are compared.

By and large, we do not have the data base necessary for laying out the differences between the various profiles of intelligence that this perspective anticipates; however, certain relevant data are already in hand and recent conceptual developments will possibly stimulate the collection of still more. McNeill (1974), for example, has observed that although chimpanzees (*Pan*) are intensely aware of one another, engaging in nearly continuous interactions when together, they seem to be much less curious about objects unless those objects relate at a very practical level to such matters as assessing the condition of feeding trees, collecting and preparing materials for "fishing termites" (van Lawick-Goodall, 1970), and attacking threatening predators (Kortlandt, 1965). McNeill felt that this might help account for the indication that Washoe chimpanzee (Gardner & Gardner, 1971) was not as adept at encoding relationships among objects as she was at encoding relationships between individuals.

Abstract or rule learning is herein considered to be the foundation of the private or covert dimension of intelligence and language referred to earlier. Learning of this type was probably necessary for the accretion of skills which allowed for the elaboration of public language, the type of language which in its decontextualized form becomes "the medium for passing on knowledge" (Bruner, 1974, p. 38). The reader is referred to Rumbaugh (1970, 1971) Warren (1973, 1974), and Mason (1976) for reviews which bear upon comparative learning and representational processes from a comparative perspective.

D. Cross-modal Perception

The capacity to equate stimuli on the basis of independent input from diverse sensory modalities may also have become progressively refined as the primate brain evolved. (See chapter 3 by Ettlinger for a review of this topic.) Davenport and Rogers (1970) demonstrated that great-ape subjects are able to select one of two haptically sensed stimuli and match them to a visual sample in tests using novel materials. They have also shown that without special training apes are able to use high-quality photographic representations as the visual stimuli to be matched through haptic choice, and that apes are also able to negotiate at least a 20-second delay prior to haptic choice. They interpreted these findings to mean that the apes are able to store symbolic information beyond the commonly accepted limits of short-term memory without the benefit of formal verbal competencies to mediate that storage (Davenport, Rogers, & Russell, 1973, 1975).

Attempts by Davenport and others to establish cross-modal competencies with rhesus macaque (*Macaca mulatta*) subjects have succeeded only marginally. Rhesus do have at least circumscribed skills of this type, however, for Cowey and Weiskrantz (1975) have demonstrated their ability to visually select edible from inedible foods with distinctive shapes subsequent to haptic experience with them during feeding sessions in the dark. In this writer's opinion, extant data demonstrating abilities for cross-modal perception more clearly differentiate great apes from rhesus macaques than do any other type of data obtained in formal test situations.

Deficiencies in cross-modal perceptual skills can apparently serve to restrict the perceptual processes necessary to process sensory inputs from diverse environmental sources efficiently. Such deficits would seem to hamper the organism's ability to monitor events in a highly dynamic environment and to automatize patterned behavior (Lieberman, 1975, p. 92), and they would also seem to preclude the decontextualized use of language described by Bruner. Formal language systems may quite possibly serve to integrate environmental events and concurrently enhance the options for adaptive behavior. As Bruner sees it, ". . . though language springs from and aids action, it quickly becomes self-contained and free of the context of action. It is a device, moreover, that frees its possessor from the immediacy of the environment not only by pre-emption of attention during language use but by its capacity to direct attention toward those aspects of the environment that are singled out by language" (1974, p. 37).

E. The Evolution of Human Speech

Animals have relatively sophisticated communication channels which are used in ways that enhance the probabilities of survival. But while some of their species-typical signals might be altered through imitation, stimulation, and learning, ". . . there is no evidence that [animals] continue to recombine qualitatively different vocal units, separately meaningful, into new messages with new meanings. In other words, they have no syntax" (Marler, 1975, p. 33). According to Marler, is was the early evolutionary emergence of "templates" into the perception and learning of speech that facilitated the human child's mastery of speech by imitation and the segmentation of highly dynamic speech sounds and prepared as well for "the syntactical openness that made our speech such a powerful force in social evolution" (1975, p. 34). Marler's comparative studies with song sparrows and chimpanzee vocalization patterns and his review of studies dealing with animal communication and human speech perception led him to suggest "that speech arose not just from a general increase in human intellectual capacity, but from a distinctive concatenation of specific physiological abilities on the one hand, and behavioral and ecological opportunities on the other, pressing the exploitation of these abilities to the utmost. Though human in detail, none of the basic physiological mechanisms is in principle unique to man" (1975, p. 34). In Marler's opinion it was probably the discovery and exploitation of the tools used in cooperative hunting that selected for those processes which collectively constitute human language.

The development of competent speech surely followed a gradual evolutionary course, and one which perhaps faltered along the way. The great apes never have evolved the cortical control allowing for the graded repertoire of vocalizations necessary for speech. Various studies (see Kellogg, 1968, for a review), notably the one by Hayes and Nissen (1971, reviewed below), have demonstrated that the ape can master only the most rudimentary skills of speech. Thoughts concerning the evolution of human speech are found in theoretical articles and research reports by Liberman, Cooper, Shankweiler, and Studdert-Kennedy (1967), Nottenbohm (1972), Lieberman (1975), Hamilton (1974), Falk (1975), Pribram (1971, 1976), and Dingwall (1975). The work of these investigators suggests that the evolution of human speech involved a number of coordinated evolutionary developments, including the following: refined neocortical control over the movements of the tongue, jaw, lips, larynx, and vocal cords; alterations in the anatomy of the larynx and the relative positions of the epiglottis and velum which facilitate the articulation of a broad range of sounds; cytoarchitectural areas of special control for speech (Broca's area) and word comprehension (Wernicke's area), and the requisite neural tracts for their coordinated function (notably the arcuate fasciculus and the angular and supramarginal gyri); hemispheric asymmetry in sensitivity for auditory speech perception; enhanced neural associations for commerce between the visual, auditory, sensory, and motor cortices; and possibly neurological feature detectors which predispose even the human infant to attend selectively to certain sounds used in speech, to discriminate similar phonemes, and to emulate selectively certain sounds that are germane to natural speech. These and other evolutionary developments are rather reliably associated with hemispheric asymmetry of the planum temporale, which is very pronounced in man, extant but not as extensive in the great apes, and possibly absent in the rhesus monkey (Yeni-Komshian & Benson, 1976).

Apart from the above developments and the development of the frontal lobes, there are relatively few characteristics of the human brain which differentiate it from the apes', except for its extraordinary size. For man's average body weight, his brain is approximately 3 to 3-1/2 times greater than what would be predicted from the brain/body-weight regression line for primates in general (Radinsky, 1975).

F. Summary

The conceptual foundations of ape-language projects are in line with the evolutionary framework of comparative psychology (Church, 1971; Riesen, 1974; Savage & Rumbaugh, 1977). The projects all rest on the assumption that animals are capable of behaviors which form a continuum with human language functions. Speech has been rejected as a requisite to language, despite its refinement for linguistic communication among humans. Artificial or other "silent" language systems have been devised to circumvent the inability of the apes to master human speech. And apes have been the preferred choice for these projects of animals to date because their behavior and brains bear such close resemblance to ours.

II. THE LANGUAGE PROJECTS

The origin of the idea that the chimpanzee and the other great apes might be capable of learning a natural human language is perhaps impossible to identify. Hewes (1976, 1977) provides a detailed historical account of the theories of glottogenesis and of speculations regarding the possibility that apes might learn language. This writer is indebted to Hewes for bringing to his attention the conjecture of La Mettrie in 1748 (published in 1912) that it might be possible to teach language to an ape. La Mettrie indicated that he would choose a young ape, one with "the most intelligent face," and one whose mastery of tasks confirmed that it was indeed intelligent. He would pair the ape with an excellent teacher, Amman, whose ability to discover "ears in eyes" of humans born deaf (to teach them language despite their handicap) had left a lasting impression on him. La Mettrie thought that apes might even be taught literally to speak and that if they could learn to do so, they would then know "a language." Unlike the other "true" philosophers of his time, he viewed the transition from animals to man as a continuum, not a "violent" break. And he speculated on the state of man before "the invention of words and the knowledge of language," concluding that man was then but another animal species, though one with less instinct than other animals. La Mettrie viewed language skills as the origin of law, science, and the fine arts and held that they had served to polish "the rough diamond of our mind." Should the ape master language, he too would be gentled; he would no longer be "a wild man, nor a defective man, but he would be a perfect man, a little gentleman. . . ." Nearly two centuries later Yerkes (1927) also speculated that apes might master a gestural, nonvocal language system.

Kellogg's review (1968) provides the reader with a comprehensive account of early attempts to teach apes to speak. At the turn of the century, efforts by Witmer (1909) and Furness (1916) netted only the slightest suggestion of success—despite arduous effort, their chimpanzee and orangutan subjects mastered only one or two approximations of words. In their own work, the Kelloggs demonstrated that the chimpanzee does have a rather well developed ability to "understand" simple voiced commands; Gua, their subject, was able to respond appropriately to 68 specific commands. In brief, their chimpanzee appeared to have at least a receptive competence for language if not an expressive one. Gua was not subject to extensive, systematic training to develop language, but there was nothing to prevent her from developing an expressive linguistic competence on her own in the enriched home environment in which she was kept had she been so disposed and able to do so. Neither Gua nor any other ape kept as a research subject in a home situation nor any ape kept as a pet has developed a voiced language competence on its own initiative. Although apes do communicate by combinations (not syntactically arranged) of vocalizations, gestures, movements, and facial expressions, they do not develop human language skills simply by living with humans in a linguistically saturated milieu.

A. Project Viki

The Hayeses (Hayes & Nissen, 1971) were the first to conduct a prolonged program with a chimpanzee that included an attempt to teach it to communicate via speech. Their chimpanzee, Viki, was kept in their home and was subject to a wide variety of ingeniously cast projects to tap her "higher mental functions." Tasks entailing the use of instruments; the perception of numbers in a manner that suggests rudimentary counting skills; and the mastery, use, and generation of concepts are lucidly reported by Hayes and Nissen. Viki's limited success in learning sequences of responses in string-pulling tasks was taken to suggest a barrier caused by her lack of language skills. Efforts to teach her speech met with only a modicum of success. Viki chimpanzee mastered four voiceless approximations of "mama," "papa," "cup," and "up." She also used "clicking of the teeth" for a ride in the car, "tsk" to get a cigarette, and another sound, said to be reminiscent of the "clicks" used in certain non-European languages, for requesting to go outdoors (Hayes & Hayes, 1950). Ironically, the Hayeses' failure did lead them to consider the use of a gesture language, in part because of a written suggestion by Hewes (see Hewes, 1977, for an account of the correspondence); ultimately, however, they did not attempt to teach Viki a gestural language, though their reports of her behavior are replete with instances where she used gestures of her own initiative to attempt communication. For instance, Viki would "ask" for a ride by gesturing toward the car outside, by leading one of the Hayeses by the hand to the drawer which contained the key to the front door, by bringing them a purse always taken along on car rides, and by either showing a picture of a car to the Hayeses or by clicking her teeth together as a "word" for this request. Systematic use of a gestural language with an ape was not implemented until 1966 with the launching of Project Washoe, described below (also see Gardner & Gardner, 1971).

The study by the Hayeses was not a failure, however, for it served to underscore the advanced cognitive skills possessed by their subject, Viki. It also served to indicate that if the chimpanzee were capable of language as used by man, its language would not be likely to take the form of speech. Since the time of the study with Viki, a great deal has been learned about the anatomic restrictions of the chimpanzee's vocal tract as far as the production of human phones and phonemes is concerned (Lieberman, 1968). Had these limitations been understood in 1947 when the study began, the Hayeses would probably not have used speech as the language medium for training. That probability notwithstanding, we are fortunate that an able pair of researchers did attempt what is now viewed as impossible—the instruction of a chimpanzee in human speech.

B. Project Washoe

The project undertaken by Beatrice T. and R. Allen Gardner (1971) in June, 1966, provided the first strong evidence that the chimpanzee has the potential to master at least the rudiments of a language system devised and used by man. From the Hayeses' project with Viki, the Gardners had concluded that either the chimpanzee did not possess the capacity for significant two-way communication or that, though the capacity was indeed present, human speech was not a feasible medium for such communication.

For them it seemed reasonable to expect that "behavior that is at least continuous with human language can be found in other species" (Gardner &

Gardner, 1971, p. 118). This perspective, fundamental to the field of comparative psychology, is held in common by all investigators who study the potentials of the chimpanzee for language. More critical, however, are the questions: What is the linguistic domain? and, What is language? For the Gardners, any system is a language if ". . . it is used as a language by a group of human beings" (1971, p. 122).

Speech was ruled out as a feasible choice for cultivating two-way communication skills in their chimpanzee subject, Washoe, a female estimated to be between 8 and 14 months of age when the project began. (The subject was named after Washoe county in which the Gardners' academic home, the University of Nevada, is situated.) The American Sign Language (Ameslan) was selected as the linguistic medium for the project (1) because it met their definition of a language in that it is used widely by one group of human beings, the deaf in the United States, (2) because the chimpanzee in the field is reported to use gestures in social communications, and (3) because the use of gestures would obviate the many difficulties in the invention of a synthetic language. In view of the lack of a generally accepted set of criteria for determining when a given human being has language competence, the Gardners refused to commit themselves to performance criteria for concluding that their chimpanzee had mastered language; however, they did anticipate that meaningful comparisons might be made between the signing skills of the chimpanzee and those of children.

The diverse aspects of Ameslan and questions regarding its structure, syntax, and production are to be found in Stokoe, Casterline, and Croneberg (1965), Bellugi and Klima (1975), and Stokoe (1975). For this author, the appropriateness of Ameslan for the Gardners' project, given what was then *not* known about the chimpanzee's propensities for learning language skills, was vindicated not only by their project's results, but by Stokoe's (1975, p. 210) report that, according to their parents' reports, the hearing children of deaf parents have *signed sentences* prior to learning to talk! Such observations seemingly attest to the "naturalness" of communicating by manual gestures and support Hewes's theory (1973, 1976) that manual gesturing was possibly the original medium of linguistic communication among the precursors of man.

To date, all of the ape-language projects have made varying, but nonetheless significant, demands on the subjects' use of hands. The ability to gesture or to sign with facility is contingent, in part, upon a highly mobile hand, the evolution of which is fairly well understood. Through the course of primate evolution the hand has undergone radical modifications (Schultz, 1969; Steklis & Harnad, 1976) which have made it quite versatile for gesturing. The thumb in the Old World monkeys (*Cercopithecoidea*) evolved to a point of rotation so that between its transverse axis and the transverse axis of the other digits an angle approximating 90° was formed. It also branched more proximally to the second phalangeal joint and acquired increased mobility, thereby allowing for the hand to generate a greater repertoire of finely controlled movements. These trends produced remarkable manual skills in the chimpanzee and the gorilla, many of which are of nearly human quality. The late scientist-philosopher J. Bronowski, in reference to the productions of the human hand, noted that "man alone leaves traces of what he created" (1973, p. 38). For him, "The hand is the cutting edge of the mind," and the ascent of man's civilization ". . . is the refinement of the hand in action" (p. 116).

1. Washoe's Laboratory

The Gardners were determined to provide, insofar as resources would permit, a rich, stimulating environment within which their subject would live and learn. A trailer home surrounded by a large fenced yard comprised the laboratory context. Within this context, Washoe was treated in many ways as though she were a human child—not with the intention of simulating a human family-life condition as with the Kelloggs and the Hayeses, but to provide a challenging milieu within which she might learn and apply language skills in an adaptive manner.

The trailer and the yard were equipped with a variety of materials to stimulate Washoe's attention, activity, and language-learning. In addition, trips to various parts of the city, the university, and the country were provided. The goal was to immerse Washoe in a linguistically enriched style of living that would foster whatever language skills her *Pan troglodytes* genetic endowment might support. The linguistic context was restricted to Ameslan, except for the inevitable speech sounds of the neighborhood and the occasional outings. No deliberate attempt was made to keep Washoe's milieu silent, but every effort was made to restrict communications between persons in her presence to Ameslan so that she would have only one linguistic system to imitate.

2. Teaching Methods

Various methods of teaching signs to Washoe were employed. Initially, attempts were made to shape responses from gestures which in some manner suggested that target sign to be mastered. Efforts to capitalize on Washoe's manual "babbling" were also made initially, but these were abandoned as relatively futile. Guidance was found to be perhaps the best method of all; it entailed holding Washoe's hand, forming her fingers in the desired fashion and moving her hand thus formed through the movement appropriate to the sign-to-be-learned, and then giving her a reward such as food or tickling. Washoe also acquired a few signs through observation (e.g., *sweet:* contact of tongue and lower lip with first and second fingers) of those signing about her and even invented a few signs of her own (e.g., *bib:* drawing the outline of one with index fingers on the chest) which, interestingly, proved to be valid Ameslan signs (Gardner & Gardner, 1971, p. 139).

Detailed daily records were kept of Washoe's spontaneous signing and her responses to questions such as *What is it*? or *What do you want*? Only when three observers reported Washoe to have signed spontaneously and appropriately to the context was the introduction of a sign recorded. The criterion for determining that a given sign had been *reliably* mastered by Washoe was extremely, and perhaps overly, stringent. It required that Washoe generate at least one observed appropriate and spontaneous use of a sign for 15 *consecutive* days. McNeill (1974, p. 77) concludes, based on his own work and L. Bloom's, that the object-words that children acquire are highly transitory and that substitutions across days are the rule. By implication, the stringent criterion employed for defining a sign as reliable for Washoe might well have served to exclude object-words in early stages. This risk was perhaps minimized by the Gardners when they began to conduct two formal sessions daily during which time stimuli were introduced for the possible elicitation of those signs not otherwise observed. Although the rationale for the criterion of reliability of Washoe's signs was fundamentally sound, it in no way ensured that the initial corpus was comprehensive; other criteria would have resulted in different definitions of Washoe's lexicon. Consequently, its exact composition may be compared with those of the human child but only with a certain risk of lack of definition.

A self-paced, double-blind testing situation was devised by the Gardners to establish Washoe's signs unequivocally in reference to an array of exemplars. High reliability was reported. Within limits, the semantic value of each sign was inferred as it was or was not given in response to novel exemplars of the referent.

It bears noting, however, that the test procedures did not provide for a way to determine the degree to which Washoe's signs were essentially generalized responses to stimuli similar to those used in prior training. Her competence in the use of her signs syntactically in order to generate and transmit truly novel messages, information, or requests was not tapped by this or any other test. Instances of her using signs in these ways were reported separately; however, they may have been fortuitous productions.

Her extensions of certain "word-signs" to exemplars quite foreign to those used initially in training are, nonetheless, quite impressive in many instances and should be accepted as evidence that Washoe did conceptualize the meanings of certain signs in a semantic sense. A prime example is in her use of the sign for *open*. Initially she learned this word in reference to a door of the trailer in which she lived. Its use was extended spontaneously (i.e., without special training) to various doors of buildings, to the lids of briefcases and boxes, and, most impressively of all, to a water faucet apparently as part of a request that she be given a drink of water (Gardner & Gardner, 1969). Extensions of the use of signs in response to other than the exemplars or contexts in which they were initially used were recognized by the Gardners as constituting the best opportunity for inferring the meaning which the words had for Washoe.

Significantly, Washoe not only imitated but did so on a deferred basis. One morning, for example, the Gardners tried unsuccessfully to give Washoe an injection. Later on that same morning, Washoe was observed to be sticking the inside of her thigh with a long nail which she found, her actions not unlike those she saw the Gardners attempting to carry out on her with the hypodermic needle (1971, p. 178). This episode is apparently a remarkable instance of a chimpanzee engaging in an activity that would suggest both a representation of the initial shot-giving episode and the metaphorical use of a nail.

On the question of whether or not Washoe gave evidence of using syntax, the Gardners were properly guarded in their 1971 report. Nonrandom patterns of stringing signs were not necessarily taken to mean that Washoe had some sense or mastery of syntactic principles. After all, no rules for the stringing of signs were required in Washoe's training. In addition, there was always the possibility that generalized imitation of combinations of signs used by the humans might have determined Washoe's patterns. Those views and possibilities notwithstanding, it is impressive and, I believe, highly significant that Washoe did spontaneously string signs together; she did so selectively and in many instances very appropriately (signing at a locked door–*gimme key, more key, open more, open key please, in open help;* requesting soda pop ["sweet drink"]–*please sweet drink, gimme sweet, please hurry sweet drink, please gimme sweet drink* [Gardner & Gardner, 1971, p. 167]). It would also seem that her use of signs was characterized by certain consistencies idiosyncratically determined. In short, Washoe's use of signs in some degree suggests extended linguistic functions, as seen in her propensity for stringing words as though to form phrases, and also an inkling of syntactic sensitivity. At no point, however, was Washoe highly productive in forming and transmitting novel statements in the diverse situations available to her; nonetheless, we cannot assume on the basis of her performance that the mastery of these skills is beyond the competence of the chimpanzee, be it Washoe or any other subject.

At the conclusion of the 1971 report, the Gardners reasserted their reluctance to join the debate on the capacity of an animal (Washoe) to acquire language. They acknowledged that in the final analysis language can be defined so as either to include or exclude a given set of data, and they left it to others to conclude for themselves whether or not Washoe had achieved language.

A later report by the Gardners (1975a) on Project Washoe builds upon the hypothesis that the best evidence of vocabulary use by young children lies in their composition of sentences in response to "wh" (who, what, where, and whose) questions. They predicted that because Washoe was maintained under conditions similar to those of a child, her responses to wh questions would be similar to those of children. From the 50th and 51st months of the project, Washoe's responses to 50 wh questions of 10 different question-frame types were examined. The Gardners made a variety of analyses to determine whether ". . . the replies were grammatically controlled by the questions" (1975a, p. 251). The words of Washoe's responses were categorized into proper names, pronouns, possessives, locative verb phrases, etc., for the 10 different question frames; a significant relationship was statistically established, and Washoe was adjudged to be relatively advanced compared to young children (Stage III, Brown, 1968). But whether this level of mastery constitutes "grammatical" control is a real question, for grammar subsumes word-order effects. The constituents of Washoe's responses to the wh questions (e.g., Q. *Who you*? A. *Linn;* Q. *Whose that*? A. *Shoes you;* Q. *Where we go*? A. *You me out*) were by and large appropriate, but the report and its analyses did not address questions regarding the logic inherent in the organization of responses that entailed *more* than one word–a relevant issue in the evaluation of "grammatical control."

The Gardners have been sensitive, and quite responsibly so, to the possibility that Washoe's responses might have been inadvertently cued by the questioners. They conclude that their double-blind testing situation for tests of vocabulary ". . . must be the rock-bottom definition of verbal behavior" (1975a, p. 256). They argue further that, in their requirements for "production" by Washoe (i.e., that she form the hand signs for responding) and for other tasks as described above, inherent control against cueing her responses was built in: the cues would have to ". . . contain as much information as the correct replies" (1975a, p. 256). But in instances where her replies consisted of only one or two words, it is possible that cues, *if extant,* might have provided all the information necessary for correct responses: production does not *necessarily* preclude all risk of inadvertant cueing of the subject.

Interestingly, in their most recent article the Gardners refer to Köhler's (1925) early work in which Köhler demonstrates that chimpanzees are able ". . . to combine and recombine their learned responses in meaningful sequences" (Gardner & Gardner, 1975 a, p. 245). Since chimpanzees had long been known to possess this type of ability, the Gardners state that they, unlike other researchers, saw no need to determine the chimpanzee's capacity for language. Consequently, they designed their research to determine whether a chimpanzee might use a *bona fide* human language, i.e., Ameslan. Support for their train of reasoning, that chimpanzees were already *known* to possess the capacity for "language," is generally lacking, for language is surely more than the mere recombination of responses. If it is no more than that, then every animal form that has been conditioned to chain responses in sequences and that modified those sequences might be said to have language. The question of whether or not the chimpanzee is capable of language admittedly revolves around definitional problems just as the Gardners assert–of that there is no doubt. Until those definitional problems are resolved, the question of the chimpanzee's capacity for language should remain open.

C. Project Sarah

A precursor to Premack's work with Sarah chimpanzee was his earlier work (Premack & Schwartz, 1966) designed to determine whether a chimpanzee might master a joy-stick control so as to modulate the generation of electronically produced sounds for communication purposes. This study, while not successful, was an admirable attempt to circumvent the chimpanzee's limitations in the production of vocal sounds for linguistic exchange.

Premack's work with Sarah contrasts sharply with the methods employed by the Gardners in Project Washoe. In contrast to the Gardners' requirements that work begin with an infant chimpanzee, that the chimpanzee be maintained in a linguistically saturated and generally stimulating environment, and that it be signed to in the course of social exchanges throughout the waking hours, Premack's work with Sarah (1970, 1971a, 1971b) was modeled after the general approach and methods employed by experimental psychologists in laboratory animal research projects. Sarah, like Washoe, was feral-born and was but an infant (estimated 9 months old) when received by Premack. For the first year, she was raised in a home where she could be given the personalized care necessary for normal healthy development. Beyond that point she was maintained in a laboratory setting and served in various research projects. Nonetheless, her social contacts with humans continued to be close and until she was about seven years old she enjoyed the probable benefits of daily outings, which included romps on the beach. Her linguistic training sessions took place during specified and limited hours of each day, and the methods employed in those sessions were more of a discrete-trial type than of the social-interactional type used with Washoe. All of these differences notwithstanding, Sarah did exceedingly well in her mastery of language skills. How and why she did so warrants the closest attention, because the results contain clear implications for our understanding of the roots of language and how it should be defined.

The methods devised for Sarah's training sessions were precise. Each one was intended to inculcate a specific linguistic function. Premack was interested in the chimpanzee's intelligence and did not intend that his chimpanzee simulate human language (as the Gardners had hoped Washoe would do in the mastery of Ameslan). Rather, he wished to demonstrate experimentally a functional analysis of language skills.

For Premack, language training was in essence (1) the mapping of existing knowledge through the acquisition of word meanings, (2) the mastery of a set of concepts (e.g., name-of, color-of, same-as, different-than, relations between things in space, etc.), and (3) the learning of rules for relating words to one another for the purpose of constructing and decoding the internal organization of sentences, in which word order is relevant, (Premack, 1970, p. 113). As important as vocabulary is, by itself it is not language. Premack never pressed his subject for the mastery of a large vocabulary; throughout training he stressed the basic functions of productive, syntactic language.

Sarah's language was a synthetic one, its words consisting of pieces of plastic of various colors and random shapes. The words could be securely placed on a magnetized board, a feature which allowed for the possibility of sustained visual access to compensate for possible limitations in chimpanzees' short-term memory (see Rumbaugh, 1970, for a review) and also for total control over the linguistic options afforded the subject. Although it is reasonable to conclude that effective social relationships between Sarah and her testers did exist (chimpanzees just don't work well for people they dislike!), they were probably not as pervasive as those between the Gardners and Washoe.

Premack's basic strategy assumed that every complex rule of language can be analyzed into simpler units. By defining these units and devising a procedure for teaching them, one may inculcate language in organisms that do not otherwise have it.

Sarah's first words were taught by pairing agents, objects, and actions with corresponding language elements. Strings of two or more words were then built; by restricting the word options available but nonetheless requiring that Sarah eventually fill in every empty slot in the sentence, word meanings were taught. The negation "No" was introduced as an injunction against certain actions, as in, for example, "No Sarah take banana." Through the presentation of pairs comprised of identical and nonidentical members coupled with the marker for the interrogative and a word to specify either "same" or "different," Sarah learned to respond appropriately by selecting the word for either "yes" or "no," depending both on the members of a pair in a given presentation and on whether the question-word was "same" or "different." Thus if the two members were identical and Sarah was asked if they were "different," her correct answer was "no."

Through extensions of these procedures, Sarah learned "name-of" as a concept which facilitated her mastery of new names. Language also was used to teach additional language. Dimensional class words for color, shape, and size were likewise used to teach Sarah still other specific words. Quite impressively, the property name "brown color-of chocolate," was used at a time when both "chocolate" and "color-of" were familiar words and "brown" was new. On the basis of that metalinguistic event, Sarah was able to select the "brown" disc (from a set of four distinctively colored ones) and to insert it in a specific dish when commanded, "Sarah insert brown [in] red dish" (Premack, 1971b, p. 211).

Sarah also learned to describe whether a card of a given color was on, under, or to the side of a card of another designated color, and she learned to place them correctly in response to requests such as, "red on green." Sentences were built up through the acquisition of unit skills which could be hierarchically organized into logically structured strings of words. Subsequently, mastery of the conditional "if-then" allowed for appropriate performance in response to statements such as, "[If] Sarah no take red [then] Mary give Sarah cracker," (1971b, p. 222; bracketed expressions added by this author).

Premack was and continues to be sensitive to fundamental questions such as, "When does something come to serve as a word?" In addition to demonstrating that pieces of plastic functioned as words in naming tasks and in requests by Sarah for different items, Premack demonstrated that in response to an item identified only by its plastic word piece, the object itself being absent, Sarah could describe its features. For example, in response to the blue piece of plastic which functioned as the word for "apple," Sarah described "apple" as red (not green), round (not square), and as having a stem. Also, she seemingly inferred that a knife had caused an apple to be sectioned and demonstrated an ability to represent or infer the name of the various fruits from which seeds, stems, etc., came (Premack, 1975, 1976).

Premack's work with Sarah made a powerful impact on other researchers, not only because of the impressive empirical data it produced but also because of the perceptive theory regarding the nature and acquisition of language which it generated. He demonstrated that through use of a functional and analytical approach, novel insights about an exceedingly complex set of phenomena can be gained. At the same time, interestingly, he has retained a willingness to speak both mentalistically and nativistically, as, for example, when he states that "The mind appears to be a device for forming internal representations. If it were not, there could be neither words nor language . . . every response is a potential word. The procedures that train animals will also produce words" (1971b, p. 226). A remarkable blend of apparent mentalism, nativism, and functionalism!

This author agrees with McNeill's conclusion: "Thus, Premack's experiment complements the Gardners' by showing a difference between chimpanzees and children that is correlated with the ability to perceive and presumably use, syntactic patterns that encode conceptual relations. The conceptual relations themselves appear to be available to both species, a conclusion that Sarah's performance reinforces quite strongly" (McNeill, 1974, p. 88).

D. The Lana Project

The germinal idea for the Lana Project came to this author in the fall of 1970 as a direct consequence of the research reports emanating from Projects Washoe and Sarah. The basic motivation behind the Lana Project was to obviate the extraordinary investments of human time and effort required in one-on-one research with single chimpanzee subjects. Alternative methods to those previously employed had to be devised if researchers were to expedite investigation into the nature of language and the capacity for language by life forms other than man. Automation of training procedures seemed the obvious answer. It would serve both to enhance the efficiency of training and to objectify the procedures; it would allow for the automatic recording of all linguistic events and for computerized summary and analysis thereof, and in due course it would provide for a technology with which to support systematic study of the parameters controlling the emergence of initial language skills. Success in this undertaking would also allow for the eventual extension of the training system to research with alinguistic mentally retarded children, who for a variety of reasons find the acquisition of expressive language skills very difficult.

Consultation with a creative bioengineer, Harold Warner, led to the conclusion that such an undertaking was feasible and later to the formation of an interdisciplinary team that worked to define the myriad facets such a system might have. Research resources became available to the project in January, 1972, and by February, 1973, the system was in operation.

The entire system has been summarized elsewhere (Rumbaugh, von Glasersfeld, Warner, Pisani, Gill, Brown, & Bell, 1973), and recent articles by Warner, Bell, Rumbaugh, and Gill (1976) and by von Glasersfeld (1977) provide technical details of the electronics and of the synthetic language termed "Yerkish" which was devised specifically for the Lana Project. Consequently, only its most salient features will be described here.

The system was designed to provide around-the-clock operations that would not require the presence of a human operator or experimenter. The subject's room, built of plastic and glass, permitted excellent two-way visual access. The subject was provided with a keyboard console equipped with keys, each one serving as the functional equivalent of a word.

The keys were differentiated by unique geometric configurations embossed on their surfaces to designate specific objects, animates, edibles, colors, prepositions, activities, and so forth. Each class of words had a distinctive color for its keys to help the subject learn the various word classes. The keyboard console and the keys themselves were designed to provide for the ready relocation of the keys so that their locations alone would never provide cues as to their function or meaning, and the subject would have to attend to the geometric configurations, termed "*lexigrams,*" which were to serve as formal, functional words. The keys were back-lighted when in an active state (i.e., when their depression would be sensed by the computer); when depressed, a key became brighter in order to allow the subject to review what she had linguistically produced. When a key was depressed, a facsimile of the lexigram on its surface was produced in an overhead row of projectors. The net result was the production, from left to right in a row of projectors, of a visual portrayal of the sentence or word string.

Outside Lana's room, another keyboard was accessible to the experimenter. Its function was identical to that of her keyboard; the use of either keyboard resulted in the transmission of the visually portrayed sentences to allow for two-way communication and also potentially for conversation. Situated between these keyboards was a PDP-8E computer with the necessary interfacing. It served to monitor all linguistic events, to evaluate their grammar in accordance with the rules of the Yerkish language, and to record via the activation of a teleprinter and a punched paper tape all communications and the time of day they occurred. Syntactically correct requests for a variety of foods and drinks or for a variety of events (such as a movie, projected slides, music, or the opening of a window) were rewarded automatically by the language-training system. Other requests for social interactions (grooming, tickling, swinging, a trip outdoors) were honored if the person named was present and had the time to honor the request.

Initial training began with Lana's learning to use a single key, followed by her mastery of what were termed "stock sentences," sentences which reliably served to net for the subject drinks or foods of certain types, various types of entertainment, etc. These sentences were taught through essentially standard operant conditioning techniques; at the time of their initial mastery, there was no reason to believe that Lana possessed semantic meanings for any of the keys. Special training procedures instituted to teach her not only the names of things, but also the concept that things do have names (Gill & Rumbaugh, 1974) served initially to instruct her, within limits, in the meanings of the various keys. Similarly, Lana was taught eight colors, the names of various items, and several prepositions so as to expand her working vocabulary and to allow her to make reference to things either by name, by attribute, or by location.

On her own initiative, Lana extended her use of "stock sentences" for other than the originally intended single purposes (Rumbaugh & Gill, 1976, 1977). Furthermore, she extended the use of "no," as taught within the context of answering "yes" or "no" to questions about whether the window or door were shut or open, to include "no" as meaning "don't do that." The initial occasion for her doing so was to protest a technician's drinking of a Coca-cola when she had none. Still later, she spontaneously used "no" to produce the meaning "it is not true that [food's name] is in the machine for vending" (Rumbaugh & Gill, 1976).

Through the course of other studies (Rumbaugh & Gill, 1976), it was determined that Lana's familiarity with items facilitated her execution of cross-modal judgments of sameness-difference, and that apart from familiarity, names seemingly made their separate contribution to the accuracy of the judgments. But the primary goal was to cultivate in Lana the desire and the skills needed to converse with us about a wide variety of subjects. After all, most everyday language of humans occurs in the context of conversation, in the course of which attempts are made to exchange the proper social amenities, to define topics or problems that need mutual attention, to evaluate alternative courses of action or methods of solving problems, to plan for the future relative to the experiences of the past, and so forth. Significantly Lana began to enter into conversation without any formal training to do so. Her first conversation was to ask, in essence, whether she might come out and drink some Coca-cola (Rumbaugh & Gill, 1975). Her exact formulation, novelly composed from words and phrases of stock sentences and requests used in the naming training sessions was, "Lana drink this out-of room?" The subsequent question put to Lana, "Drink what?" led to an appropriate refinement, "Lana drink coke out-of room?"

Conversations with Lana have been examined in detail (Gill, 1977; Rumbaugh, Gill, von Glasersfeld, Warner, & Pisani, 1975; Rumbaugh & Gill, 1975, 1976, 1977). It seems clear that Lana has been prone to converse whenever she must do so in order to receive something exceptional, or whenever something not in accordance with the routine delivery of foods and drinks has occurred—in short, when some practical problem arises for her. She has never *in conversation* commented extensively on this or that as children and adults are inclined when their attention or motivation shifts unpredictably. For Lana, language is an adaptive behavior of considerable instrumental value for achieving specific goals not readily achieved otherwise. To date, at least, she has not used expressive language to expand her horizons except to ask for the name of something which she then requested by the name given (Rumbaugh et al., 1975).

Color terms in those natural languages which possess them serve as conceptual codes for describing variations in hue and brightness. Such color-naming systems are not arbitrarily derived; rather, the opponent-process underpinnings of hue perception apparently provide for the evolution of color terms based on physiological contingencies (Bornstein, 1973; Bornstein, Kessen, & Weiskopf, 1976; Hurvich & Jameson, 1974). A human, given the necessary visual apparatus, the necessary linguistic environment, and the requisite cognitive capacity, will develop an arbitrary conceptual code which serves reliably to denote non-arbitrary portions of color-space. Essock (1977) asked if Lana, given the fact that she possesses color vision which is extremely similar to that of a normal human (Grether, 1940), would do the same.

Subsequent to Lana's acquisition of eight color terms following training with eight arbitrarily selected training colors (red, orange, yellow, green, blue, purple, black, white), Essock presented Lana with over 350 different Munsell color chips to determine whether she would use her color terms reliably to describe colors perceptually distant from her training colors. Over the course of the experiment, each chip was presented for identification on three widely separated occasions. Lana's response distribution resembled that of human subjects tested under similar conditions. Over 99% of the time only two responses at most competed as possible labels for a given color chip, and when two responses competed, they were always the names for spectrally adjacent hues. Lana's assignment of color names to various areas of color-space did *not* produce areas labeled by a given color term surrounded by increasingly variable responses to colors perceptually distant from the training colors, as should be the case following stimulus generalization. Rather, her responses formed well-defined areas in which a single color name was given to a particular hue despite wide changes in brightness and saturation. This finding is further evidence that Lana does possess sufficient cognitive capabilities to assimilate and adopt arbitrary conceptual codes and to use such codes to describe her perceptual world.

The methods of the Lana Project fall between those of Project Washoe (where the emphasis with an infant chimpanzee was on linguistic saturation, socialization, close human-chimpanzee interactions, and discourse) and those of Project Sarah (where the emphasis was on the design and implementation of rigorous, step-by-step training procedures designed to cultivate well-specified language skills with a juvenile subject). Lana was just two years old when formal work with her began. She had been laboratory-born and reared, and as a result she was probably less advantaged than either Washoe or Sarah, since both were feral-born and home-reared as well. Nonetheless, Lana has both mastered and initiated an impressive array of linguistic skills and performances, as have Washoe and Sarah. Why and how all three have succeeded so well is an interesting question when one juxtaposes the diverse characteristics of the training principles.

E. Other Ape Language Projects

The projects described above are, at present, all being continued, and since their inception, about a dozen additional projects have begun which extend the original research in various directions. Roger Fouts, initially with Project Washoe, has continued to study Washoe after she was moved to the Institute for Primate Studies of the University of Oklahoma. His studies (Fouts, 1974) have included assessments of individual differences in the acquisition of signs (Fouts, 1973), assignments of examplars to conceptual categories, chimpanzee-chimpanzee communication, and the teaching of Ameslan through spoken English.

The last of these studies by Fouts (1974) provides an impressive demonstration of how language mediates the acquisition of new information—in this instance, the meanings of words. Ally, a three-year-old Ameslan-trained chimpanzee, was tested for his understanding of 10 spoken English words used in commands to bring specified items to the experimenter. After he had demonstrated receptive competence with those 10 words, they were divided into two lists of five words each. For one of these lists, Ally then had special training, which consisted of seeing the Ameslan sign for each word for the first time while hearing the word through the modeling and speech of the experimenter. For the second list, no special instruction in Ameslan was provided. Ally was then asked to name via Ameslan each ten objects in a controlled test. He was able to name the five objects for which he had had prior training but not the five objects for which he had had no such training. Fouts's experiment serves as an important demonstration of linguistic instruction with a chimpanzee in which productive competence emerged from initial auditory receptive competence through the contiguous pairings of auditory and visual stimuli.

Additional projects in which Ameslan is being used include the work with Nim chimpanzee by Terrace and Bever (1976) and Patterson's work (1977) with Koko gorilla (*Gorilla g. gorilla*). Terrace and Bever are concentrating upon the ability of Nim to combine words in accordance with syntactical rules and are hoping to determine the abilities of chimpanzees for linguistic communication and for the report of memories, moods, and other private events. Their study is, at the writing of this chapter, in its early stages.

Patterson's study is unique in that to date it is the only one with a gorilla. Koko gorilla's progress has been as orderly and as rapid as was Washoe's at comparable stages of training. Koko's performance has corroborated essentially all of Washoe's proclivities for acquiring new signs, for extending their usage, and for appropriately chaining them together (as suggested by the context). Patterson concludes that both the chimpanzee and the gorilla parallels the human child in the early development of semantic relations.

F. Chimpanzee Language Skills and Intelligence

In conclusion, a word regarding the chimpanzee and intelligence is in order. Intelligence is admittedly a highly problematic and controversial concept. Though it is beyond the scope of this paper to review the diverse perspectives regarding intelligence and its worth as a concept, reference to Wechsler's thoughts on the question might assist in the interpretation of data emanating from the chimpanzee language projects. For Wechsler, intelligence is "the capacity of an individual to understand the world about and his resourcefulness to cope with its challenges" (1975, p. 139). In his view, its components are numerous and diverse; its reference systems include (1) awareness of what is being done and why; (2) meaningfulness, in the sense that intelligent behavior is goal-directed and not random; (3) rationality, in that intelligent behavior can be logically deduced and is consistent; and (4) usefulness, in that intelligent behavior is deemed worthwhile by the consensus of the group—i.e., the assessment of intelligence inevitably entails value judgments.

If Weschler's reference system is used to define the intelligent behaviors of the chimpanzees in language-training projects, it is not difficult to select several behaviors which seem to be meaningful and worthwhile adaptations and that are also reflections of awareness, goal-directedness, and rationality. These systems of reference are admittedly elusive, but they do serve to bring attention to the possibility that the operations of intelligence in chimpanzee and human have close resemblance. Despite the fact that the chimpanzee brain is much smaller than the human brain, its basic functions, are not, in all likelihood, totally unique.

III. A COMPARISON OF THE LANGUAGE PROJECTS

The chimpanzee language projects, particularly Projects Washoe, Sarah, and Lana, were characterized by major differences in their subjects' ages, in the languages employed, and in maintenance and training procedures. Nevertheless, all the chimpanzee subjects trained in these projects were able to master significant aspects of linguistic communication. All proved to be relatively adroit at mastering a basic working vocabulary, for example, so that at the end of their training they were able upon the presentation of an examplar to give a reliably correct response of identification (sign, plastic piece, key depression) through the use of their hands.

Admittedly, a problem exists in defining with any degree of precision the *meanings* of each and every "word" in the respective vocabularies of the various subjects. That problem notwithstanding, each subject did give clear evidence of appropriately extending word usage beyond the specific exemplars of vocabulary training. To review a few of the more important illustrations, Washoe used the word "open" first in connection with one door, then with all doors, then with the lids of briefcases, boxes, and jars, and finally as part of a request that a water faucet be turned on (Gardner & Garnder, 1971). Washoe also aptly termed a duck a "water bird," and the brazil nut a "rock berry" (Fouts, 1974). Sarah was taught the meanings of new words through instructions and information given her through the use of familiar words; she also was observed both to formulate and then to answer questions in isolation. Lana extended the meaning of "no" from "it's not true," to "don't do that," and to "there is no [food-name] in machine." Also, she has spontaneously asked for things for which she had no formal name by creating metaphorical or descriptive labels. For example, she referred to a bottled Fanta soft drink as "coke which-is orange [colored]"; she asked for an overly ripe banana as "banana which-is black"; and she has variously requested an orange as "apple which-is orange" and "ball in bowl." Fouts (1974) has reported on work with still another chimpanzee, Lucy. In the course of her training, Lucy labeled four citrus fruits "smell fruits," radishes "cry hurt food," and watermelon "drink fruit" and "candy drink." Perceptually salient characteristics apparently served as the natural bases for naming.

Both the extended usage of words and the compositions of descriptive new labels should be accepted as evidence of semanticity, both receptive and expressive. Perhaps the most convincing evidence of semanticity, however, is found in the *productive* use of words in syntactic relationships with other words. Evidence that at least rudimentary mastery of syntax was achieved is much stronger for both Sarah and Lana than for Washoe. Sarah's appropriate, differential responses to requests and to if-then conditional communications implied some understanding of syntax, as did Lana's composition of syntactically correct sentences to request that she be allowed to do something new ("Lana drink coke out-of room?" etc., [Rumbaugh & Gill, 1975, 1976]) and her ability to interact competently through the course of protracted conversations that were problem-solving in their orientation (Gill, 1977). It should also be noted that, apart from such extensions and generative usages, it is problematic to infer semanticity when the sole evidence consists of a correct response of "identification" to a single exemplar.

All of the chimpanzees have shown a readiness either to use words in chains or to attend to words in sentences. This readiness is possibly significant in that it suggests an informational capacity in the chimpanzee which is a necessary condition for the syntactic production and interpretation of signal chains, a clear requisite to the openness of language discussed earlier in this chapter and in the discussion section which follows.

IV. DISCUSSION

"In cognitive psychology, the instigation to begin peeking behind the curtain of the abstract organism has begun to arise under the influence of developments in ethology, cross-cultural research, and linguistics" (Estes, 1975, p. 6). The chimpanzee language projects might well call for a complete opening of that curtain for a variety of reasons.

A. Implications for the Definition of Language

Despite the problem that at present no definition of *language* is generally accepted, there are indications of an increasing acceptance within a variety of disciplines–psychology, anthropology, psycholinguistics, communication–that Washoe, Sarah, Lana, Lucy, Koko, and other animals have demonstrated communication skills which resemble the language used by man much more than the essentially closed (as far as we now know), non-syntactic signal systems of animals in the field. Continued studies with chimpanzees in language projects should eventually lead to an acceptable definition of language, one cast in nonanthropocentric terms (e.g., Segal, 1977).

As stated earlier, language, in this author's view, is most clearly distinguished from other forms of communication by a single attribute–its openness, one of several terms used by Hockett (1960) in his descriptive system of natural languages (see also Altmann, 1967; Hockett & Altmann, 1968). Openness here refers to the introduction of new lexical units (i.e., words) with the possibility that a totally arbitrary relationship might exist between the morphology of the lexical units (sounds, gestures, geometric patterns, etc.) and their accrued meanings. It also refers to the generation of new sentences that convey new information as old and new words are used in interaction (i.e., syntactically) so as to modulate their meanings for the encoding of information covertly selected for public transmission. The openness of language allows for all of the other characteristics of language described by Hockett, including displacement, reflexiveness, and lying, which are not otherwise specifically attributable to the physics of propagation and sound conduction (as are, for example, rapid fading and broadcasting). Because of its openness, language stands in sharp contrast with the stereotypy of most animal communication, in which there are few lexical elements and no evidence of any recombination of "qualitatively different vocal units, separately meaningful, into new messages with new meanings" (Marler, 1975, p. 33).

B. Implications for Learning Research

The chimpanzee language projects should, in due course, lead to a clarification of a number of problems in the area of learning and of the processes entailed in formulating adaptive behavior patterns (such as in the production of sentences).

Years ago, Miller (1959, p. 247) speculated that perhaps it is the enhanced capacity of man ". . . to respond selectively to more subtle aspects of the environment as cues" in an abstract manner that makes his mental processes appear to be much "higher" than those of other animals. Another explanation for the same phenomenon, he felt, might lie in man's enhanced "capacity to make a greater variety of distinctive central cue-producing responses, and especially a greater capacity to respond with a number of different cue-producing responses simultaneously so that further responses may be elicited on the basis of a pattern of cues representing several different units of experience" (1959, p. 247).

A concerted effort is now underway to effect a rapprochement between cognitive psychology and the more traditional models of S-R learning theory (e.g., Estes, 1975, 1976; Mason, 1970; Restle, 1975a, 1975b). Single-unit S-R models, where single responses are assumed to be evoked by single stimuli, cannot account for all behavioral changes that are known to take place within learning experiments (Estes, 1975). But if experiments are viewed ". . . as ways of transmitting information about the environment that, if learning occurs, will be incorporated by the animal" (Bolles, 1975, p. 272), then one might be able to explain how certain information might not only be used for the determination of an immediate response, but stored for possible reference at some future time.

Bolles considers, for example, that animal subjects might learn at least two types of predictive relationships within conditioning contexts–relationships between the stimuli and the consequences (i.e., light is followed by shock) and between responses and their consequences (i.e., if "such-and-such" responses are made, shock will be attenuated or avoided). He further proposes that animal species differ in terms of their capacities to learn predictive relationships between responses and consequences.

Bolles suggests that the learning of predictive relationships between stimuli and consequences is the more pervasive type and that species are preferentially sensitive to stimuli that are relatively important to them in their natural habitats; in other words biological constraints partially determine what will be readily attended to and learned. By extension, animal species might well differ in terms of their readiness and capacity to integrate sensory events which occur together in time or to integrate motor patterns for responding (Osgood, 1957).

The predictive learning abilities of a given species and its mediating capabilities are all important in determining its ability to receive, process, and use information advantageously in formulating novel response patterns, particularly as called for in concept-based behaviors and language. Expressions based on language skills entail the coordination of several complex functions. Problem situations must be defined and analyzed. Their dimensions must receive selective attention. Words must be called up for possible use, and their concatenation must adhere to certain sets of rules. Seemingly, identical problem situations confronted by linguistically trained subjects of various genera might reveal differences in terms of what is perceived or defined as a problem, how it is attended to and analyzed, and how response tactics are deliberated and selected for use. This would be the case, of course, only to the degree that the linguistic expressions would correspond with the psychological processes activated by systematic variations in problem situations—not an unreasonable assumption; but the possibility that language-type training programs and test situations might be uniquely sensitive to species differences in propensities for attending to and for analyzing various classes of problems for the determination of response tactics should not be overlooked. To the degree that species differences in the formulation of linguistic responses would prove relatively insensitive to wide variations in rearing and experience, basic biological differences in proclivity to respond would be implicated.

C. Language Acquisition and the Formation of Concepts

Language skills are widely believed to facilitate mediating processes, for they provide, among many things, formal labels for organizing related items into conceptual classes. The word-labels of languages are thought to facilitate reference to information units in memory and to facilitate the definition of new relationships between those units as the exigencies of new situations might require. But according to S-S (stimulus-stimulus) theories, as noted by the Kendlers (Kendler & Kendler, 1975, p. 236), it is possible for a child, even before he begins to talk, to learn that a given sound pattern refers to a given visual pattern simply by hearing and seeing the two patterns together in time. This type of association requires no labeling response, either overt or implicit. These kinds of associations, the Kendlers hold, might well account for the fact that in most children receptive or comprehension language skills antedate production skills.

On the other hand, the acquisition of productive public language does entail both the learning and the appropriate use of relatively specific words and meanings. How are word concepts formed and how are word meanings agreed upon for public use? Language learning is not a totally arbitrary process. Rosch (1973) has contributed important work and ideas concerning these questions. According to Rosch, perceptual domains exist within which the *core* meaning is not arbitrary but rather is dictated by the nature of the perceptual system. The use of "clearest cases" or "best examples" facilitates the learning of both color and form categories. Rosch obtained evidence to support the hypotheses that (1) it is easier to learn color and form categories in which natural as opposed to distorted prototypes are used as central prototypes in sets of variations, (2) the natural prototype will usually be learned first regardless of whether it is central to the category, and (3) subjects tend to define a given category as a set of variations about the "most typical" or natural prototype. Rosch suggests the possibility that these findings might indicate that even "nonperceptual" semantic categories of languages might adhere to certain general principles of internal structure (with a focal center and nonfocal surrounds) and that these, in turn, might be the key to certain universals of natural language systems. Rosch predicts " . . . that children will be similar to adults in tasks where adults use *internal* structure as the basis for processing . . . , but different from adults in tasks for which adults use *abstract* criterial attributes" (1973, p. 142). Essock's study (1977) of Lana's color classification skills strongly suggests that chimpanzees and man have comparable internal structures for colors.

Extensions of Rosch's ideas and methods might assist us in understanding the degree to which man and apes share the basic processes and structures that are used in learning concepts and categories. To the degree that such research yields positive results, support will be given for the interpretation that apes can master bona fide language skills.

Indirect evidence relative to this point is already in hand. It has been pointed out that Washoe was very young, about one year old, when her language training began (the Gardners now hold that training should start at birth [Gardner & Gardner, 1975b); Lana was about two years old when her formal training began; and Sarah was about six years old. Despite these major differences in ages, *all* of the chimpanzees accomplished basically similar linguistic feats. That they all did so despite substantial age differences might be taken as a reflection of their having similar concept-formation processes and structures which were equivalently functional despite their different rearing conditions prior to language training.

D. Underlying Processes—Homologous or Analogous?

Extension of Rosch's tactics into developmental-comparative studies of the human child and the chimpanzee would help to answer a key question: Are the processes which support the acquisition of linguistic-type skills in men and in apes homologous or analogous? To the degree that both ape and child perfect their language-relevant skills in the same basic developmental pattern, to the degree that training methods have relatively the same supportive or deterring effects upon the development of those skills, and to the degree that both ape and child have seemingly the same internal structures for their concepts and categories, homologous processes would be indicated. To this author, it seems quite probable that homologous processes are involved because of the very close biological similarity and relationship established between man and chimpanzee (King & Wilson, 1975).

V. PROJECTIONS

A. Animal-model Studies and Perspectives of Language

Research directed toward accurately assessing the several dimensions of the capacities of chimpanzees and other great apes for linguistic functions (e.g., Wicklegren, 1974) will undoubtedly continue. Ultimately, if this research is successful, young apes may come to serve as surrogates for human children in research on the parameters of language acquisition. Such a development would permit the investigation of certain basic questions which have been precluded to date because of the ethical constraints which we place upon research with human subjects. But the use of apes as substitutes for human children in linguistic projects can be justified in the long term only on the basis of convincing evidence that the chimpanzee's language-learning processes are homologous to those used by the human child.

Should such evidence be forthcoming, one important topic which would then be open to research in ways now impossible is the relative efficacy of various methods of cultivating *initial* language functions in human retardates (for suggested prototypes see Brown, 1970, 1973; Fouts, 1973, 1974; Fox & Skolnick, 1975). Other important questions include how one language skill builds on other skills and how extralinguistic experiences contribute to language learning. These two questions might be investigated by systematically depriving different ape subjects of various opportunities to learn and experience. Questions regarding apes' abilities to tell us about their internal states, to teach artificial languages to their offspring, and to translate their natural communication networks to us will be answered only after many, many years of additional research.

Extended comparative research with apes should also provide us with a better understanding of (1) the role of language functions in thought and in problem-solving activities, (2) the relationship between intelligence and language-skill acquistion, (3) the contributions of social experience to language functions (Lewis & Cherry, 1977) and to concept of self (Gallup, 1969), and (4) the bases for the so-called universals of natural languages. Regarding the last of these, Chomsky (1968) has been credited, perhaps inaccurately, with the theory that the normal human child possesses a genetically predicated grammar system which shapes his language-learning efforts. But even "the rankest nativist would not claim that the child is genetically endowed with a complete grammatical system" (Moore, 1973, p. 4). The few language universals that can be taken as evidence for the genetic view are seemingly secondary to the diverse networks of rules which facilitate language learning in the broad array of human cultures (Schlesinger, 1970). Ape language research should eventually yield a much clearer perspective on the interaction of biological and environmental factors as they influence the acquisition of language.

B. Language Research and Psychology

In reflecting upon the probable effects which research on language will have on psychology, Slobin concluded that "what is bound to emerge will be a more complex image of the psychological nature of man, involving complex internal mental structures, in part genetically determined, in part determined by the subtlety and richness of the environment provided by human culture, and probably only minimally determined by *traditional* sorts of reinforced stimulus-response connections" (1971, p. 61). Comparative psychological studies will be of critical importance in testing such hypotheses.

ACKNOWLEDGMENTS

Preparation of this manuscript was supported by grants NICHD–06016 and RR–00165 from the National Institutes of Health.

REFERENCES

Altmann, S. A. The structure of primate social communication. In S. A. Altmann (Ed.), *Social communication among primates.* Chicago: University of Chicago Press, 1967.

Bellugi, U., & Klima, E. S. Aspects of sign language and its structure. In J. F. Kavanagh & J. E. Cuttings (Eds.), *The role of speech in language.* Cambridge, Massachusetts: MIT Press, 1975.

Bolles, R. C. Learning, motivation, and cognition. In W. K. Estes (Ed.), *Handbook of learning and cognitive processes* (Vol. 1). New York: Wiley, 1975.

Bornstein, M. Color vision and color naming. *Psychological Bulletin,* 1973, **80,** 257–285.

Bornstein, M., Kessen, W., & Weiskopf, S. Categories of hue in infancy. *Science,* 1976, **191,** 201–202.

Bronowski, J. *The ascent of man.* Boston: Little, Brown, 1973.

Brown, R. The development of wh questions in child speech. *Journal of Verbal Learning and Verbal Behavior,* 1968, **7,** 277–290.

Brown R. The first sentences of child and chimpanzee. In R. Brown (Ed.), *Psycholinguistics: Selected papers.* New York: Free Press, 1970.

Brown, R. Development of the first language in the human species. *American Psychologist,* 1973, **28,** 97–106.

Bruner, J. S. Nature and uses of immaturity. In K. Conolly & J. Bruner (Eds.), *The growth of competence.* New York: Academic Press, 1974.

Chomsky, N. *Language and mind.* New York: Harcourt, Brace, Jovanovich, 1968.

Church, J. Ontogeny of language. In H. Moltz (Ed.), *The ontogeny of vertebrate behavior.* New York: Academic Press, 1971.

Cowey, A., & Weiskrantz, L. Demonstration of cross-modal matching in rhesus monkeys, macaca mulatta. *Neuropsychologia,* 1975, **13,** 117–120.

Davenport, R. K., & Rogers, C. M. Intermodal equivalence of stimuli in apes. *Science,* 1970, **168,** 279–180.

Davenport, R. K., Rogers, C. M., & Russell, I. S. Cross-modal perception in apes. *Neuropsychologia,* 1973, **11,** 21–28.

Davenport, R. K., Rogers, C. M., & Russell, I. S. Cross-modal perception in apes: Altered visual cues and delay. *Neuropsychologia,* 1975, **13,** 229–235.

Dingwall, W. O. The species-specificity of speech. In D. Dato (Ed.), *Developmental psycholinguistics: Theory and applications.* Washington, D.C.: Georgetown University Round Table, 1975.

Essock, S. Color perception and color classification of Lana chimpanzee. In D. M. Rumbaugh (Ed.), *Language learning by a chimpanzee: The LANA project.* New York: Academic Press, 1977.

Estes, W. K. The state of the field: General problems and issues of theory and metatheory. In W. K. Estes (Ed.), *Handbook of learning and cognitive processes* (Vol. 1). New York: Wiley, 1975.

Estes, W. K. (Ed.). *Handbook of learning and cognitive processes* (Vol. 2). New York: Wiley 1976.

Falk, D. Comparative anatomy of the larynx in man and the chimpanzee: Implications for language in Neanderthal. *American Journal of Physical Anthropology*, 1975 **43**, 123–132.

Fouts, R. S. Acquisition and testing of gestural signs in four young chimpanzees. *Science*, 1973, **180**, 978–980.

Fouts, R. S. Language: Origins, definition and chimpanzees. *Journal of Human Evolution*, 1974, **3**, 475–482.

Fox, M. J., & Skolnick, B. P. Language in education: Problems and prospects in research and training. New York: The Ford Foundation, 1975.

Furness, W. H. Observations of the mentality of chimpanzees and orangutans. *Proceedings from the American Philosophical Society*, 1916, **55**, 281.

Gallup, G. G., Jr. Chimpanzees: Self-recognition. *Science*, 1969, **167**, 86–87.

Gardner, B. T., & Gardner, R. A. Two-way communications with an infant chimpanzee. In A. M. Schrier & F. Stollnitz (Eds.), *Behavior of nonhuman primates* (Vol. 4). New York: Academic Press, 1971.

Gardner, B. T., & Gardner, R. A. Evidence for sentence constituents in the early utterances of child and chimpanzee. *Journal of Experimental Psychology: General*, 1975, **104**, 244–267. (a)

Gardner, R. A., & Gardner, B. T. Teaching sign language to a chimpanzee. *Science*, 1969, **165**, 664–672.

Gardner, R. A., & Gardner, B. T. Early signs of language in child and chimpanzee. *Science*, 1975, **187**, 752–753. (b)

Gill, T. V. Conversations with Lana (*Pan*). In D. M. Rumbaugh (Ed.), *Language learning by a chimpanzee: The LANA project*. New York: Academic Press, 1977.

Gill, T. V., & Rumbaugh, D. M. Mastery of naming skills by a chimpanzee. *Journal of Human Evolution*, 1974, **3**, 483–492.

Grether, W. Chimpanzee color vision. *Journal of Comparative and Physiological Psychology*, 1940, **29**, 167–192.

Hamilton, J. Hominid divergence and speech evolution. *Journal of Human Evolution*, 1974, **3**, 417–424.

Hayes, K. J., & Hayes, C. *Vocalization and speech in chimpanzees*. State College, Pennsylvania: Psychological Cinema Register, 1950. (film)

Hayes, K. J., & Nissen, C. H. Higher mental functions of a home-raised chimpanzee. In A. M. Schrier & F. Stollnitz (Eds.), *Behavior of nonhuman primates* (Vol. 4). New York: Academic Press, 1971.

Hewes, G. W. Primate communication and the gestural origin of language. *Current Anthropology*, 1973, **14**, 5–32.

Hewes, G. W. The current status of gestural origin theory. In H. Steklis, S. Harnad, & J. Lancaster (Eds.), *Origins and evolution of language and speech*. New York: New York Academy of Sciences, 1976. (*Annals of the New York Academy of Sciences*, Vol. 280.)

Hewes, G. W. Language origin theories. In D. M. Rumbaugh (Ed.), *Language learning by a chimpanzee: The LANA project*. New York: Academic Press, 1977.

Hill, O. *Evolutionary biology of primates*. London: Academic Press, 1972.

Hockett, C. F. Logical considerations in the study of animal communication. In W. E. Lanyon & W. N. Tavolga (Eds.), *Animal sounds and communication*. Washington, D.C.: American Institute of Biological Sciences, 1960.

Hockett, C. F., & Altmann, S. A. A note on design features. In T. A. Sebeok (Ed.), *Animal communication*. Bloomington, Indiana: Indiana University Press, 1968.

Hurvich, L., & Jameson, D. Opponent processes as a model of neural organization. *American Psychologist,* 1974, 29, 88–102.
Jerison, H. J. *Evolution of the brain and intelligence.* New York: Academic Press, 1973.
Kellogg, W. N. Communication and language in the home-raised chimpanzee. *Science,* 1968, **162,** 423–438.
Kendler, H. H., & Kendler, T. S. From discrimination learning to cognitive development: A neobehavioristic odyssey. In W. K. Estes (Ed.), *Handbook of learning and cognitive processes* (Vol. I). New York: Wiley, 1975.
King, J. E., & Fobes, J. L. Evolutionary changes in primate sensory capacities. *Journal of Human Evolution,* 1974, **3,** 435–443.
King, M. C., & Wilson, A. C. Evolution at two levels in humans and chimpanzees. *Science,* 1975, **186,** 107–116.
Köhler, W. *The mentality of apes.* London: Routledge & Kegan Paul, 1925.
Kortlandt, A. How do chimpanzees use weapons when fighting leopards? In *Year book* of the American Philosophical Society. Philadelphia: The American Philosophical Society, 1965.
La Mettrie, J. O. *Man a machine.* Chicago: Opencourt, 1912.
Lewis, M., & Cherry, L. Social behavior and language acquisition. In M. Lewis & L. Rosenblum (Eds.), *Communication and language: The origins of behavior.* New York: Wiley, 1977.
Liberman, A. M., Cooper, F. S., Shankweiler, D. P., & Studdert-Kennedy, M. Perception of the speech code. *Psychological Review,* 1967, **74,** 431–461.
Lieberman, P. *Intonation, perception and language.* Cambridge, Massachusetts: MIT Press, 1967.
Lieberman, P. Primate vocalizations and human linguistic ability. *Journal of the Acoustical Society of America,* 1968, **44,** 1574–1584.
Lieberman, P. The evolution of speech and language. In J. F. Kavanagh & J. E. Cutting (Eds.), *The role of speech in language.* Cambridge, Massachusetts: MIT Press, 1975.
Lieberman, P., Crelin, E. S., & Klatt, D. H. Phonetic ability and related anatomy of the newborn and adult human, Neanderthal man, and the chimpanzee. *American Anthropologist,* 1972, **74,** 287–307.
Marler, P. On the origin of speech from animal sounds. In J. F. Kavanagh & J. E. Cutting (Eds.), *The role of speech in language.* Cambridge, Massachusetts: MIT Press, 1975.
Marshack, A. Some implications of the paleolithic symbolic evidence for the origin of language. In H. Steklis, S. Harnad, & J. Lancaster (Eds.), *Origins and evolution of language and speech.* New York: New York Academy of Sciences, 1976. (*Annals of the New York Academy of Sciences,* Vol. 280.)
Mason, W. A. Information processing and experiential deprivation: A biologic perspective. In F. A. Young & D. B. Lindsley (Eds.), *Early experience and visual information processing in perceptual and reading disorders.* Washington, D.C.: National Academy of Sciences, 1970.
Mason, W. A. Environmental models and mental modes: Representational processes in the great apes and man. *American Psychologist,* 1976, **31,** 284–294.
Mayr, E. Behavior programs and evolutionary strategies. *American Scientist,* 1974, **62,** 650–659.
McNeill, D. Chimpanzee communication. In K. J. Connolly & J. S. Bruner (Eds.), *The growth of competence.* London: Academic Press, 1974.
Menzel, E. W. Chimpanzee spatial memory organization. *Science,* 1973, **182,** 943–946.
Menzel, E. W. A group of young chimpanzees in a one-acre field. In A. M. Schrier & F. Stollnitz (Eds.), *Behavior of nonhuman primates* (Vol. 5). New York: Academic Press, 1974.
Menzel, E. W., & Halperin, S. Purposive behavior as a basis for objective communication between chimpanzees. *Science,* 1975, **189,** 652–654.

Menzel, E. W., & Johnson, M. C. Communication and cognitive organization in humans and other animals. In H. Steklis, S. Harnad, & J. Lancaster (Eds.), *Origins and evolution of language and speech.* New York: New York Academy of Sciences, 1976. (*Annals of the New York Academy of Sciences,* Vol. 280.)

Miller, N. E. Liberalization of basic S-R concepts: Extensions to conflict behavior, motivation and social learning. In S. Koch (Ed.), *Psychology: A study of a science* (Vol. 2). New York: McGraw-Hill, 1959.

Moore, T. E. Introduction. In T. E. Moore (Ed.), *Cognitive development and the acquisition of language.* New York: Academic Press, 1973.

Nottebohm, F. The origins of vocal learning. *The American Naturalist,* 1972, **106,** 116–140.

Osgood, C. E. A behavioristic analysis of perception and language as cognitive phenomena. *Contemporary approaches to cognition: A symposium held at the University of Colorado.* Cambridge, Massachusetts: Harvard University Press, 1957.

Parker, C. E. The antecedents of man the manipulator. *Journal of Human Evolution,* 1974, **3,** 493–500.

Patterson, F. The gestures of a gorilla: Language acquisition in another pongoid species. In D. Hamburg, J. Goodall, & R. E. McCown (Eds.), *Perspectives on human evolution* (Vol. 5). Menlo Park, California: Benjamin, 1977.

Premack, D. A functional analysis of language. *Journal of the Experimental Analysis of Behavior,* 1970, **14,** 107–125.

Premack, D. Language in chimpanzee? *Science,* 1971, **172,** 808–822. (a)

Premack, D. On the assessment of language competence in the chimpanzee. In A. M. Schrier & F. Stollnitz (Eds.), *Behavior of nonhuman primates* (Vol. 4). New York: Academic Press, 1971. (b)

Premack, D. Putting a face together. *Science,* 1975, **188,** 228–236.

Premack, D. Learning and cognition. In H. Steklis, S. Harnad, & J. Lancaster (Eds.), *Origins and evolution of language and speech.* New York: New York Academy of Sciences, 1976. (*Annals of the New York Academy of Sciences,* Vol. 280.)

Premack, D., & Schwartz, A. Preparations for discussing behaviorism with chimpanzee. In F. L. Smith & G. A. Miller (Eds.), *The genesis of language.* Cambridge, Massachusetts: MIT Press, 1966.

Pribram, K. H. Languages of the brain. Englewood Cliffs, New Jersey: Prentice-Hall, 1971.

Pribram, K. H. Neural parallels and continuities. In H. Steklis, S. Harnad, & J. Lancaster (Eds.), *Origins and evolution of language and speech.* New York: New York Academy of Sciences, 1976. (*Annals of the New York Academy of Sciences,* Vol. 280.)

Radinsky, L. Primate brain evolution. *American Scientist,* 1975, **63,** 656–663.

Restle, F. Cognitive structures. In F. Restle, R. M. Shiffrin, N. J. Castellan, H. R. Lindman, & D. B. Pisoni (Eds.), *Cognitive theory* (Vol. 1). New York: Wiley, 1975. (a)

Restle, F. *Learning: Animal behavior and human cognition.* New York: McGraw-Hill, 1975. (b)

Riesen, A. H. Comparative perspectives in behavior study. *Journal of Human Evolution,* 1974, **3,** 433–434.

Rosch, E. H. On the internal structure of perceptual and semantic categories. In T. E. Moore (Ed.), *Cognitive development and the acquisition of language.* New York: Academic Press, 1973.

Rumbaugh, D. M. Learning skills of anthropoids. In L. A. Rosenblum, (Ed.), *Primate behavior: Developments in field and laboratory research* (Vol. 1). New York: Academic Press, 1970.

Rumbaugh, D. M. Evidence of qualitative differences in learning processes among primates. *Journal of Comparative and Physiological Psychology,* 1971, **76,** 250–255.

Rumbaugh, D. M., & Gill, T. V. Language, apes and the apple which-is orange, please. In S. Kondo, M. Kawai, A. Ehara, & S. Kawmure (Eds.), *Proceedings from the Symposia of the*

Fifth Congress of the International Primatological Society. Tokyo: Japan Science Press, 1975.

Rumbaugh, D. M., & Gill, T. V. Language and the acquisition of language type skills by a chimpanzee *(Pan). Psychology in Progress: An Interim Report,* 1976, **270,** 90–135.

Rumbaugh, D. M., & Gill, T. V. Lana's mastery of language skills. In D. M. Rumbaugh (Ed.), *Language learning by a chimpanzee: The LANA project.* New York: Academic Press, 1977.

Rumbaugh, D. M., Gill, T. V., von Glasersfeld, E., Warner, H., & Pisani, P. Conversations with a chimpanzee in a computer-controlled environment. *Biological Psychiatry,* 1975, **10,** 627–641.

Rumbaugh, D. M., von Glasersfeld, E. C., Warner, H., Pisani, P., Gill, T. V., Brown, J. V., & Bell, C. L. A computer-controlled language training system for investigating the language skills of young apes. *Behavior Research Methods and Instrumentation,* 1973, **5,** 385–392.

Savage, E. S., & Rumbaugh, D. M. Communication, language, and Lana: a perspective. In D. M. Rumbaugh (Ed.), *Language learning by a chimpanzee: the LANA Project.* New York: Academic Press, 1977.

Schlesinger, I. M. The grammar of sign language and the problems of language universals. In J. Morton (Ed.), *Biological and social factors in psycholinguistics.* Urbana, Illinois: University of Illinois Press, 1970.

Schultz, A. H. *The life of primates.* New York: Universe Books, 1969.

Segal, E. Toward a coherent psychology of language. In W. K. Honig & J. E. R. Staddon (Eds.) *Handbook of operant behavior.* New York: Prentice-Hall, 1977.

Shantha, T. R., & Manocha, S. L. The brain of chimpanzee. In G. Bourne (Ed.), *The chimpanzee* (Vol. 1). Basel: S. Karger, 1969.

Slobin, D. I. *Psycholinguistics.* Glenview, Illinois: Scott, Foresman, 1971.

Steklis, H. D., & Harnad, S. R. From hand to mouth: Some critical stages in the evolution of language. In H. Steklis, S. Harnad, & J. Lancaster (Eds.), *Origins and evolution of language and speech.* New York: New York Academy of Sciences, 1976. (*Annals of the New York Academy of Sciences,* Vol. 280.)

Stokoe, W. C., Jr. The shape of soundless language. In J. F. Kavanagh & J. E. Cutting (Eds.), *The role of speech in language.* Cambridge, Massachusetts: MIT Press, 1975.

Stokoe, W. C., Jr., Casterline, D., & Croneberg, C. G. *A dictionary of American sign language.* Washington, D.C.: Gallaudet College Press, 1965.

Terrace, H., & Bever, T. *What might be learned from studying language in a chimpanzee.* In H. Steklis, S. Harnad, & J. Lancaster (Eds.), *Origins and evolution of language and speech.* New York: New York Academy of Sciences, 1976. (*Annals of the New York Academy of Sciences,* Vol. 280.)

Toulmin, S. Brain and language: A commentary. *Synthèse,* 1971, **22,** 369–395.

van Lawick-Goodall, J. Tool-using in primates and other vertebrates. *Advances in the Study of Behavior,* 1970, **3,** 195–249.

von Glasersfeld, E. C. The Yerkish language and its automatic parser. In D. M. Rumbaugh (Ed.), *Language learning by a chimpanzee: The LANA project.* New York: Academic Press, 1977.

Warner, H., Bell, C. L., Rumbaugh, D. M., & Gill, T. V. Computer-controlled teaching instrumentation for linguistic studies with great apes. *IEEE Transactions on Computers,* 1976, **C-25,** 38–43.

Warren, J. M. Learning in vertebrates. In D. A. Dewsbury & D. A. Rethlingshafer (Eds.), *Comparative psychology: A modern survey.* New York: McGraw-Hill, 1973.

Warren, J. M. Possibly unique characteristics of learning by primates. *Journal of Human Evolution,* 1974, **3,** 445–454.

Wechsler, D. Intelligence defined and undefined: A relativistic appraisal. *American Psychologist,* 1975, **30,** 135–139.

Wickelgren, W. Memory. In J. A. Swets & L. L. Elliot (Eds.), *Psychology and the handicapped child.* Washington, D.C.: U.S. Government Printing Office, 1974.

Witmer, L. *Psychological Clinic,* 1909, **3**, 179–205.

Yeni-Komshian, G. H., & Benson, D. A. Anatomical study of cerebral asymmetry in the temporal lobe of humans, chimpanzees and rhesus monkeys. *Science,* 1976, **192,** 387–389.

Yerkes, R. M. *Almost human.* New York: The Century Company, 1927.

Young, F. A., & Farrer, D. N. Visual similarities of non-human and human primates. In E. I. Goldsmith & J. Moor-Jankowski (Eds.), *Medical primatology.* Basel: S. Karger, 1971.

5

Sociosexual Behaviors of Nonhuman Primates During Development and Maturity: Social and Hormonal Relationships

David A. Goldfoot

Wisconsin Regional Primate Research Center, Madison

I. INTRODUCTION

Many nonhuman primates, including all Old World monkeys and apes, share with the human a particular social characteristic which accounts for both the fascination and difficulty of the study of sexual behavior in these animals. Monkeys, apes, and humans have incorporated sexual displays and copulation into their social lives *outside of restricted periods of fertility* more fully and with more diversity than any other vertebrates. Several nonprimate species do display behavioral patterns that are fragments of courtship or mating sequences outside of estrous periods, but these behaviors are interpreted to serve social functions other than procreation, such as greeting, dominance assertion or acquiescence, and group cohesiveness (Wickler, 1973), and in any event rarely if ever result in copulation. Primates, however, not only exhibit a variety of sexual postures and sequences of sexual display outside of periods of fertility with great frequency, but under several social conditions they actually copulate to ejaculation at times far removed from ovulation. Of course, the possibility is strong that the coitus engaged in by primates at times outside of conceptual periods serves social functions similar to those described for other species (Wickler, 1973).

The regular appearance of complete or nearly complete copulation in contexts not limited to specific gonadal conditions constitutes a unique feature of primate behavior. Sometimes referred to as "gonadal emancipation," the display of coitus during infertile states, although often still under hormonal influences, is mediated by a variety of nonhormonal factors, with complex social pressures being the most obvious. Because social context plays such an important role for the evocation of sexual behavior in primates, and since the behaviors are quite clearly not solely the result of hormonal factors, Hinde (1974) has reminded us that the sexual behavior of nonhuman primates is not a clearly defined category, and can occur as a result of more than one underlying motivational cause. Therefore, Hinde emphasizes that *any generalization made about observed sexual behavior of primates demands great interpretive caution.*

Several excellent discussions considering relationships between primate sexual behavior and endocrine factors are available which summarize much of the current data (Baum, Everitt, Herbert, & Keverne, in press; Eaton, 1973; Goy & Resko, 1972; Hanby, in press; Keverne, in press; Luttge, 1971; Michael, 1971, 1972, 1973; Michael, Wilson, & Plant, 1973; Michael, Zumpe, Keverne, & Bonsall, 1972; Rowell, 1972). Taken together, with each review emphasizing one or more aspects of theoretical interest, a representative impression of the field can be rather easily obtained. Missing from most reviews, however, or, more correctly, from many of the studies treated in the reviews, is the interpretive caution of which Hinde speaks. For reasons perhaps more clear to philosophers of science than to scientists themselves, behavioral problems of significant complexity, represented here by primate sexual behavior, are often characterized by data bases of incredible variance, and yet, at the same time, by theoretical frameworks of optimistic oversimplification. This chapter, rather than trying to reduce, generalize, or simplify the field, will attempt only to sensitize the reader to the difficulties the area has had with regard to data collection, to theoretical interpretation, and to integration of information from relevant disciplines.

As a first exercise in sensitization, the reader is reminded that writing about behaviors of "the primate" is much like writing about behaviors of "the carnivore," in that the species constituting the order Primates are not only numerous, but also extremely varied in morphological, endocrinological, and behavioral characteristics. While some generalizations are certainly possible concerning all primates, the details of behavioral and endocrine factors that act to support sexual behavior are quite individualistic. Thus, for example, results of studies of the rhesus monkey (*Macaca mulatta*) often have only superficial resemblance to those obtained with the hamadryas baboon (*Papio hamadryas*) and share even less commonality with talapoins (*Cercopithecus talapoin*) or vervets (*C. aethiops*) or hanuman langurs (*Presbytis entellus*). Moreover, the common notion of increased behavioral automony from endocrine influences as the phylogenetic scale is ascended is not clearly supported by data available thus far for many primate species. Although the problems of generalizing too broadly among primate species is recognized by most researchers, it is also the case that the majority of the data concerning hormonal and social variables influencing sexual behaviors of primates comes from studies using macaque species, and primarily rhesus macaques. Discussions of the primate, therefore are often reduced to discussions of the rhesus monkey, lamentably even in the chapter presented here. When appropriate, I have attempted to contrast data obtained with more than one species to illustrate this fact, but, nonetheless, knowledgeable primatologists will recognize that the chapter is heavily influenced by what is known about the rhesus monkey, and not necessarily about the hypothetical nonhuman primate.

II. DEVELOPMENTAL ORIGINS OF SOCIOSEXUAL BEHAVIOR

A striking feature of the behavioral interactions displayed by many nonhuman primate species is the unmistakable occurrence of an adultlike form of mounting behavior developing in infancy (see Figure 5.1). Both the mount and presentation displayed by infants of most macaque species, for example, are virtually indistinguishable from the adult copulatory postures which precede intromission. This has been shown for rhesus monkeys (Goy, Wallen, & Goldfoot, 1974; Lindburg, 1971; Wallen, Bielert, & Slimp, in press), stump-tailed monkeys (*M. arctoides*; Trollope & Blurton Jones, 1972), Japanese monkeys (*M. fuscata;* Hanby & Brown, 1974), and bonnet monkeys (*M. radiata;* Rosenblum & Nadler, 1971). Early development of adultlike mounting similarly occurs in infants or juveniles of species which do not assume the foot clasp posture in adulthood,

FIG. 5.1 Double foot clasp mount of an infant male rhesus monkey. The pattern is nearly indistinguishable from the adult mount except that intromissions rarely occur before $2\frac{1}{2}$ years of age.

such as marmosets (*Callithrix jacchus*; Rothe, 1975), squirrel monkeys (*Saimiri sciureus;* Baldwin & Baldwin, 1973), and chimpanzees (*Pan;* van Lawick-Goodall, 1968). Provided that appropriate social rearing conditions exist for the infants, well-executed, properly oriented foot clasp mounts, usually with pelvic thrusting but not including penile intromission, are displayed by macaques regularly before the first year of life and often as early as 2 to 4 months of age (Goy, Wallen, & Goldfoot, 1974). The initial appearance of presentation responses in infants, which are either elicited in response to a contact or mount attempt (present-to-contact) or displayed at some distance from a partner (present-at-distance) under a variety of social situations, accompanies the display of foot clasp mounting or develops somewhat earlier than foot clasp mounting. The development of adultlike copulatory elements in both sexes at such early ages is quite remarkable, since physiological puberty does not begin in rhesus monkeys until about 30 months of age for females and about 36 months of age for males (Resko, 1967; van Wagenen & Simpson, 1954). Moreover, castration of the male or ovariectomy of the female at birth does not appear to significantly alter frequencies with which these behaviors are displayed by infants and juveniles (Goy, 1966, 1968; Joslyn, 1973; Phoenix, Goy, & Young, 1967). This demonstrates that postnatal gonadal secretions are not necessary for the display of these behaviors prior to puberty.

The possible ramifications of nonhuman primate species exhibiting major features of copulatory behavior years before puberty constitutes an intriguing question which has only recently been the focus of experimental investigation. A point of confusion or controversy that has often been raised in research of this kind and is in need of further clarification is whether mounting and presenting behaviors are correctly classified as sexual behaviors at these early ages, especially when a good case can be made for their expression within agonistic or dominance-related contexts. Hinde's (1974) suggestion represents the most reasonable course to follow to approach this problem: namely, it is better to consider which social circumstances influence the probability of display of these responses, rather than to attempt to strictly categorize a motor pattern as sexual, affiliative, agonistic, etc., thereby realizing from the outset that behaviors such as mounts and presentations can be displayed for more than one "purpose." This strategy does not necessarily sidetrack the issue; rather, it allows the problem to be taken a step further. For me, a far more exciting problem is not to consider whether a mount by an infant is a "dominance mount" or a "sexual mount," but rather to realize that behaviors used in copulation by the adult may have associative (learned) histories relating to quite specific emotional and social conditions that existed when the behaviors were first developed in infancy. Some infants may have developed the mounting pattern primarily during highly aggressive interactions with peers, whereas others may have displayed the behavior primarily during affiliative play episodes. Thus, because the prototypical behavioral patterns develop early in the life of the individual it seems logical to hypothesize that major aspects of the copulatory patterns of adults have been previously associated with various types of affiliative or agonistic social conditions, depending largely upon the rearing history of the individual, and that these previous associations may have strong influences on the subsequent sexual activities of the adult via learned emotional associations. While this hypothesis is highly speculative at present, it nevertheless seems possible that components of sexual behavior can be acquired and are displayed by infants or juveniles in dramatically different emotional climates, i.e., under hostile and tense social conditions, or, alternatively, in social environments nearly devoid of aggressive encounters.

A. Influence of Conditions of Rearing on Subsequent Sexual Behavior

The necessity of adequate early social rearing conditions for the eventual display of complete sexual activities in adulthood has long been recognized, especially for males (Harlow & Harlow, 1965, 1971; Mason, 1960; Missakian, 1969; Riesen, 1971), but it has only recently been found that conditions of early social restriction far less severe than those produced by social isolation can nonetheless disrupt the development and expression of copulation to a significant degree (Goy & Goldfoot, 1974; Senko, 1966; Wallen et al., in press). Unfortunately, the discussion of the phenomenon of sociosexual behavior displayed in the early periods of development in primates has been hampered by the fact that, with few exceptions, most investigators have failed to distinguish the adult form of the mount (foot clasp mounting for most species studied; see Figure 5.1) in infants from abortive (improperly oriented) or standing (properly oriented but lacking the foot clasp; see Figure 5.2) types of mounting, and similarly, many have failed to categorize different presenting forms such as present-on-contact versus present-to-approach or present-at-distance (for definitions, see Goy, Wallen & Goldfoot, 1974). Some studies, in fact, have not differentiated mounting from presenting, and simply indicated that "sexual behavior" was displayed. Several conclusions are nonetheless evident, especially with regard to the rhesus monkey.

1. Severity of Social Deprivation

There are four consistent findings reported in the literature dealing with early social deprivation and the development of sexual behavior. First, the male is more severely affected by social deprivation than the female with regard to the eventual display of coitus. Second, there is a direct relationship between the severity of early social restriction and subsequent disruption of adult sexual function in the individual. Third, the failure to display foot clasp mounting during infant or juvenile (prepuberal) periods in males is largely predictive of later deficient or nonexistent sexual behavior in adulthood. Fourth, rehabilita-

FIG. 5.2 One of several forms of abortive mounting involving pelvic thrusting, in which the mounter fails to achieve a foot-clasp orientation. The mount is correctly oriented here, but it is sometimes directed to the head or side of the partner.

tion efforts directed at restoring or establishing sexual function in adulthood have not been successful with severely socially deprived animals, but some degree of recovery has been obtained with animals subjected to more moderate social restrictions early in life. The following discussion illustrates these findings.

Total social isolation during the first year of life almost always prevents the later display of foot clasp mounting (Harlow & Harlow, 1966). When eventually given social opportunities, either prepuberally or in adulthood, some isolates try repeatedly to mount, but these attempts usually result in improperly oriented or otherwise bizarre mount forms. Other isolates never attempt any mounting whatsoever. Isolate-reared animals are, of course, severely disturbed emotionally and are incapable of almost any type of cooperative social interaction (Mason, 1961; Sackett, 1965); therefore the inability to display foot clasp mounts with peers, which involves considerable cooperative effort (Wallen et al., in press), is not surprising. Extensive efforts to rehabilitate such animals have met with partial success for certain social responses (Novak, 1974), but efforts to establish foot clasp mounting have been conspicuously unsuccessful thus far (Missakian, 1969; Senko, 1966; S. Suomi, personal communication, 1976).

Less severe conditions of social restriction produce more moderate and sometimes partially reversible sexual deficits. When male rhesus infants are allowed access to peers for a 1/2-hour period each day after permanent separation from mothers at 3 to 6 months of age (peer-group rearing), foot clasp mounting develops in about 30% of the cases, but usually not before 18 to 24 months of age (Goy & Goldfoot, 1974). The remaining 70% of males display abortive and/or properly oriented, but nonclasping, mounts through their first 2 to 3 years of life, but they fail to develop the foot clasp form of the mount during this period of time. The development of foot clasp mounting in infancy appears to be significant to later adult copulatory behaviors, since its absence in the yearling or juvenile is predictive of deficient sexual behavior in adulthood (Goy & Goldfoot, 1974). The few animals which develop the foot clasp response prior to puberty with peer-group rearing as described above are found to copulate in adulthood, although not with the proficiency of feral-reared males. Males which do not develop foot clasp mounting as infants or young juveniles, in contrast, fail to copulate in adulthood (Goy & Goldfoot, 1974). Similar findings of deficient adult sexual behavior following early social restriction have been reported in several other laboratories (Bingham, 1928; Mason, 1960; Missakian, 1969; Riesen, 1971). Significantly, no evidence has been collected which suggests that these deficits in behavior involve hormonal dysfunction. While the issue is not completely answered, it appears that social rather than hormonal anomalies account for the failure of the deprived male to perform sexually as an adult.

Extensive socialization opportunities following the first year of life can partially alleviate the detrimental effects of social restriction on mounting responses. Animals reared for the first year of life with only limited access to peers (1/2-hour per day) and then allowed access to peers for 24 hours a day in their second year, have a higher probability of acquiring the foot clasp mount than animals not afforded this delayed socialization (Goy, Wallen, & Goldfoot, 1974; Wallen et al., in press). Thus some social rehabilitation is possible under these less severe conditions of rearing while the animals are still prepuberal. It is significant that the peer-rearing systems considered here do not produce the marked stereotypes and neurotic behaviors seen in animals subjected to severe forms of social isolation. Integrated social patterns develop and varied play patterns appear in virtually all animals given 1/2-hour daily peer experiences, but foot clasp mounting clearly suffers. Thus the display of integrated play does not predict later copulatory success, as has been previously suggested (Harlow, 1965). The development of foot clasp mounting seems particularly dependent for its expression upon extensive socialization opportunities which go beyond the requirements for the development of play responses.

When the laboratory social environment approaches conditions found in the wild, integrated mounting patterns are seen for most males quite early. For example, when infants are reared in communal pens with mothers and peers for their first year of life, foot clasp mounting develops in more than 90% of the males prior to 12 months of age, and is displayed by more than half of the males before 6 months (Goy, Wallen, & Goldfoot, 1974). In addition, several other rearing strategies that allow for extensive interactions with both mothers and peers similarly produce mounters at early ages (Hanby & Brown, 1974; Trollope & Blurton Jones, 1972). The early development of these behaviors should not be considered precocious, but instead appears to reflect patterns of development which normally occur within naturalistic social environments (Lindburg, 1971; Wallen, unpublished observations, cited in Wallen et al., in press). Finally, results available at present indicate that males reared in the laboratory with extensive socialization opportunities experience little difficulty with adult sexual performance. Kim Wallen of our laboratory has studied the oldest three males which had been reared with mothers and peers for the first year of life and subsequently kept in communal cages with peers. All three males copulated to ejaculation at 3-1/2 to 4 years of age. It appears, therefore, that a group living situation in which both peers and mothers are consistently available for at least the first year of life provides the minimal conditions which allow adultlike mounting behavior to develop in young males at rates seen in the field or in seminatural environments (Hanby & Brown, 1974) and which lead to successful copulations in adulthood. Future work will determine whether this rearing procedure will be adequate to insure a vigorous breeding program of this species without reliance on importation of feral-reared animals.

2. *Modeling of Adult Patterns*

Infant macaques demonstrate considerable interest in adult copulatory sequences. For example, they often stop play and watch intensely when heterosexual copulations occur among adults. De Benedictis (1973), in a carefully executed study, suggested that observational learning might be a very important element in the acquisition of copulatory postures for developing infant male cynomolgus monkeys (*Macaca fascicularis*). While this may indeed be the case, it is of both theoretical and practical interest that adult or subadult males need not be present in social rearing paradigms for foot clasp mounting to develop in young male rhesus monkeys (Goy, Wallen, & Goldfoot, 1974), and therefore modeling experiences, e.g., opportunities to observe copulatory behaviors in older individuals, are not a prerequisite for its development. In our laboratory, James Cohn and R. W. Goy have recently examined in detail the question of modeling opportunities for the development of foot clasp mounting in rhesus infants living under seminatural conditions. Infant males living in a natural troop housed at the Vilas Park Zoo, Madison, Wisconsin, displayed foot clasp mounts with peers as early as 2 to 3 months after birth, several months in advance of the adult breeding season. A marked increase in mounting by infants corresponded with the onset of adult breeding activity, but this level of mounting did not subside following the decrease in copulation by adults at the end of the season, and occurred without measurable changes in androgen levels of the infants. Furthermore, the age at which the increased levels of foot clasp mounts occurred in infants (5 to 7 months) corresponded to ages at which infants reared under constant environmental conditions in mother-peer groups with no adult or subadult males present showed moderate increases in foot clasp mount frequencies. The latter groups never saw foot clasp mounting executed by older individuals. The presence of adult mounting activity as well as the presence of adult females near ovulation might have stimulated or facilitated mounting in infants in the Vilas Zoo study, but, on the other hand, the developmental mounting rates were not significantly different from mounting rates of infants reared away from such experiences. Therefore, while observational learning of sexual behavior may have important influences of an undetermined nature, it is not necessary for infants to see adult heterosexual coitus in order to become proficient foot clasp mounters.

3. Maternal versus Peer Contributions to Mounting Development

To determine in more detail the social dynamics of mother-infant groups which permit the development of foot clasp mounting, Kim Wallen and I have recently studied four mother-infant groups (three male and two female infants per group) of rhesus monkeys housed so that each infant for the first year of life had continuous access to its mother and either 1/2-hour or 24 hours per day access to other infants in its group. This was accomplished by constructing individual cages within a large pen. The cages were fitted with small doors which, when opened, allowed the infant, but not the mother, to leave the cage and enter the pen. Thus, animals in both conditions had access to mothers at all times, but only one condition allowed for extensive (24 hours per day) socialization with peers. In the second year of life, infants from both groups were permanently removed from their mothers and allowed access to peers for 1/2 hour per day. None of the six males receiving 1/2-hour per day access to peers in Year 1 have ever displayed foot clasp mounts with peers, whereas all six males receiving 24-hour access to peers in their first year of life have become mounters. Mere access to its mother, therefore, apparently is not enough to allow an infant to display foot clasp mounting with peers. A similar conclusion was reached by Harlow, Joslyn, Senko, and Dopp (1966). Infant males in that study were housed with their mothers for the first year of life but denied peer access. The males failed to show adult mounting forms with peers when given opportunities to do so later.

The absence of foot clasp mounting by males restricted to 1/2-hour per day group interactions is not due to a simple inability to perform the motor patterns required, since two of the six males in Wallen and Goldfoot's study given restricted peer access were observed to mount their mothers. Deutsch and Larsson (1974) have similarly shown that the motor skills for foot clasp mounting are present even in isolate-reared juveniles, since these animals will mount a cloth dummy of the appropriate shape to allow foot clasp mounts, but will not mount other monkeys. Therefore, isolated or socially restricted animals are sufficiently coordinated to achieve adult mounting forms, but they almost always fail to display the behavior with peers.

4. Hypothesized Emotional Elements Required for Foot Clasp Mounting

What, then, are the social requirements for the acquisition or display of the foot clasp mount? Goy, Wallen, and Goldfoot (1974) indicate that peer-reared groups of infant rhesus monkeys (mothers absent) have a near "Lord of the Flies" aspect about them, in that displays of threat, aggression, and submission are frequent, daily occurrences and are exaggerated compared to levels shown by infants in mother-infant groups (Table 5.1; Figure 5.3). Furthermore, grooming behaviors and other indices of positive affect are displayed at low levels in such groups. Infant rhesus monkeys living without adult intervention do not become socially disorganized; rather, they become overzealous in forming rigid dominance orders, which are then harshly maintained. Moreover, the infants often seem stressed as a result of this premature and severe social ranking. Animals ranked low in such hierarchies live under particularly difficult social conditions, and are often subject to "bullying" behaviors of more dominant members of the group. Thus, even though many socially integrated patterns of play and dominance develop in the absence of mothers, the absence of a social atmosphere in which many of the animals can interact without excessive fear may be causally related to the mounting deficiencies which usually develop. In contrast, mothers in mother-infant group-rearing conditions reduce aggression and fear among infants to a significant degree, probably by serving as a base of security and by directly interceding during infant social interactions. However, previous studies by Wallen and Goldfoot, in which infants could leave and return to their mothers for restricted periods, illustrate that the security provided by the presence of mothers is not by itself adequate to insure that foot clasp mounting will occur; infants seem to need extensive time with one another to develop these patterns, and without sufficient exposure, only abortive foot clasp mounts are manifest. Therefore, Goy, Wallen, and Goldfoot (1974) suggest, as does

TABLE 5.1
Average Frequency per Male Rhesus Monkey of Agonistic Behaviors Shown during 100 Days of Observation in the First Year of Life[a]

		Fear grimace		Aggression		Woofing threat[b]	
Rearing condition	*N*	Mean ± S.E.	% Displaying	Mean ± S.E.	% Displaying	Mean ± S.E.	% Displaying
Peer-reared	31	16.4 ±4.2	68	12.8 ±2.4	97	12.5 ±4.3	89
Mother-Infant	14	0.3 ±0.15	36	0.06 ±0.04	14	0.40 ±0.2	21

[a]From Goy, Wallen, and Goldfoot, 1974. Each male was scored for 5 min of the daily 30-min observation period.

[b]Data on this behavior were obtained for only 19 of the peer-reared males during the first year of life.

FIG. 5.3 A low-ranking member of a peer-reared group of infant rhesus monkeys being attacked by other members of the group. Her facial expression is an exaggerated fear grimace. This level of aggression is not uncommon in peer-related groups, whereas it is extremely rare in mother-infant-reared animals of similar ages.

Harlow (1965), that an affectional system in which infants learn something akin to trust, or at least learn not to be fearful of one another, appears to be an important prerequisite for the establishment of the adult mount form. Deficiencies in emotional relationships between age-mates rather than deficiencies in presumed fundamental or prototypical motor response patterns seem to account for the failure to develop foot clasp mounting. Wallen et al. (in press), moreover, suggest that foot clasp mounting, more than other social behaviors of infants, takes the active cooperation of two animals, and that the failure of foot clasp mounting may, in part, reflect the partner's unwillingness, because of fear or other deficiencies in affect, to hold the presentation posture long enough or adequately enough for a foot clasp mount to be executed. Regardless of the degree to which this factor determines the outcome of the developmental process, researchers are in agreement that it is the quality of an animal's emotional relationship with age-mates that appears to be the fundamental factor governing the display of this response.

B. Dimorphic Aspects of Mounting and Presenting

1. Social Influences

Since the original observations of Rosenblum (1961), many workers (Goy, 1968, 1970; Harlow & Lauersdorf, 1974; Phoenix, Goy, & Resko, 1968; Sackett, 1965) have recognized that several social behaviors, including mounting, play, threatening, and overt aggression (attacks), are displayed by male and female infants and juveniles with differing probabilities of occurrence. Responses such as these which are displayed significantly more frequently, more readily, or with greater vigor by one sex than the other are called "dimorphic" behaviors (see Goy & Goldfoot, 1973). The term usually reflects quantitative rather than qualitative sex differences, since no behaviors displayed by monkeys, except perhaps penile erections, are exclusive to one sex alone. In fact, even this last statement may not be accurate for spider monkeys (*Ateles*) and other species in which the clitoris is peniform and large. There seem to be exceptions to *everything* in primatology!

Furthermore, when behavior patterns are found to be dimorphically expressed, it should be understood that the observation applies only to the social and experimental environments in which they are seen to occur, and cannot be extended unreservedly to more general conditions (see Goy & Goldfoot, 1973, for discussion of this point). Failure to heed this warning can sometimes generate quite misleading interpretations. For example, Harlow, Harlow, Hansen, and Suomi (1972) concluded that the presenting behavior of rhesus juveniles is displayed much more by females than males on the basis of data collected in dyads and in four-animal groups of surrogate-reared animals. The observation was generalized to the species as a whole, rather than being restricted to surrogate-reared animals tested under very specific, restricted circumstances.

Later work has now shown, however, that many categories of behavior are dimorphically expressed in some conditions of rearing or testing but not in others, and that presenting is an excellent example of such a behavior. Various studies on presenting behavior in infants and juveniles have found that the response is displayed (a) more by males than by females, (b) less by males than by females, or (c) equally by both sexes, depending on rearing and/or testing conditions, independent of hormone manipulations (Goldfoot & Wallen, in press).

Many of the dimorphic behavioral systems studied in the laboratory have been related to prenatal hormonal conditions (Goy & Phoenix, 1971; Goy & Resko, 1972). Nonetheless, from what has just been mentioned of the role of social influences in modifying many forms of dimorphic response, it seems clear that before questions of hormonal mediation of sex differences can be properly considered, social contributions to dimorphic displays must be better understood. In regard to presenting and mounting in rhesus monkeys, the following study demonstrates that situational factors have marked influences on both of these behaviors in males and females, determining the degree and even the direction of the sexual dimorphism.

Goldfoot and Wallen (in press) utilized heterosexual and isosexual peer groups of infant rhesus monkeys to investigate social factors which might possibly contribute to dimorphic patterns of play, sex, and aggression. While not discounting the obvious and important organizing influences of the the prenatal hormonal environment previously shown to influence dimorphic expression, these investigators tested the possibility that groups of infants composed entirely of males or entirely of females might develop social interactions different from those seen in heterosexual peer groups. The authors reasoned that males perhaps have social advantages over females in early interactions with peers because of biological factors such as strength, activity level, or other unidentified aspects of behavioral interactions. Therefore, early encounters with males might suppress or otherwise influence some social behaviors in females reared with the males. Obviously, an all-female group would eliminate such influences of the males. In turn, it was thought that the psychosexual development of males placed in all-male infant groups, and especially those males receiving many mounts and aggressive encounters from peers, might resemble the developmental pattern of normal females reared in heterosexual groups.

These hypotheses were largely supported by the data. In three isosexual groups of female infants ($N = 14$) reared with mothers absent, much higher threatening and somewhat elevated abortive mount frequencies were displayed, compared to levels shown by females in heterosexual groups (Table 5.2). Abortive rather than foot clasp mounts were analyzed in this study since, in this rearing situation, in which mothers were absent, foot clasp mounting was not displayed at this age by either sex. An isosexual group of five females reared with mothers present has now been studied to overcome this limitation, and under these conditions all five

TABLE 5.2
Mean Frequencies Per Partner of Four Types of Male-Male and Female-Female Interactions in Hetero- and Isosexual Peer Groups (1st 50 Day Run).

	Abortive Mounts		Presenting		Threat		Attack	
	Hetero	Iso	Hetero	Iso	Hetero	Iso	Hetero	Iso
Male-Male	8.2	6.5	4.4	14.3	8.0	5.4	6.9	1.2
Female-Female	0.6	1.2	2.3	1.9	0.8	3.1	0.7	0.1

infant females displayed foot clasp mounting, with three of the five showing the response regularly (Figures 5.4 and 5.5). This is in dramatic contrast to only 5 of 28 females from 12 heterosexual mother-infant groups which have ever displayed this response. Thus, under special conditions of rearing, it is obvious that females have considerably more potential to display "male patterns" of sexual activity than previously suspected. Nonetheless, the mounting rates displayed by isosexually reared females were much lower than those found for most heterosexually reared males. Therefore, while considerable potential to display foot clasp mounting exists in normal female infants given very special early rearing

FIG. 5.4 A lie-on foot-clasp mount displayed by an isosexually reared female rhesus monkey. This mount form was shown by all five female infants in an isosexual mother-infant group. Three of the infants subsequently developed the more typical foot-clasp mount posture.

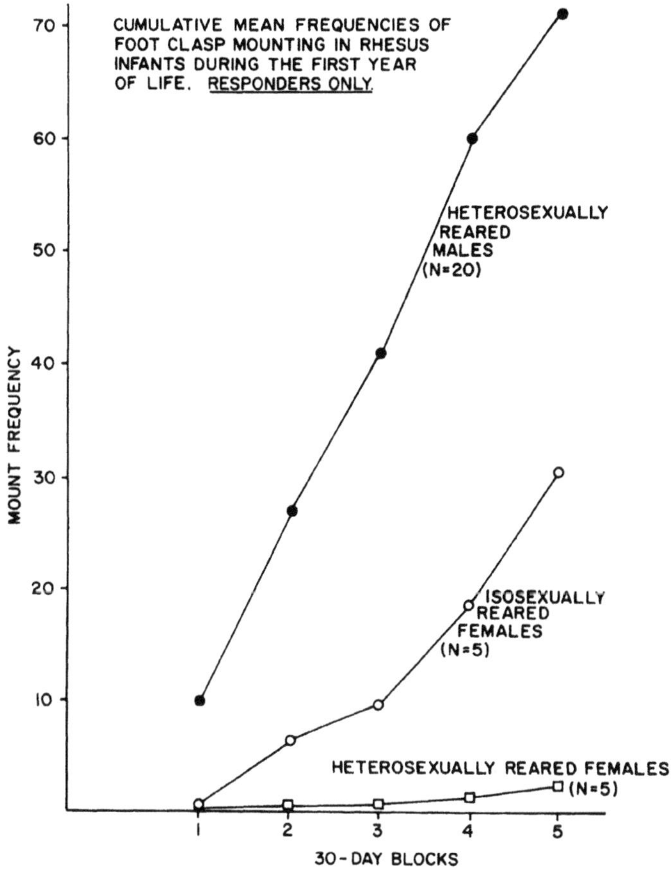

FIG. 5.5 Comparison of foot-clasp mounts by heterosexually reared males and females in contrast with those shown by isosexually reared females. All animals were from mother-infant groups. About 50% of the mounting of the isosexually reared females was of the variety illustrated in Figure 5.4.

experiences, biological factors are still clearly important for influencing response probabilities.

The conclusion that biological and social mechanisms jointly determine response probabilities was further emphasized when isosexual groups of males were studied. It was found that, overall, mounting rates were actually somewhat lower than those shown by males in mixed-sex groups, but that presenting behaviors were elevated, in some instances to levels nearly 10 times higher than those shown by males in mixed-sex groups. Thus, as a function of the sexual composition of these isosexual groups and relative to heterosexually reared age-mates, females tended to show more "masculine sexual patterns," whereas males showed more "feminine sexual responses."

Data from both hetero- and isosexual groups suggest that an individual's dominance rank in these artificial rearing paradigms is correlated with probabilities of displaying mounting and presenting. Animals in subordinate social positions tended to display presenting at high rates and mounts at low rates, whereas dominant animals showed the opposite tendencies. Dominance position was inferred primarily by fear grimace (see Figure 5.5) and displacement matrices (Goy & Goldfoot, 1974) and hence is in conformance with Rowell's (1974) suggestion to use "subordination" rather than "dominance" behaviors for such questions.

The way in which social dominance status relates to the occurrence of mounting and presenting in infants is extremely complex, and not well understood. The following facts emerge from our work at Wisconsin, however. First, in groups in which agonistic encounters are infrequent among infants, as, for example, in mother-infant groups, there is no clear relationship between social rank and mounting or presenting. The relationship is fairly obvious, however, in groups such as those with peer-rearing (mother absent) conditions, in which there are exaggerated dominance encounters. Figure 5.6 shows that high-ranking animals from such groups tend to mount with greater frequency than low-ranking

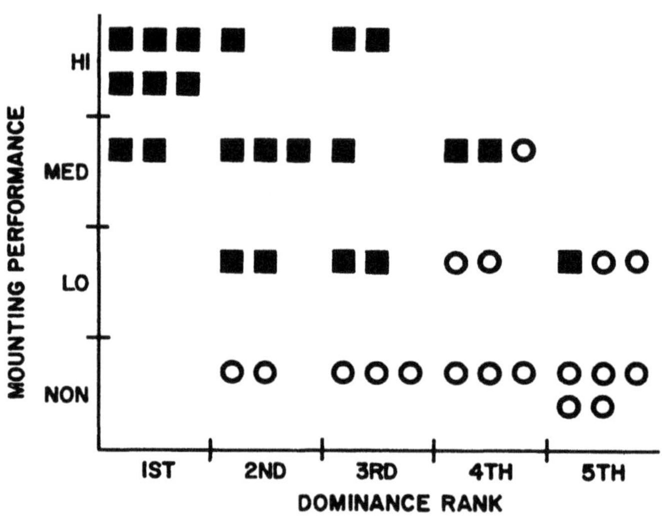

FIG. 5.6 Relationship between mounting performance and dominance for peer-reared rhesus monkeys in the first year of life. The data are from eight five-member groups, consisting of 22 males (filled squares) and 18 females (open circles). Mounting performance was based on relative mounting rank frequencies, using all forms of mounting. Animals were classified from these ranks as high, medium, low, or non-mounters.

animals. Conversely, high-ranking animals tend to present with lower frequencies than low-ranking animals. In addition, data from heterosexual peer groups (mothers absent) reveal that males have much greater chances of occupying the higher positions of social rank than do females (Table 5.3). While this is a fascinating observation, it also brings forth some difficult experimental problems, since we are now left with the following nonindependent conclusions: (a) the higher positions of social dominance are occupied primarily by males, and (b) high-ranking animals display mounting more frequently than low-ranking animals. For presenting responses, a similar confounding relationship exists: animals of low dominance tend to be females, and low-ranking individuals tend to present most frequently. Thus, without further analysis, it becomes difficult, if not impossible, to label either mounting or presenting as "dimorphic" until the problem of dominance confounded with genetic sex is experimentally separated.

For the immediate problem of unraveling the confounded nature of this sex versus dominance interaction, the isosexual data can be extremely useful, since both isosexual male and female peer groups form clear dominance hierarchies. Thus, the social dynamics of the isosexual groups insure the production of some low-ranking males and some high-ranking females. Using these data, then, we can specifically relate questions of dominance to the behaviors in question for each genotype without dealing with sex bias in these social relationships. Table 5.4 shows that most of the mounting in isosexual female groups was displayed by the higher-ranked females, and that most of the presenting in all-male groups was done by lower-ranked males. The mounting rates by isosexual females are lower than the mean levels seen in males, but they are considerably higher than those normally achieved by females in heterosexual contexts. In turn, the presenting rates of low-ranking males from isosexual groups are as high if not higher than those displayed by either sex in heterosexual groups. Clearly, dominance posi-

TABLE 5.3
Dominance Ranks of Male and Female Infant Rhesus Monkeys Reared in Heterosexual Peer Groups

	Dominance Rank Within Peer Group				
	1	2	3	4	5–6
Males (N = 33)	10	10	8	4	1
Females (N = 26)	0	1	3	7	15

Note. The data are based on 11 groups, 5 to 6 animals per group, during the first year of life. The table indicates that a male occupied the highest position of dominance in 10 of 11 groups. (In one group this position could not be discriminated unequivocally.) In contrast, most females ranked much lower in dominance in all 11 groups.

TABLE 5.4
Sexual Behaviors of Isosexual Peers Analyzed by Dominance Rank

	N	Abortive Mounts	Presents
High-ranked Males	4	11.9	10.6
High-ranked Females	6	1.9	1.5
Low-ranked Males	4	1.7	19.1
Low-ranked Females	6	0.8	2.3

tion as well as genetic sex has an influence on the probability of displaying these behaviors.

At this point the reader is cautioned that there is a disturbing circularity inherent in these demonstrations, since it is not known, for example, if "being dominant" leads to mounting or if mounting somehow leads to the establishment or maintenance of dominance. Furthermore, "dominance" may not in fact be the operating variable that is responsible for these observations, but may only be an experimental abstraction that reflects one aspect of the complex social interactions which we have been able to quantify with existing techniques.

Despite current problems of interpretation, experimental methods of evaluating behavior for dimorphic quality in more than one social setting now seem mandatory. The strategy of analyzing dimorphic displays in more than one rearing condition has already revealed for us that a sex difference in one condition of assessment, even though directly related to physiological differences, may not be as potent, or may in fact reverse direction, under different social or environmental conditions. That such a position can be taken from data on nonhuman primates in which cultural attitudes, verbal behavior, and sex bias are nonexistent, indicates that for the human, in which all of these factors obviously contribute to gender role, social learning must be expected to be extremely influencial (e.g., Money & Ehrhardt, 1968).

2. *Hormonal Influences*

a. Concurrent hormonal stimulation in infant and juvenile periods. As mentioned earlier, mounting behavior of infant and juvenile rhesus males appears to be independent of postnatal steroids, since castration at birth or within the first 90 days of life does not reduce abortive or foot clasp forms of this response prior to the fourth year of life. In addition, rough play frequencies are not significantly affected by castration, and aggressive responses actually seem slightly elevated in castrates, so that the development of male "gender role" apparently does not operate through mechanisms which rely on postnatal gonadal steroids (Bielert, 1974; Goy & Phoenix, 1971). The question then arises as to the influence of exogenous androgens: can augmented frequencies of these male gender role responses occur with precocious androgen stimulation? Can females given androgens postnatally show male gender role behaviors?

Bielert (1974) attempted to augment male gender role behaviors (mounting, rough play, threat, and aggression) in peer-reared male castrate juveniles by injecting testosterone propionate for 50 consecutive days, but found changes only in erection frequency and in yawning behavior, thus reinforcing the concept that the formerly mentioned responses are not dependent upon or easily modified by concurrent androgen stimulation. A second series of testosterone injections to these castrates ($N = 4$) 6 months subsequent to the first testosterone treatment caused the display of intromission in two of the animals, however, suggesting that the consummatory aspects of male sexual behavior, i.e., intromission and ejaculation, can be influenced by testosterone, and that this behavior can be precociously elicited by concurrent hormonal manipulation. It is very interesting to note, given the earlier discussion, that the males which had never shown foot clasp mounting prior to steroid administration were not stimulated to do so with exogenous steroids. Similarly, Joslyn (1973) was unable to augment mounting in any form in spayed female juveniles with testosterone propionate administration, although changes in dominance did occur during the course of treatment. In both studies, the dominance changes coincident with testosterone propionate administration occurred during the initial days of re-forming groups which had been separated, which is a particularly stormy period for primate groups (Bernstein, Gordon, & Rose, 1974). Dominance shifts were not seen under any conditions in which androgens were given following the establishment of the social structure. Androgenic stimulation, therefore, does not always lead to changes in dominance status or in the display of aggressive behaviors (Green, Whalen, Rutley, & Battie, 1972), but positive effects seem to be obtained when the group is first formed or is experiencing volatile or ambiguous dominance relations. Furthermore, androgenic stimulation cannot at present be interpreted to be a cause for the normal dominance advantage expressed by intact juvenile males, since the amount of testosterone propionate given in these experiments resulted in circulating levels of the hormone that were orders of magnitude higher than those encountered from endogenous sources.

The relative lack of contribution of concurrent hormonal influence on socio-sexual responses in infants and juveniles found thus far should not be considered to entirely close the question of a role for postnatal steroids, since it has recently been found by W. Bridson and J. Robinson of the Wisconsin Primate Center that elevated circulating plasma levels of testosterone in intact males—but not in females or castrated males—occurs during the first 3 months of life. A similar postnatal androgen rise has been observed in human male neonates (Forest, Cathiard, & Bertrand, 1973). No physiological or behavioral consequences of this neonatal elevation have been identified, but such endocrine events rarely are found to be capricious or without function. It could possibly be the case, therefore, that some aspects of subsequent social behaviors may be influenced by early postnatal gonadal steroids, but other conditions of evaluation will be necessary before differing behavioral potentials of intact and castrated infants may be revealed.

b. Prenatal influences of steroids on dimorphic behaviors. The propionates of testosterone (Goy & Phoenix, 1971; Goy & Resko, 1972) and dihydrotestosterone (Goy, Wolf, & Eisele, in press; R. W. Goy, personal communication, 1976) given to rhesus monkeys during the second third of pregnancy have been repeatedly shown to augment mounting, rough play, threat, and aggression in the resulting female offspring. However, prenatal androgens given to female rhesus monkeys have neither suppressed presenting behavior nor altered the potential to ovulate (Goy & Resko, 1972). In this regard, the nonhuman primate is markedly different from the rat and other short-gestation mammals in which the ability to ovulate and to display lordisis are both severely inhibited by estrogens and aromatizable androgens during critical periods of differentiation (Luttge & Whalen, 1970; Naftolin, Ryan, & Petro, 1971; Whalen, 1968, 1971). Normal male and female rhesus monkeys, as well as prenatally androgenized females, retain the ability to display presenting responses, and recent work has shown that males and prenatally androgenized females release substantial amounts of luteinizing hormone in response to acute estrogen stimulation, as well (Karsch, Dierschke, & Knobil, 1973). This indicates that, in primates, prenatal hormonal influences do not depress a hypothalamic-pituitary positive feedback response in either sex. Therefore, while prenatal steroids in rhesus monkeys are associated with behavioral "masculinization," which can be considered to be an augmentation of several behaviors in a given environment, they have not been found to cause "defeminization" either of behavior (e.g., depression of receptive postures) or of brain-pituitary relations.

Prenatal steroid treatments in rhesus monkeys, in addition to clearly changing subsequent response patterns, masculinize the urogenital sinus, genital tubercule, and Wolffian ducts of genetic female fetuses, so that a penis, scrotum, prostate and seminal vesicles are formed (Goy, Wolf, & Eisele, in press; Wells & van Wagenen, 1954). Since the administration of testosterone propionate does not influence gonadal changes or Müllerian duct differentiation, the females possess ovaries rather than testes and a well-formed uterus and oviducts in addition to the male secondary sex organs. Postnatal ovarian secretion patterns are not different from those of normal females, except that menarche is somewhat delayed (Goy & Resko, 1972). Testosterone propionate treatment beginning at 42 days of gestation and terminating 16 days later is sufficient to induce the behavioral changes, although the external genitalia are not fully masculinized (Goy, Wolf, & Eisele, in press). Theory would predict that depriving the male fetus of androgens at a critical fetal period should result in a pseudohermaphroditic or "feminized" male syndrome, but such experiments have not yet been conducted. Phoenix (1974) has shown that *in utero* castration of a male fetus at

100 days gestation does not prevent the offspring from displaying foot clasp mounting behavior as a juvenile. Thus, it can be concluded both from injections of androgens and from *in utero* castration studies that the period of maximum sensitivity for behavioral changes in response to steroids occurs before Day 100 of gestation in rhesus monkeys, and probably after Day 40. This developmental period corresponds to times when exogenous steroids have effectively altered later behavioral patterns, and similarly, to the period of gestation in which the fetal rhesus testis is producing large amounts of steroids (Goy & Resko, 1972; Resko, 1975).

Data from our laboratory show that prenatally androgenized female monkeys respond to social limitations of rearing exactly as do males. If a pseudohermaphrodite is in a low social position, especially the Omega position, mounting behavior is much less likely to develop. Compared to untreated females reared similarly, prenatally androgenized females have a greater likelihood of being in the higher positions of social dominance in their groups, but those who do not attain these ranks show decidedly poorer mounting development.

Again, the problem of relating dominance position to mounting behavior becomes circular if a causal mechanism is proposed from the observation. We cannot say whether common factors determine a position of dominance and the display of mounting. Nonetheless, the correlation of rank with this response is found for normal males, normal females, castrated males, and now for female pseudohermaphrodites as well. Perhaps the most conservative statement that can be made from these data is that the prenatal androgens experimentally evaluated to date predispose an individual to display many social responses, including mounting and rough play, but that a predisposition to display a response is obviously tempered by the opportunities or limitations imposed by the social environment.

III. TRANSITION FROM JUVENILE TO ADULT DISPLAYS OF SOCIOSEXUAL BEHAVIOR

In most nonhuman primates, the mounting and presenting behaviors which occur in infancy and juvenile periods of development are not the result of concurrent hormonal stimulation from gonadal sources. Males castrated shortly after birth not only mount with frequencies similar to intact peers, but also occasionally obtain intromissions and even display ejaculatory responses by 2-1/2 to 3-1/2 years of age (Bielert, 1974). Moreover, decreases in rough play behavior as adolescence approaches occur in both intact and castrated males (Bielert, 1974; Goy, 1968). Thus many of the alterations in behavior attributed to the adolescent periods are not the exclusive result of increased gonadal secretions. Nonetheless, with the onset of puberty and its accompanying gonadal maturation, hormonal secretions increase to adult levels over the course of several months to a year, and hence an additional potent factor influencing copulatory behavior, *hormonal activation,* becomes manifest. It might be expected that the behavioral transition from preadolescence to adulthood would be fairly straightforward in animals that have been "practicing" sexual skills since early childhood. The male, it would seem, simply needs to acquire a larger penis and to practice the motor skills involved in obtaining intromissions, while the female needs to learn parallel skills of facilitating intromission and receiving intravaginal stimulation. Both sexes, furthermore, would need to acquire additional behaviors of solicitation which typically precede mate selection and copulation, since under peer or mother-infant rearing conditions, we have never observed in rhesus females the typical solicitation gestures of the female, such as the head duck, hand slap, etc., prior to menarche. However, presenting postures, as mentioned previously, are thoroughly part of the behavioral repertoire very early. But reports from the field suggest that things are not all that simple for the maturing monkey: adolescence can be as stormy an adjustment for some nonhuman primates as it is for many human teenagers, and the assumption of an adult role within the group and the display of complete copulatory sequences is influenced by virtually all aspects of social structure as well as by hormonally induced alterations in sociosexual behaviors (Hanby, in press; Rowell, 1973; Stephenson, 1975; van Lawick-Goodall, 1968). For example, some primate species have social structures which result in partially isolating or "peripheralizing" subadult and young adult males, so that animals of this age class are often denied access to receptive females capable of conception (Norikoshi & Koyama, 1975; Stephenson, 1975). In some species, this process is severe, starting well before puberty, and young males form unisexual groups with few opportunities to engage in heterosexual activities (Goy & Goldfoot, 1975). Direct competition with established adult males is usually avoided in social systems which foster male peripheralization, and in some cases males do not have more than occasional opportunities for heterosexual coitus until many years after physiological puberty. The social organization of langurs (Hrdy, 1974; Rowell, 1974) probably represents an extreme form of this type of peripheralization, although in this case the process begins years before puberty and well before the time when the young male in any way competes with an adult male. Baboons and most macaques exhibit less severe, but nonetheless rather consistent, forms of the phenomenon. Several species, however, show no evidence of peripheralization of young males.

Laboratory data suggest that a second social phenomenon, namely low sexual "attractivity" of young males, may operate to reduce the copulating potentials of young animals in some primate species. Bielert (1974) found that young adult male rhesus monkeys paired with fully adult females were rarely successful in copulating, in part because the females characteristically threatened and refused mount attempts by their young partners. These rejection behaviors were not displayed by the same females when given older males as partners. Similar observations have been made with stump-tailed (Goldfoot, Slob, Scheffler, Robinson, Wiegand, & Cords, 1975) and bonnet macaques (Rosenblum & Nadler, 1971), while adult talapoin females have been observed not only to threaten, but even to *kill* young adult males which have attempted sexual encounters with them (Rowell, 1973). In this case, the females had accepted the young males as sexual partners earlier but became intolerant of them in early pregnancy.

Females of most species usually do not ever leave the central organization of the troop (the chimpanzee being a marked exception), so that adolescent peripheralization does not usually occur for females; but female-female competition for male partners might be expected to discourage adolescent females from copulating in at least some social structures. This influence might result in a mild version of social "peripheralization," at least for a short period. Unfortunately, very little data are available to confirm this possibility at present. A mechanism of low sexual attractiveness of adolescent females may operate as well for several primate species, including the chimpanzee (Tutin & McGrew, 1973), but few data are available. In a study of marmosets, adolescent females were not preferred as sexual partners by adult males in group situations (Rothe, 1975). Perhaps this was a result of complex social interactions, such as female-female dominance relations, but it is also possible that it reflected more basic physiological differences influencing female attractiveness. The date of first parturition for feral-living females is often later than would be expected on the basis of the date of menarche or of first ovulation (Stephenson, 1975). This delay may be due, at least in part, to social mechanisms discouraging conception, but other physiological mechanisms of early puberty, such as, so-called adolescent sterility, are clearly involved as well.

When studied in a laboratory situation in which concurrent group social factors can be eliminated, feral-born or group-reared adolescent males copulate to ejaculation with relatively little difficulty (Erwin & Mitchell, 1975; Loy & Loy, 1974), although a period of transition from sexual "ineptness" to increased efficiency in obtaining intromissions is quite evident. The exact time intervals from the onset of physiological pubertal changes to the display of full copulatory behavior have not been fully determined. In the case of stump-tailed monkeys, Trollope and Blurton Jones (1972) report that males copulate to ejaculation by the age of 3 years or earlier. Michael and Wilson (1973) observed four feral-reared subadult male rhesus monkeys of undetermined ages in the laboratory during their presumed first several ejaculatory experiences, and reported that these animals needed more time per test to ejaculate and displayed more mounts without intromissions than did experienced adult males. Moreover, when intromissions were obtained, these young animals showed higher frequencies of pelvic thrusting prior to ejaculation than adults do. Comparable studies on adolescent females have not been reported, although Bielert (1974) used premenarchial female rhesus monkeys implanted with estradiol capsules as stimulus animals in parts of his study and observed copulations to ejaculation with these young animals.

As is evident from the above discussion, the subject of the adolescence and sexual behavior of nonhuman primates has thus far received relatively little attention from scientists, which is rather surprising given the importance of more fully understanding the social and hormonal factors involved in this phase of development. Several nonhuman primate models might be profitably studied to reveal basic concepts that could conceivably be applied to humans. To cite just one example, Bielert (1974) found no difference in aggression or sexual activity between intact and castrated male rhesus monkeys prior to puberty. With the onset of puberty, however, very high levels of aggression were seen in intacts during the first few days of reestablishing a social group. The intact males showing the most aggression were those with socially restricted rearing histories (peer-reared animals), but intact males with more extensive socialization prior to puberty were not different from castrate males during comparable periods. Thus, the puberal rise in testosterone may contribute to increased aggression, but the overt display of violence will be expected to be a function of socialization histories.

IV. ADULT SEXUAL BEHAVIOR

A. Problems of Behavioral Analysis

1. Definitions and Scoring Procedures

Adult sexual interactions of nonhuman primates have been extensively studied from both field and laboratory perspectives. In addition to multiple hormonal factors that influence courtship and copulatory episodes, it seems that with each study the list of factors that have influence on sexual activity, including several interactive aspects of social structure, geneology, and even culture, is expanded (Hanby, in press; Loy & Loy, 1974; Missakian, 1972; Stephenson, 1973, 1975). Social ranks of males and females (or alternatively age-sex class roles) are found to have important influences on reproductive events in many investigations (Gartlan, 1968; Kaufmann, 1965; Stephenson, 1973; Tokuda, 1961–2), and the idea that animals have individual preferences for particular sexual partners is receiving increased emphasis (Goy & Goldfoot, 1975; Herbert, 1968; Phoenix, 1973). Effects of the presence or proximity of sexually active partners, especially as this relates to mechanisms of seasonality, are also being evaluated (Gordon & Bernstein, 1973; Vandenbergh & Drickamer, 1974).

Analysis of the various interactions of these many processes in order to obtain a more complete understanding of sexual behavior is a formidable task which has not been completed (or seriously considered!) by any laboratory to date. Needless to say, the development of behavioral observation strategies which could incorporate these many variables into a cohesive description of mating without being overwhelmed by trivial detail is an extremely difficult and ambitious project. Unfortunately, the behaviorist is far behind the biochemist in developing sophisticated analytical methods for considering discipline-related problems. In fact, the current nonuniformity of behavioral definitions, testing conditions, and data analysis seems particularly disruptive for the serious student of primate sexual behavior.

A specific example concerning attempts made to quantify sexual behavior of the adult female rhesus monkey will illustrate this problem. Many workers have come to realize that the present-at-distance response cannot be relied upon as the sole indicator of sexual solicitation on the part of the female. Although this posture is indeed a sexual solicitation, its elicitation depends on several factors, including social and physical conditions of testing. Moreover, many other behavioral patterns can serve as communicatory gestures of sexual interest, including some rather subtle head, shoulder, and hand movements described in detail by Michael and Zumpe (1970). In addition, even more subtle behaviors, such as the manner in which space is used by the female in the presence of the male–i.e., the frequency of approach and circling behaviors, standing and sitting close to the male, and eye glances with progressive decreases of interpartner distance–also serve communicative functions about sexual status. The problem for the investigator is that different monkeys use different variations and combinations of these behaviors, or sometimes they do absolutely nothing that can be reliably quantified until the male makes a move. Furthermore, the various behaviors of solicitation which have been identified do not all co-vary. Present-at-distance is displayed by most females throughout a menstrual cycle in a pair-test laboratory situation, but the behavior often decreases at ovulation for some females (Czaja & Bielert, 1975; Michael & Welegalla, 1968) and sometimes even *increases* after ovariectomy (Michael & Zumpe, 1970). The fact that other solicitation behaviors, such as head bobs, etc., usually increase at midcycle and decrease with ovariectomy would seem to indicate that these responses would be a better choice of measurement, except that many females simply do not exhibit these behaviors reliably. A combined index of solicitation including present-at-distance, head bobs, head ducks, and hand reaches (this measure is, for some reason, called "presentation" in papers by J. Herbert, and "invitation" in those by R. P. Michael), on the other hand, is a particularly difficult measure to interpret, since a given quantitative score in this combined category tells the reader little about the specific behaviors under observation. In addition, the combined measure leaves out all consideration of space utilization by the female, including proximity responses, which could in fact be the most significant aspect of sexually active individuals.

I have come to the conclusion that about the sexiest thing a female rhesus monkey can do is to sit very near the male with her back towards him, making very subtle head movements, and then begin to stand to receive the male as soon as he makes the slightest movement toward her. Unfortunately, most investigators have their own favorite measures, and very few behavioral categories are treated similarly from laboratory to laboratory. It is to be hoped that this deficiency will be corrected in the near future.

2. *Theoretical Framework: The APR Hypothesis*

If there is a relative absence of standardized definitions and standardized testing regimes in this field, it is not surprising that there is also a lack of agreement concerning interpretation of collected data. Over the last several years, various laboratories have attempted to organize data collection techniques by using the concepts of *attractiveness* and *receptivity* (Herbert & Trimble, 1967; Michael, Saayman, & Zumpe, 1967b). With this theoretical orientation, it is assumed that a male only attempts to copulate with females which are sexually attractive to him, and that females, in turn, display solicitation behaviors and accept the male only when they are receptive. Recently, Beach (1976), in considering the basic question of sexual motivation, has refined the concepts of attractiveness and receptivity and added an important new element called *proceptivity,* in an attempt to bring increased order to analysis of mechanisms of sexual response.

The theory is offered by Beach as a general mammalian model, but it is heavily influenced by the complexity of primate responses and is closely related to earlier hypotheses advanced by R. P. Michael and by J. Herbert. Beach suggests that the study of sexual interactions can be facilitated by conceptualizing the hypothetical constructs of (1) *attractivity,* which, when applied to the female, is any behavioral or nonbehavioral quality which stimulates the male to attempt copulation; (2) *proceptivity,* which is any behavioral response of the female that is sexually appetitive, i.e., behaviors which encourage the male to mount; and (3) *receptivity,* which is behavior of the female that augments the consummatory aspects of copulation, such as acceptance and facilitation of intromission, and maintenance of copulatory postures long enough to allow ejaculation to occur. Two important steps forward have been accomplished by Beach's analysis. The conceptual separation of proceptivity from receptivity is a valuable contribution to considerations of sexual motivation of the female, reflecting the active role which females assume in many sexual encounters. In addition, the notion that attractivity is composed of both behavioral and nonbehavioral (e.g., odor, color, etc.) cues is a very useful change of emphasis from earlier definitions. Previously, the term appeared to be restricted to nonbehavioral attributes of the female, with odors receiving the greatest emphasis. In spite of the clarification achieved with Beach's schema, referred to as the "APR model" in the rest of this chapter, the new definitions are not without their own problems. Beach correctly cautions that each of these concepts must be independently defined in terms of stimulus-response relationships susceptible to quantitative measurement, but herein lies a potential "catch-22," since most of the measures used in the past to define attractivity, proceptivity, and receptivity are not independent of one another.

One specific stimulus-response index recommended by Beach and used previously by other workers to operationally define attractivity (Michael & Welegalla, 1968) is the male acceptance ratio (AR), which is the number of mount attempts by the male elicited in response to the female's presentation or invitation (present-at-distance, head bob, head duck, or hand reach). But this is not a satisfactory way of measuring attractivity, because it is, as already indicated, defined as any behavioral or *nonbehavioral* aspect of the female which stimulates the male to mount; therefore, measurements of attractivity should not be limited to those cases in which the female first displays a particular behavior. When the male acceptance ratio is used to define attractivity, this means that the measure only reflects the attractivity of females which are displaying specific proceptive responses and would, among other problems, certainly not conform to the requirement of independent definitions of each of the three constructs comprising the APR model.

Other measures of attractivity can be constructed without this problem, but even when attractivity of the female is assessed by responses of the male, irrespective of the female's behavior, it is impossible to determine from such observations whether or not behavioral or nonbehavioral cues coming from the female attracted the male. This is an obvious problem since no investigator measures or claims to recognize all of the subtle behavioral cues which can occur between pairs that would facilitate the male's approach behavior. Obviously, to answer such questions, strategies other than placing a heterosexual pair together must be utilized. Studies such as those described by Keverne (in press) using bar press tasks offer much promise as an approach to this problem.

A second and more serious problem with the model is that some males may attempt to mount females without regard to their "attractiveness," choosing perhaps to see what the female will do following the male's advances. This seems to be particularly the case with stump-tailed monkeys in laboratory tests (Goldfoot et al., 1975). Also, some investigators have used the concept of attractivity with the assumption that a male is in a constant and ever-ready sexual state of preparedness, and yet many of us primates know that this is not always the case. Since attractivity of the female can only be measured by responses of the male, researchers wishing to use these concepts must make every effort to standardize conditions. Yet many workers, Beach (1976) included, report that males form individual perferences for certain females, with a surprising incidence of nonagreement among males (Goy & Goldfoot, 1975; Phoenix, 1973; see also data of Wiegand & Goy in Figure 5.7). Thus a female can be attractive to one male and unattractive to another at virtually the same time and under the same hormonal and environmental conditions.

A third problem with the model is that considerable proceptive activity of the female may in part be regulated or affected by the interest shown her by the male, such that the frequency of proceptive responding is sometimes inversely related to the sexual attention shown by the male (Baum et al., in press; Trimble & Herbert, 1968)! If a male is very persistent, the female does not show the same range of proceptive responses that she might with a more sluggish partner. On the other hand, extremely persistent males can force unreceptive females to submit to mounting attempts in certain testing situations. A "rape" can occur, especially in a cage providing minimal space, and many females will begin to present and tolerate mounts presumably in order to avoid further attacks from the male. Thus, although each concept in the APR model seems to be independently defined, they are interrelated to such a degree operationally that their use in most situations must be approached with the clear appreciation that nonhormonal factors can decidedly influence each of the measures. Perhaps the most useful result fo the introduction of the APR model will be in its effect on future research, since careful design strategies should be able to more accurately delineate these constructs than traditional pair-test paradigms now permit. Although it does not cover all conditions of sexual interactions, the APR model appears to be a strong theoretical contribution, provided that research strategies are employed which can correctly test the constructs proposed. The reader is directed to Baum et al. (in press) and Keverne (in press) for more complete and more positive treatments of the APR theory.

B. Hormonal Stimulation of Sociosexual Behavior

The analysis of hormonal factors influencing copulation present typical problems of analysis from several points of view. In general, although hormones can strongly influence copulatory events, most concurrent hormonal actions in primates appear to act much more as behavioral potentiators, changing response probabilities, than as behavioral releasors, directly "turning on behaviors." This is suggested by the fact that changes in hormone level do not invariably lead to changes of behavior. Some specific examples of response changes following castration of adults will illustrate this point most clearly. When appropriate, terms defined by the APR model will be used in these following discussions.

1. Castration Studies

Adult male rhesus monkeys respond in very individualistic manners to adult castration: some males quickly lose their capacity to achieve intromission and ejaculations, and eventually show decreased mounting behavior, whereas others continue to copulate for years after surgery although usually at reduced frequencies (Michael & Wilson, 1974; Phoenix, Slob, & Goy, 1973). Phoenix (1976) reports that 4 years postcastration, 5 of 10 males displayed ejaculatory patterns, and 70% showed intromissions, but at significantly lower levels than intact control males. Administration of testosterone or dihydrotestosterone fully restored preoperative rates of copulation in most individuals. The hormones clearly augment consummatory aspects of adult male responses, such as intromission and ejaculation, as was noted to be the case for juvenile male sexual responses, but the capacity to display these behaviors for many males is not lost following castration. In addition, there is a clear relationship between decreased circulating androgens at the end of a breeding season, and a rather abrupt loss of sexual interest on the part of the male, although steroid levels under these seasonal influences never fall to postcastration levels (Gordon, Rose, & Bernstein, 1976; Plant, Zumpe, Sauls, & Michael, 1974; Robinson, Scheffler, Eisele, & Goy, 1975). This observation creates some difficulty, because as just noted, castration does not necessarily bring about rapid changes in sexual response. Factors in addition to decreased androgen levels are therfore suggested to be involved in the seasonal termination of a male's sexual activity. Robinson et al. (1975), studying the effect of age and season on copulatory behavior and testosterone stimulation, concluded that "although both testosterone concentrations and behavior varied seasonally, there was no evidence for a direct relationship between these two variables . . . [and] . . . levels of sexual performance for individual males bore no consistent relationship to concentrations of peripheral testosterone" (p. 207). Michael and Wilson (1975), moreover, have discovered that the seasonal rise and fall of mating activity is maintained in castrates which receive constant daily injections of testosterone while paired with spayed females receiving constant exogenous estrogen stimulation. Both studies imply that other unidentified physiological factors are perhaps influencing seasonal variations of the functional activating properties of endogenous or exogenous androgen, perhaps mediated by seasonal changes in pituitary secretions or plasma binding substances, or by alterations in androgen metabolism. Nonetheless, most researchers believe that the seasonal rise of testosterone during the breeding period plays a functional role in the maintenance of sexual activity and is probably also involved in the mediation of other behavioral changes, such as increases in aggression seen at this time (Gordon et al., 1976). Researchers are also in agreement that the individual sexual performance of a male bears little or no relationship to his testosterone level, provided that some threshold of circulating androgen has been exceeded (Goldfoot et al., 1975; Gordon et al., 1976; Robinson et al., 1975).

In contrast to castration effects, medial preoptic hypothalamic lesions of adult and juvenile male rhesus monkeys promptly reduce mounting and copulation to extremely low levels without influencing testosterone titers (Slimp, 1976). Adult male rhesus monkeys living in cages masturbate to ejaculation rather frequently, though, and Slimp (1976) made the fascinating discovery that masturbation to ejaculation in lesioned adults remained at preoperative levels. This finding of maintenance of masturbation but not of heterosexual copulation following hypothalamic lesions means that new evaluations are called for with regard to the concepts of male sexual motivation and its control by hormonally dependent neural structures within the hypothalamus.

The hormone-behavior relationships of females are equally interesting and only slightly clearer. Following ovariectomy, most, but not all, experienced adult female rhesus monkeys show decreased sexual interest in male partners (loss of proceptivity), and are not as stimulating to males as intact females (loss of attractiveness). Changes in receptivity also decrease, according to several studies by Michael and colleagues, including those in which the male's interest in the female was artificially maintained by use of vaginal olfactants (Michael et al., 1972). Everitt, Herbert, and Hamer (1972) and Goldfoot, Kravetz, Goy, and Freeman (1976), however, found several instances in which receptivity of rhesus females was relatively high following ovariectomy. Baum et al. (in press) and Keverne (in press) take the position that receptivity is not markedly influenced by ovariectomy, and that adrenal steroids may contribute to the maintenance of a receptive condition following ovariectomy.

Although ovariectomy usually leads to cessation of coitus in rhesus females, whether by changes in attractivity, proceptivity, or receptivity, this is decidedly not the case for the female stump-tailed macaque. S. Wiegand, A. K. Slob, and R. W. Goy have found that copulatory levels in this species decreased only moderately following gonadectomy (Slob, 1975), and in two of five females, sexual vigor and ejaculatory frequencies returned to intact levels 2 years following surgery. Steroidal influences from the adrenal may possibly be playing some role in maintaining sexual activities of these individuals, although this has not yet been experimentally tested. However, even if true, the stump-tailed macaque seems more like the human female than other primates in its capacity to maintain copulatory behavior in the absence of ovarian secretions. Figure 5.7 illustrates that, in addition, males and females of this species exhibit strong individual preferences for specific sexual partners, even when all the females in the study had been gonadectomized at least 1.5 years earlier. Obviously "attractivity" in these instances depends upon something other than ovarian secretions.

Several investigators have shown, either directly by measurement of steroids or indirectly by changes in sex skin color and testis size (Sade, 1964; Conaway & Sade, 1965; Vandenbergh, 1965), that the presence of receptive females augments peripheral androgen levels in adult male rhesus monkeys and stimulates mounting activity "during nonbreeding periods" (Bernstein et al., 1974; Vandenbergh & Drickamer, 1974). Other work has failed to confirm elevated plasma testosterone levels shortly after coitus (Dixson & Phoenix, in press; Goldfoot, et al., 1975), but in these cases males were already evidencing high peripheral androgen levels prior to copulatory activity. Moreover, although the availability of sophisticated radioimmunoassay techniques has made it possible to determine even minor fluctuations of endogenous steroids, it is suspected that the collection of blood samples sometimes may cause spurious changes in hormone levels which do not reflect the physiological conditions prior to experimental intervention, so that what appear to be relatively simple techniques, such as taking repeated blood

FEMALES

MALES	A	B	C	D	E	$\bar{X}$
1	3.9	2.6	2.4	1.0	0.5	2.08
2	2.4	3.7	1.3	1.5	0.9	1.96
3	3.6	3.1	1.3	1.3	0.0	1.86
4	1.9	2.5	2.0	0.2	0.2	1.36
5	1.6	1.4	0.3	0.0	0.4	0.74
$\bar{X}$	2.68	2.66	1.46	0.80	0.40	

FIG. 5.7 Sexual behavior (mean number of ejaculations per test) of five male stump-tailed macaques as a function of partner. Data are means per 10 tests. All females were spayed at least $1\frac{1}{2}$ years prior to the study and were receiving no exogenous steroids. Data from an unpublished study by S. Wiegand and R. W. Goy.

samples prior to and following coitus, may sometimes seriously distort the results. In such cases, special control procedures are called for.

In short, while it is technically possible to generate hormone-behavior correlations, considerable interpretive care must be exercised, especially with regard to questions of causality, since the hormone titers might well reflect a correlated but nondeterminative relationship with the behavior in question, or alternatively might represent an effect rather than a cause of the behaviors under study (e.g., Rose, Bernstein, & Gordon, 1974).

2. *Cyclic Sexual Behavior*

Most investigators agree that there are cyclical increases and decreases in copulatory probabilities occurring within menstrual cycles for most primates studied, but with various degrees of cyclicity occurring as a function of species or even of individual pairs (see reviews by Luttge, 1971; Michael, 1973; and Rowell, 1972). When heterosexual pairs of rhesus monkeys are observed daily in the laboratory beginning with the first day of menstruation, ejaculatory series occur throughout the menstrual cycle, but there are usually progressive increases in the frequency and decreases in the latency to ejaculation through the follicular phase of the cycle, with a peak in coital performance reached near the time of expected ovulation (Figure 5.8). Ejaculatory series then diminish in frequency in luteal phases, with some pairs evidencing a secondary rise in sexual activity just before the next menstruation (e.g., Czaja, Eisele, & Goy, 1975). Two additional variations of this pattern have been reported for rhesus monkeys: cycles in which copulatory behavior is uniformly high through follicular and periovulatory stages, and then diminishes in the luteal phase, and cycles in which the behavior is quite low except during the periovulatory period. Michael (1968) estimated that only about 50% of the intact heterosexual pairs of rhesus monkeys studied in his laboratory have evidenced behavioral cycles related to ovarian events. Pig-tailed macaques (Bullock, Paris, & Goy, 1972; Eaton & Resko, 1974), chimpanzees (Young & Orbison, 1944), and chacma baboons (*Papio ursinus;* Saayman, 1970)–all species with marked cyclic perineal turgescence at midcycle,–show similar copulatory distributions to that of rhesus monkeys, except that the phase of luteal inhibition seems even more pronounced. In contrast, gorilla pairs apparently are sexually active only during a very limited periovulatory period (Nadler, 1975), whereas captive orangutans

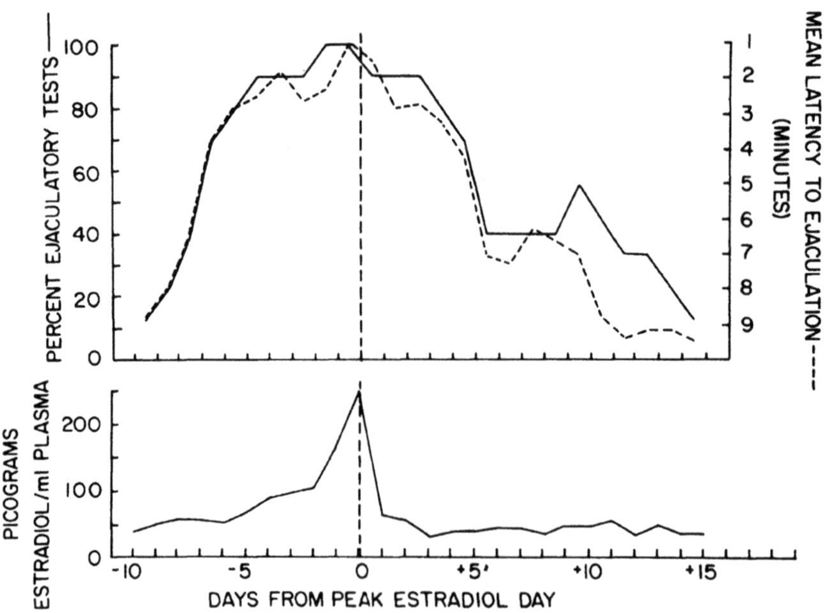

FIG. 5.8 Changes in ejaculatory probabilities of eight pairs of rhesus monkeys as a function of the stage of the ovarian cycle. Unpublished data collected by J. A. Czaja, D. A. Goldfoot, C. F. Bielert, and J. A. Robinson.

copulate steadily throughout the cycle (Nadler, in press). Japanese macaques have (Hanby, Robertson, & Phoenix, 1971) and have not (Eaton, 1973) been found to show cyclic sexual behavior, and stump-tailed macaques tested as pairs in the laboratory show extremely high rates of coitus with only minimal evidence of cyclic patterning of coital episodes (Slob, Wiegand, Scheffler, & Goy, 1975). Thus, little phylogenetic "order" can be made of the situation, especially when the cyclic activity is observed in laboratory environments.

Common to all pair test studies, regardless of species, is the observation that sexual consummatory behaviors of the male (intromission and ejaculation) rather than sexual initiation behaviors of the female are the more reliable indicators of ovarian status of the female. In contrast to the low to moderate correlations with ovarian state that are generally obtained in heterosexual pair tests using indices of invitation by the female, frequencies of ejaculation and ejaculatory latencies of males in time-limited tests are remarkably well correlated with the ovarian condition of their partners for most Old World species. Several possible hypotheses, not necessarily independent of one another, have been offered to account for this observation: (a) human observers have not been as astute as male nonhuman primates in recognizing subtle but crucial behavioral changes of the female (e.g., Czaja & Bielert, 1975); (b) nonbehavioral cues such as ovarian-induced odor or sex skin color changes stimulate the male to copulate, and therefore changes in attractiveness rather than proceptivity account for midcycle peaks in sexual behavior (Everitt, Herbert, & Hamer, 1972; Michael et al., 1972); (c) nonovarian hormones, such as adrenal androgens of the female, also determine copulatory probabilities by influencing the female's solicitation rates, thus suggesting that correlations with the ovarian cycle may not be pronounced (Everitt et al., 1972); (d) a social environment involving several animals may be necessary for the occurrence of some behavioral changes which females display near midcycle, thus rendering the standard heterosexual pair test an inappropriate or at least a very limited technique for this problem (Goldfoot, 1971); and (e) perhaps there really are no cyclical variations in the behavior of the female related to ovarian condition, especially when considered in naturalistic environments (Eaton, 1973; Rowell, 1963, 1972). Other explanations are possible, as well.

A series of studies on the pig-tailed macaque will illustrate why tempers sometime rise over this particular issue of the behavioral cyclicity of the female. Three separate studies on the very same intact male and female pig-tailed macaque subjects were conducted from 1968 to 1973 at the Oregon Regional Primate Research Center by different sets of investigators. In the first study, Bullock, Paris, Resko and Goy (1968), using heterosexual pair tests, initially reported clear evidence of a peak in ejaculatory frequencies occurring near ovulation, but found no evidence for behavioral cyclicity of the female per se. Reanalysis of the data (Bullock, Paris, & Goy, 1972), suggested, however, that presenting responses were significantly higher in the follicular phase than they were in the luteal phase, but that considerable presenting occurred any time during the cycle. Goldfoot (1971), using the same animals found clear midcycle changes not only in ejaculatory probabilities of the male, but also for a variety of behaviors of the female, including follow, proximity, present-near, present-at-distance, and a facial gesture which was referred to as "sex pout." These results were obtained by testing triads of females placed together in a large cage with the male. Each of the three females was in a different ovarian phase, i.e., follicular, preovulatory, and luteal. Triads were re-formed with different combinations of the 15 females studied until every female was tested under each of these three ovarian conditions. Thus, not only could each female's behavior be judged at three different phases of the ovarian cycle, but elements of female-female competition and male preference behavior were also present in this design. It was found that as long as a female was not in the lowest position of dominance within a triad, each of the males responded to her most frequently at midcycle, and she, in turn, displayed her highest levels of proceptive behavior at that time. If she were subordinate to the other females in the group, however, she showed little proceptive behavior, even at midcycle, and the male then copulated with either the follicular or the luteal female (Figure 5.9). When triads were formed in which all three females were in similar phases of the cycle (all follicular or all luteal), then the female ranking as most dominant received and displayed the most sexual activity.

In a third study, again with the same animals, Eaton and Resko (1974) allowed females to control a lever which released one of five males into a test arena. The female could choose which of the males to release, or she could elect not to press for any male. Under these conditions, Eaton and Resko found (1) ejaculatory probabilities highest at midcycle, (2) clear partner preferences exhibited by the females, (3) no cyclic influence on the release of males by females, and (4) no change of proceptive responding, e.g., presenting, thoughout the cycle. We have, then, three studies on the same animals, three distinctly different design strategies, and three separate and apparently contradictory conclusions regarding proceptive responses of the female.

Nonetheless, it is possible to conclude from these studies that behaviors of the female do change as a function of ovarian influences, but (and this should no longer be a surprise to the reader), many factors, including social competition, dominance rank, and perhaps even cage size, can also facilitate or inhibit the display of sexual activities for females and males, often to the point of completely obscuring the hormonal influence which is presumed to be operative and under study.

Experimental designs which separate the male from the female and/or give the female more control in the experimental setting seem to reveal behavioral inclinations of the female more readily than studies employing single pair-test designs. Czaja and Bielert (1975) found obvious changes of female proximity to the male using such a strategy, and, in an elegant series of experiments, Keverne

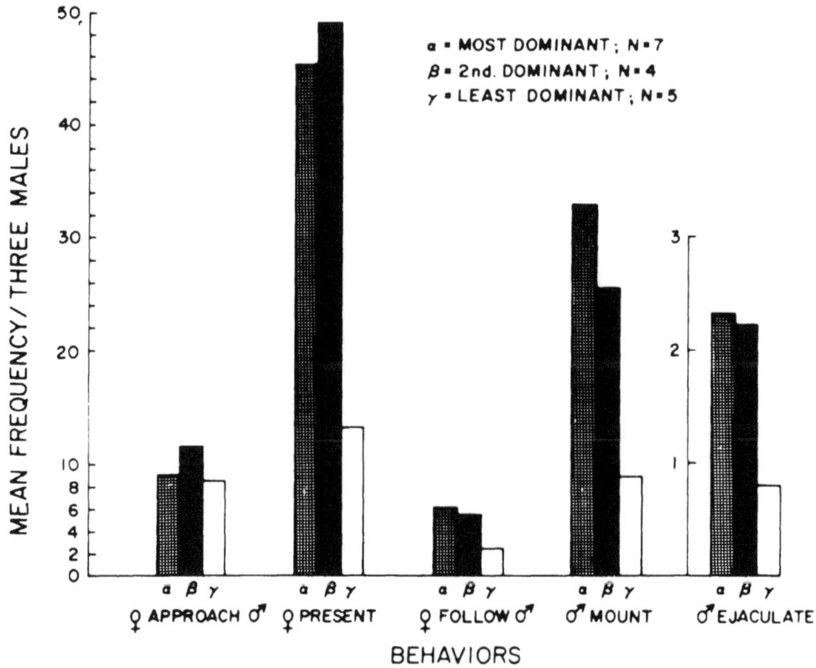

FIG. 5.9 Sexual behaviors received and displayed by maximally turgescent (presumed periovulatory) female pig-tailed macaques of differing positions of dominance in temporary groups of three females tested with three males, one after the other. Note that the periovulatory female is sexually active unless she is least dominant in the temporary groups. (Data From Goldfoot, 1971.)

(in press) has shown that females will perform an operant task (bar press) for access to males as a function of hormonal condition. As Eaton and Resko (1974) show, however, such experimental approaches do not always lead to similar results.

3. *Hypothesized Hormonal Influences on Attractivity, Proceptivity, and Receptivity*

Perhaps more work has been directed to questions involving the separation of function of various ovarian and adrenal steroids on the display of sexual activity in nonhuman primate pairs than any other single pursuit within this field. Several reviews are available (see citations in section I, as well as the summary of primate research in Beach's 1976 APR paper). Very briefly, it has been suggested that although estrogens certainly act on behavioral mechanisms, their major effect in nonhuman primates, and specifically in rhesus monkeys, is on nonbehavioral elements of attractivity, including sex skin coloration (Czaja, Eisele, & Goy, 1975), perineal turgescence (Bullock et al., 1972; Saayman, 1970), vaginal olfactants (e.g., Keverne, 1974; Michael & Keverne, 1968, 1970), and vaginal lubrication and tonus. Thus estrogens are hypothesized to change the nonbehavioral attractive qualities of the female, which in turn cause the male to attempt sexual activities. The role of vaginal olfactants (sometimes called pheromones) may indeed play an important stimulatory role for many primates (see review by Epple, 1974), but recent evidence cautions against an unqualified acceptance of the hypothesis that odor cues are either necessary or sufficient to induce coitus in rhesus monkeys. In many cases their presence or absence does not change copulatory probabilities, and, therefore, they cannot constitute a complete explanation for female attractivity (Goldfoot et al., 1976). Nonetheless, olfactory information probably contributes to sexual interactions in several specific instances, even for rhesus monkeys, but not with the effectiveness or mechanism implied in the word "pheromone."

Everitt, Herbert, and colleagues, in a series of interesting studies, have been the main supporters of the idea that proceptive and receptive responses of the female are primarily under androgenic, rather than estrogenic, control. Herbert's group bases this hypothesis on the observations that following chemical suppression (Everitt & Herbert, 1971) or surgical removal (Everitt et al., 1972) of the adrenals, more than 50% of their spayed females showed decreased proceptive and receptive behaviors, even when estrogens were exogenously administered. In these studies, testosterone or androstenedione injections reversed the influence of adrenal insufficiency. Further, Herbert and Trimble (1967) reported that administration of testosterone propionate to ovariectomized females with intact adrenals stimulated proceptive displays in 6 of 8 pairs. Under these conditions, males did not show increased attempted mounting, however, in spite of high levels of invitational displays, presumably because the spayed females were not sexually attractive, due to estrogenic insufficiency.

In its most oversimplified form, therefore, the most widely cited hypothesis now finding its way into textbooks (Schlesinger & Groves, 1976, p. 99) suggests that estrogen is primarily associated with nonbehavioral elements of attractivity, and that androgen, not estrogen, is associated with proceptivity and receptivity and is therefore the "libidinal hormone" of female primates (also, see Dixson, Everitt, Herbert, Rugman, & Scruton, 1973). If true, this represents a dramatic deviation from evolutionary history, because in all nonprimate mammals studied, estrogens, either alone or in combination with progesterone, have been found to be the primary "libidinal substances" responsible for estrous behavior in females. On the other hand, androgens have not been fully evaluated in nonprimate species, and they may in fact play a role in establishing or maintaining the sexual responses of the estrous female (Rodriguez-Sierra, Naggar, & Komisaruk, in press).

In partial contradiction of the evidence just cited, the results of two very recent studies suggest that it is an oversimplification to equate estrogen with attractivity and androgen with proceptivity and receptivity. Johnson and Phoenix (1976), studying spayed female rhesus monkeys in heterosexual pair tests and in a bar-pressing task for access to males, concluded that administration of either estradiol or low doses of testosterone increased female attractivity and that both hormones also increased proceptive responses of females. In turn, female sexual receptivity measured by the acceptance ratio was significantly augmented only by estradiol, while the removal of adrenal androgens did not affect receptivity. The authors raised three important points of discussion based on their findings.

First, they did not regard testosterone as *the* libidinal hormone for the female rhesus monkey, since estrogen and testosterone had very similar effects in the study. Instead, they suggested that both proceptivity and attractiveness are probably controlled by estrogen and androgens in appropriate balance. Second, the authors indicated that receptivity may be influenced more by extrahormonal factors such as social stimuli than by hormonal mediation in this species. Third, the authors hypothesized that testosterone is effective in stimulating sexual behavior of the spayed female only to the extent that it is partially metabolized to estradiol, thus providing both estrogen and testosterone to the spayed female.

Unpublished heterosexual pair-test data on spayed rhesus monkeys collected by Kim Wallen and R. W. Goy add further dimension to this issue, since these researchers evaluated the effects of estrone and dihydrotestosterone propionate in addition to estradiol and testosterone propionate. Dihydrotestosterone propionate is an esterfied form of a major metabolite of testosterone, which cannot be metabolized to estrogenic substances; its use was meant to reveal whether testosterone-to-estrogen conversion is an obligatory step in its mode of action for proceptive behaviors. Wallen and Goy found that (a) estradiol, estrone, and testosterone given to spayed rhesus females were all equally effective in stimulating males to copulate to ejaculation, but that (b) approach and proximity behaviors initiated by the female were affected by the estrogens, but not by either of the androgens; (c) female hand reach, head bob, and head duck measures were influenced by both of the estrogens, but even more so by testosterone; dihydrotestosterone was entirely without effect; finally, (d) present-at-distance was not significantly influenced by any hormone treatment. The only behavior change noted for dihydrotestosterone was the stimulation of yawning behavior, an effect also obtained with testosterone. Both of these studies suggest that each of the several aspects of proceptive display may be controlled by one hormone more than another. For example, testosterone increases hand reach, head bob, and other similar head and shoulder responses of solicitation, but estrogen seems to influence the way in which the female approaches and sits by the male. Both sets of behaviors, of course, are proceptive. Secondly, the complete failure of dihydrotestosterone to influence sexual behavior suggests that conversion of testosterone to estradiol may indeed be an important element in the mediation of testosterone's influence on proceptive and receptive elements previously reported. However, this issue has still not been resolved, and it would be quite incorrect to assume from the lack of response to dihydrotestosterone that the behavioral effects obtained with testosterone merely reflect estrogenic conversions. Much preliminary evidence suggests, alternatively, that estrogen and testosterone act in synergy, especially at midcycle, to influence maximal behavioral proceptivity of the female (Johnson and Phoenix, 1976; Keverne, in press), and hormonal secretory patterns at midcycle would certainly support this hypothesis (Hess and Resko, 1973).

Progesterone, the predominant hormone of the luteal phase of the menstrual cycle, is thought to inhibit either or both attractivity and receptivity mechanisms in rhesus monkeys (Michael, Saayman, & Zumpe, 1967a). Bielert, Czaja, Eisele, Scheffler, Robinson, and Goy (1976) suggest that estrogen-progesterone ratios regulate levels of sexual activity for the rhesus female except in the second half of pregnancy, when sexual behavior is not seen, in spite of favorable estrogen-progesterone ratios. The findings of Hess and Resko (1973), on the other hand, suggest that progesterone's inhibitory effects are perhaps secondary, arising from its ability to lower testosterone titers. Research with progesterone is in a more preliminary phase and presents even greater problems than research concerning the other ovarian hormones. Therefore, I will not attempt to discuss this topic further, but suggest that the reader consult Bielert et al. (1976) and Baum et al. (in press) for the most current information available on this topic.

V. SUMMARY AND CONCLUSIONS

This chapter has attempted to give detailed consideration to factors identified with the development and expression of sociosexual behavior in nonhuman primates. The picture that emerges, in spite of the great difficulties encountered in the study of this complex problem, is of an intricate balance of social, hormonal and environmental systems acting upon primates at every stage of growth to determine the behavioral expression of sexuality. Prenatal hormonal influences, interacting with the genetic substrate, predispose animals to behave along certain dimensions, but the postnatal social system, depending upon its particular characteristics, almost immediately modifies, limits, or permits full expression of the biologically set predispositions. During the period of infant and juvenile development, concurrent hormonal stimulation does not appear to play a major role in the elaboration of sexual interactions; sociosexual relationships and behavioral patterns establish themselves without hormonal activation. At puberty, however, both maturational factors and increased gonadal secretions determine the individual's potential to copulate, but in naturalistic environments social pressures exerted by adults in some primate species often segregate puberal individuals and delay their full participation in heterosexual reproductive activities, sometimes for as long as several years after the physiological onset of puberty. Finally, with the attainment of full social as well as physiological maturity, sexual expression reaches its most complex stage, being very much interrelated with other social mechanisms. Hormonal processes in adult life clearly facilitate and regulate sexual activities, but such regulation is expressed as a function of the social history of the individual and within a modulating social system.

It is hoped that the integration of social and hormonal systems will be more fully characterized and better understood with future research, because, in this author's opinion, it is likely that major aspects of human personality systems operate in response to the very same social and hormonal variables that affect other primates.

ACKNOWLEDGMENTS

This work, Publ. No. 16-038 of the Wisconsin Regional Primate Research Center, was supported by Grants MH 21312 from the National Institute of Mental Health and RR-00167 from the National Institutes of Health.

I wish to thank the entire staff of the Wisconsin Primate Center for the excellent support provided in the execution of many of the experiments reported here as well as in the preparation of this chapter. Dr. R. W. Goy is especially thanked for his support and encouragement and for his generous permission to allow me to analyze data collected from earlier work. In addition, I thank Larry Jacobsen and Hannah King for their many library services, Pat Newell and Betsy Shirah for secretarial assistance, Kim Wallen and Alan Leshner for critical readings of the manuscript, and finally Mary Collins and Jane Cords for diligently collecting substantial amounts of data reported here for the first time.

REFERENCES

Baldwin, J. D., & Baldwin, J. I. The role of play in social organization: Comparative observations on squirrel monkeys (*Saimiri*). *Primates,* 1973, **14,** 369–381.

Baum, M., Everitt, B. J., Herbert, J., & Keverne, E. B. Hormonal basis of proceptivity and receptivity in female primates. *Archives of Sexual Behavior,* in press.

Beach, F. A. Sexual attractivity, proceptivity and receptivity in female mammals. *Hormones and Behavior,* 1976, **7,** 105–138.

Bernstein, I. S., Gordon, T. P., & Rose, R. M. Aggression and social controls in rhesus monkey (*Macaca mulatta*) groups revealed in group formation studies. *Folia Primatologica,* 1974, **21,** 81–107.

Bielert, C. F. The effects of early castration and testosterone propionate treatment on the development and display of behavior patterns by male rhesus monkeys (*Macaca mulatta*) (Doctoral dissertation, Michigan State University, 1974). *Dissertation Abstracts International,* 1975, **36,** 124B–125B. (University Microfilms No. 75-14, 702).

Bielert, C., Czaja, J. A., Eisele, S., Scheffler, G., Robinson, J. A., & Goy, R. W. Mating in the rhesus monkey (*Macaca mulatta*) after conception and its relationship to oestradiol and progesterone levels throughout pregnancy. *Journal of Reproduction and Fertility,* 1976, **46,** 179–187.

Bingham, H. C. Sex development in apes. *Comparative Psychology Monographs,* 1928, **5**(1, Serial No. 23), 1–165.

Bullock, D. W., Paris, C. A., & Goy, R. W. Sexual behavior, swelling of the sex skin and plasma progesterone in the pigtail macaque. *Journal of Reproduction and Fertility,* 1972, **31,** 225–236.

Bullock, D. W., Paris, C. A., Resko, J. A., & Goy, R. W. Sexual behavior and progesterone secretion during the menstrual cycle in rhesus and pigtail macaques. In *Proceedings of the Sixth International Congress of Animal Reproduction and Artificial Insemination* (Vol. 2), Paris, 1968.

Conaway, C. H., & Sade, D. S. The seasonal spermatogenic cycle in free ranging rhesus monkeys. *Folia Primatologica,* 1965, 3, 1–12.

Czaja, J. A., & Bielert, C. F. Female rhesus sexual behavior and distance to a male partner: Relation to stage of the menstrual cycle. *Archives of Sexual Behavior,* 1975, **4,** 583–597.

Czaja, J. A., Eisele, S. G., & Goy, R. W. Cyclical changes in the sexual skin of female rhesus: Relationships to mating behavior and successful artificial insemination. *Federation Proceedings,* 1975, **34,** 1680–1684.

De Benedictis, T. The behavior of young primates during adult copulation: Observation of a *Macaca irus* colony. *American Anthropologist,* 1973, **75,** 1469–1484.

Deutsch, J., & Larsson, K. Model-oriented sexual behavior in surrogate reared rhesus monkeys. *Brain, Behavior and Evolution,* 1974, **9,** 157–164.

Dixson, A. F., Everitt, B. J., Herbert, J., Rugman, S. M., & Scruton, D. M. Hormonal and other determinants of sexual attractiveness and receptivity in rhesus and talapoin monkeys. In C. H. Phoenix (Ed.), *Symposia of the Fourth International Congress of Primatology* (Vol. 2). Basel: Karger, 1973.

Dixson, A., & Phoenix, C. H. The effects of ejaculation on levels of testosterone, cortisol and luteinizing hormone in peripheral plasma of rhesus monkeys. *Journal of Comparative and Physiological Psychology,* 1977, **90,** 120–127.

Eaton, G. G. Social and endocrine determinants of sexual behavior in simian and prosimian females. In C. H. Phoenix (Ed.), *Symposia of the Fourth International Congress of Primatology* (Vol. 2). Basel: Karger, 1973.

Eaton, G. G., & Resko, J. A. Ovarian hormones and sexual behavior in *Macaca nemestrina. Journal of Comparative and Physiological Psychology,* 1974, **86,** 919–925.

Epple, G. Pheromones in primate reproduction and social behavior. In W. Montagna & W. A. Sadler (Eds.), *Reproductive behavior: Advances in behavioral biology* (Vol. 2). New York: Plenum Press, 1974.

Erwin, J., & Mitchell, G. Initial heterosexual behavior of adolescent rhesus monkeys (*Macaca mulatta*). *Archives of Sexual Behavior,* 1975, **4,** 97–104.

Everitt, B. J., & Herbert, J. The effects of dexamethasone and androgens on sexual receptivity of female rhesus monkeys. *Journal of Endocrinology,* 1971, **51,** 575–588.

Everitt, B. J., Herbert, J., & Hamer, J. D. Sexual receptivity of bilaterally adrenalectomized female rhesus monkeys. *Physiology and Behavior,* 1972, **8,** 409–415.

Forest, M. G., Cathiard, A. M., & Bertrand, J. A. Total and unbound testosterone levels in the newborn and in normal and hypogonadal children: Use of a sensitive radioimmunoassay for testosterone. *Journal of Clinical Endocrinology and Metabolism,* 1973, **36,** 1132–1142.

Gartlan, J. S. Structure and function in primate society. *Folia Primatologica,* 1968, **8,** 89–120.

Goldfoot, D. A. Hormonal and social determinants of sexual behavior in the pigtail monkey (*Macaca nemestrina*). In G. B. A. Stoelinga & J. J. van der Werff ten Bosch (Eds.), *Normal and abnormal development of brain and behaviour.* Leiden: University of Leiden Press, 1971.

Goldfoot, D. A., Kravetz, M. A., Goy, R. W., & Freeman, S. K. Lack of effect of vaginal lavages and aliphatic acids on ejaculatory responses in rhesus monkeys: Behavioral and chemical analyses. *Hormones and Behavior,* 1976, **7**, 1–27.

Goldfoot, D. A., Slob, A. K., Scheffler, G., Robinson, J. A., Wiegand, S. J., & Cords, J. Multiple ejaculations during prolonged sexual tests and lack of resultant serum testosterone increases in male stumptail macaques (*M. arctoides*). *Archives of Sexual Behavior,* 1975, **4**, 547–560.

Goldfoot, D. A., & Wallen, K. Gender role development in rhesus infants as a function of rearing conditions. In D. J. Chivers (Ed.), *Recent advances in primatology–behaviour* (Vol. 1). (Proceedings of the Sixth Congress of the International Primatological Society.) New York: Academic Press, in press.

Gordon, T. P., & Bernstein, I. S. Seasonal variation in sexual behavior in all-male rhesus troops. *American Journal of Physical Anthropology,* 1973, **38**, 221–227.

Gordon, T. P., Rose, R. M., & Bernstein, I. S. Seasonal rhythm in plasma testosterone levels in the rhesus monkey (*Macaca mulatta*): A three year study. *Hormones and Behavior,* 1976, **7**, 229–243.

Goy, R. W. Role of androgens in the establishment and regulation of behavioral sex differences in mammals. *Journal of Animal Science,* 1966, **25** (Suppl.), 21–35.

Goy, R. W. Organizing effects of androgen on the behaviour of rhesus monkeys. In R. P. Michael (Ed.), *Endocrinology and human behaviour.* London: Oxford University Press, 1968.

Goy, R. W. Experimental control of psychosexuality. *Philosophical Transactions of the Royal Society of London* (Series B), 1970, **259**, 149–162.

Goy, R. W., & Goldfoot, D. A. Hormonal influences on sexually dimorphic behavior. In R. O. Greep & E. B. Astwood (Eds.), *Handbook of physiology: Endocrinology* (Vol. 2, Part 1). Baltimore: Williams & Wilkins, 1973.

Goy, R. W., & Goldfoot, D. A. Experiential and hormonal factors influencing development of sexual behavior in the male rhesus monkey. In F. O. Schmitt & F. G. Worden (Eds.), *The neurosciences: Third study program.* Cambridge, Massachusetts: MIT Press, 1974.

Goy, R. W., & Goldfoot, D. A. Neuroendocrinology: Animal models and problems of human sexuality. *Archives of Sexual Behavior,* 1975, **4**, 405–420.

Goy, R. W., & Phoenix, C. H. The effects of testosterone propionate administered before birth on the development of behavior in genetic female rhesus monkeys. In C. H. Sawyer & R. A. Gorski (Eds.), *Steroid hormones and brain function.* Berkeley: University of California Press, 1971.

Goy, R. W., & Resko, J. A. Gonadal hormones and behavior of normal and pseudohermaphroditic nonhuman female primates. In E. B. Astwood (Ed.), *Recent progress in hormone research* (Vol. 28). New York: Academic Press, 1972.

Goy, R. W., Wallen, K., & Goldfoot, D. A. Social factors affecting the development of mounting behavior in male rhesus monkeys. In W. Montagna & W. A. Sadler (Eds.), *Reproductive behavior.* New York: Plenum Press, 1974.

Goy, R. W., Wolf, J. E., & Eisele, S. G. Experimental pseudohermaphroditism in rhesus monkeys: Anatomical and psychological characteristics. In J. Money & H. Musaph (Eds.), *Handbook of sexology.* Amsterdam: Elsevier/North-Holland Biomedical Press B. V., in press.

Green, R., Whalen, R. E., Rutley, B., & Battie, C. Dominance hierarchy in squirrel monkeys (*Saimiri sciureus*): Role of the gonads and androgen on genital display and feeding order *Folia Primatologica,* 1972, **18**, 185–195.

Hanby, J. Social factors affecting primate sexual behaviour. In J. Money & H. Musaph (Eds.), *Handbook of sexology*. Amsterdam: Elsevier/North-Holland Biomedical Press B. V., in press.

Hanby, J. P., & Brown, C. E. The development of sociosexual behaviours in Japanese macaques, *Macaca fuscata*. *Behaviour*, 1974, **49**, 152–196.

Hanby, J. P., Robertson, L. T., & Phoenix, C. H. The sexual behavior of a confined troop of Japanese macaques. *Folia Primatologica*, 1971, **16**, 123–143.

Harlow, H. F. Sexual behavior in the rhesus monkey. In F. A. Beach (Ed.), *Sex̂ and behavior*. New York: John Wiley & Sons, 1965.

Harlow, H. F., & Harlow, M. K. The affectional systems. In A. M. Schrier, H. F. Harlow, & F. Stollnitz (Eds.), *Behavior of nonhuman primates* (Vol. 2). New York: Academic Press, 1965.

Harlow, H. F., & Harlow, M. K. Learning to love. *American Scientist*, 1966, **54**, 244–272.

Harlow, H. F., & Harlow, M. K. Psychopathology in monkeys. In H. D. Kimmel (Ed.), *Experimental psychopathology: Recent research and theory*. New York: Academic Press, 1971.

Harlow, H. F., Harlow, M. K., Hansen, E. W., & Suomi, S. J. Infantile sexuality in monkeys. *Archives of Sexual Behavior*, 1972, **2**, 1–7.

Harlow, H. F., Joslyn, W. D., Senko, M. G., & Dopp, A. Behavioral aspects of reproduction in primates. *Journal of Animal Science*, 1966, **25**, 49–67.

Harlow, H. F., & Lauersdorf, H. E. Sex differences in passion and play. *Perspectives in Biology and Medicine*, 1974, **17**, 348–361.

Herbert, J. Sexual preference in the rhesus monkey, *Macaca mulatta*, in the laboratory. *Animal Behaviour*, 1968, **16**, 120–128.

Herbert, J., & Trimble, M. R. Effect of oestradiol and testosterone on the sexual receptivity and attractiveness of the female rhesus monkey. *Nature*, 1967, **216**, 165–166.

Hess, D. L. and Resko, J. A. The effects of progesterone on the patterns of testosterone and estradiol concentrations in the systemic plasma of the female rhesus monkey during the intermenstrual period. *Endocrinology*, 1973, **92**, 446–453.

Hinde, R. A. *Biological bases of human social behaviour*. New York: McGraw-Hill, 1974.

Hrdy, S. B. Male-male competition and infanticide among the langurs (*Presbytis entellus*) of Abu, Rajasthan. *Folia Primatologica*, 1974, **22**, 19–58.

Johnson, D. F., & Phoenix, C. H. The hormonal control of female sexual attractiveness, proceptivity and receptivity in rhesus monkeys. *Journal of Comparative and Physiological Psychology*, 1976, **90**, 473–483.

Joslyn, W. D. Androgen-induced social dominance in infant female rhesus monkeys. *Journal of Child Psychology and Psychiatry*, 1973, **14**, 137–145.

Karsch, F. J., Dierschke, D. J., & Knobil, E. Sexual differentiation of pituitary function: Apparent difference between primates and rodents. *Science*, 1973, **179**, 484–486.

Kaufmann, J. H. A three-year study of mating behavior in a free-ranging band of rhesus monkeys. *Ecology*, 1965, **46**, 500–512.

Keverne, E. B. Sex attractants in primates. *New Scientist*, 1974, **61**, 22–24.

Keverne, E. B. Sexual receptivity and attractiveness in the female rhesus monkey. In J. S. Rosenblatt & R. Hinde (Eds.), *Advances in the study of behaviour* (Vol. 7). New York: Academic Press, in press.

Lindburg, D. G. The rhesus monkey in North India: An ecological and behavioral study. *Primate Behavior*, 1971, **2**, 1–106.

Loy, J., & Loy, K. Behavior of an all-juvenile group of rhesus monkeys. *American Journal of Physical Anthropology*, 1974, **40**, 83–95.

Luttge, W. G. The role of gonadal hormones in the sexual behavior of the rhesus monkey and human: A literature survey. *Archives of Sexual Behavior*, 1971, **1**, 61–88.

Luttge, W. G., & Whalen, R. E. Dihydrotestosterone, androstenedione, testosterone: Comparative effectiveness in masculinizing and defeminizing reproductive systems in male and female rats. *Hormones and Behavior,* 1970, **1**, 265–281.

Mason, W. A. The effects of social restriction on the behavior of rhesus monkeys: I. Free social behavior. *Journal of Comparative and Physiological Psychology,* 1960, **53**, 582–589.

Mason, W. A. The effects of social restriction on the behavior of rhesus monkeys: II. Tests of gregariousness. *Journal of Comparative and Physiological Psychology,* 1961, **54**, 287–290.

Michael, R. P. Gonadal hormones and the control of primate behaviour. In R. P. Michael (Ed.), *Endocrinology and human behaviour.* London: Oxford University Press, 1968.

Michael, R. P. Neuroendocrine factors regulating primate behavior. In L. Martini & W. F. Ganong (Eds.), *Frontiers in neuroendocrinology.* London: Oxford University Press, 1971.

Michael, R. P. Determinants of primate reproductive behavior. *Acta Endocrinologica* (Suppl.), 1972, **166**, 322–361.

Michael, R. P. The effects of hormones on sexual behavior in female cat and rhesus monkey. In R. O. Greep (Ed.), *Handbook of physiology, Section 7: Endocrinology* (Vol. 2, Part 1). Washington, D.C.: American Physiological Society, 1973.

Michael, R. P., & Keverne, E. B. Pheromones and the communication of sexual status in primates. *Nature* (London), 1968, **218**, 746–749.

Michael, R. P., & Keverne, E. B. Primate sex pheromones of vaginal origin. *Nature* (London), 1970, **225**, 84–85.

Michael, R. P., Saayman, G. S., & Zumpe, D. Inhibition of sexual receptivity by progesterone in rhesus monkeys. *Journal of Endocrinology,* 1967, **39**, 309–310. (a)

Michael, R. P., Saayman, G. S., & Zumpe, D. Sexual attractiveness and receptivity in rhesus monkeys. *Nature,* 1967, **215**, 554–556. (b)

Michael, R. P., & Welegalla, J. Ovarian hormones and the sexual behaviour of the female rhesus monkey (*Macaca mulatta*) under laboratory conditions. *Journal of Endocrinology,* 1968, **41**, 407–420.

Michael, R. P., & Wilson, M. Changes in the sexual behaviour of male rhesus monkeys (*M. mulatta*) at puberty: Comparisons with the behaviour of adults. *Folia Primatologica,* 1973, **19**, 384–403.

Michael, R. P., & Wilson, M. Effects of castration and hormone replacement in fully adult male rhesus monkeys (*Macaca mulatta*). *Endocrinology,* 1974, **95**, 150–159.

Michael, R. P., & Wilson, M. Mating seasonality in castrated male rhesus monkeys. *Journal of Reproduction and Fertility,* 1975, **43**, 325–328.

Michael, R. P., Wilson, M., & Plant, T. M. Sexual behaviour of male primates and the role of testosterone. In R. P. Michael & J. H. Crook (Eds.), *Comparative ecology and behaviour of primates.* London: Academic Press, 1973.

Michael, R. P., & Zumpe, D. Sexual initiating behaviour by female rhesus monkeys (*Macaca mulatta*) under laboratory conditions. *Behaviour,* 1970, **36**, 168–186.

Michael, R. P., Zumpe, D., Keverne, E. B., & Bonsall, R. W. Neuroendocrine factors in the control of primate behavior. *Recent Progress in Hormone Research,* 1972, **28**, 665–706.

Missakian, E. A. Reproductive behavior of socially deprived adult male rhesus monkeys (*Macaca mulatta*). *Journal of Comparative and Physiological Psychology,* 1969, **69**, 403–407.

Missakian, E. A. Genealogical and cross-genealogical dominance relations in a group of free-ranging rhesus monkeys (*Macaca mulatta*) on Cayo Santiago. *Primates,* 1972, **13**, 169–180.

Money, J., & Ehrhardt, A. A. Prenatal hormonal exposure: Possible effects on behaviour in man. In R. P. Michael (Ed.), *Endocrinology and human behaviour.* London: Oxford University Press, 1968.

Nadler, R. D. Sexual cyclicity in captive lowland gorillas. *Science,* 1975, **189**, 813–814.

Nadler, R. Sexual behavior of orang-utans in the laboratory. In D. Chivers (Ed.), *Recent Advances in Primatology–Behavior* (Vol. 1). (Proceedings of the Sixth Congress of the International Primatological Society.) New York: Academic Press, in press.

Naftolin, F., Ryan, K. J., & Petro, Z. Aromatization of androstenedione by the diencephalon. *Journal of Clinical Endorcinology and Metabolism,* 1971, **33**, 368–370.

Norikoshi, K., & Koyama, N. Group shifting and social organization among Japanese monkeys. In S. Kondo, M. Kawai, A. Ehara, & S. Kawamura (Eds.), *Proceedings from the Fifth Congress of the International Primatological Society.* Tokyo: Japan Science Press, 1975.

Novak, M. Fear-attachment relationships in infant and juvenile rhesus monkeys (Doctoral dissertation, University of Wisconsin-Madison, 1973). *Dissertation Abstracts International,* 1974, **34**, 5227B. (University Microfilms No. 74-00490)

Phoenix, C. H. Ejaculation by male rhesus as a function of the female partner. *Hormones and Behavior,* 1973, **4**, 365–370.

Phoenix, C. H. Prenatal testosterone in the nonhuman primate and its consequences for behavior. In R. C. Friedman, R. M. Richart, & R. L. Vande Wiele (Eds.), *Sex differences in behavior.* New York: John Wiley & Sons, 1974.

Phoenix, C. H. Sexual behavior of castrated male rhesus monkeys treated with 19-hydroxytestosterone. *Physiology and Behavior,* 1976, **16**, 305–310.

Phoenix, C. H., Goy, R. W., & Resko, J. A. Psychosexual differentiation as a function of androgenic stimulation. In M. Diamond (Ed.), *Perspectives in reproduction and sexual behavior.* Bloomington: Indiana University Press, 1968.

Phoenix, C. H., Goy, R. W., & Young, W. C. Sexual behavior: General aspects. In L. Martini & W. F. Ganong (Eds.), *Neuroendocrinology* (Vol. 2). New York: Academic Press, 1967.

Phoenix, C. H., Slob, A. K., & Goy, R. W. Effects of castration and replacement therapy on the sexual behavior of adult male rhesus. *Journal of Comparative and Physiological Psychology,* 1973, **84**, 472–481.

Plant, T. M., Zumpe, D., Sauls, M., & Michael, R. P. An annual rhythm in plasma testosterone of adult male rhesus monkeys maintained in the laboratory. *Journal of Endocrinology,* 1974, **62**, 403–404.

Resko, J. A. Plasma androgen levels of the rhesus monkey: Effects of age and season. *Endocrinology,* 1967, **81**, 1203–1212.

Resko, J. A. Fetal hormones and their effect on the differentiation of the central nervous system in primates. *Federation Proceedings,* 1975, **34**, 1650–1655.

Riesen, A. H. Nissen's observations on the development of sexual behavior in captive-born nursery-reared chimpanzees. *The Chimpanzee,* 1971, **4**, 260–270.

Robinson, J. A., Scheffler, G., Eisele, S., & Goy, R. W. The effects of age and season on the sexual behavior and plasma testosterone and dihydrotestosterone concentrations of laboratory-housed rhesus monkeys (*Macaca mulatta*). *Biology of Reproduction,* 1975, **13**, 203–210.

Rodriguez-Sierra, J. F., Naggar, A., & Komisaruk, B. R. Monoaminergic mediation of masculine and feminine copulatory behavior in female rats. *Pharmacology, Biochemistry and Behavior,* 1976, **15**, 457–463.

Rose, R. M., Bernstein, I. S., & Gordon, T. P. Consequences of social conflict on plasma testosterone levels in rhesus monkeys. *Psychosomatic Medicine,* 1974, **37**, 50–61.

Rose, R. M., Gordon, T. P., & Bernstein, I. S. Plasma testosterone levels in the male rhesus: Influences of sexual and social stimuli. *Science,* 1972, **178**, 643–645.

Rosenblum, L. A. The development of social behavior in the rhesus monkey (Doctoral dissertation, University of Wisconsin-Madison, 1961). *Dissertation Abstracts International,* 1961, **22**, 926. (University Microfilms No. 61-03158).

Rosenblum, L. A., & Nadler, R. D. The ontogeny of sexual behavior in male bonnet macaques. In D. H. Ford (Ed.), *Influence of hormones on the nervous system.* Basel: Karger, 1971.

Rothe, H. Some aspects of sexuality and reproduction in groups of captive marmosets (*Callithrix jacchus*). *Zeitshrift für Tierpsychologie,* 1975, **37**, 255–273.

Rowell, T. E. Behaviour and female reproductive cycles of rhesus macaques. *Journal of Reproduction and Fertility,* 1963, **6**, 193–203.

Rowell, T. E. Female reproduction cycles and social behavior in primates. *Advances in the Study of Behavior,* 1972, **4**, 69–105.

Rowell, T. E. Social organization of wild talapoin monkeys. *American Journal of Physical Anthropology,* 1973, **38**, 593–597.

Rowell, T. E. The concept of social dominance. *Behavioral Biology,* 1974, **11**, 131–154.

Saayman, G. S. The menstrual cycle and sexual behavior in a troop of free ranging chacma baboons (*Papio ursinus*).*Folia Primatologica,* 1970, **12**, 81–110.

Sackett, G. P. Effects of rearing conditions upon the behavior of rhesus monkeys (*M. mulatta*). *Child Development,* 1965, **36**, 855–868.

Sade, D. S. Sèasonal cycle in the size of the testes of free-ranging *Macaca mulatta. Folia Primatologica,* 1964, **2**, 171–180.

Schlesinger, K., & Groves, P. M. *Psychology, a dynamic science.* Dubuque: William C. Brown, 1976.

Senko, M. G. The effects of early, intermediate and late experiences upon adult macaque sexual behavior. Unpublished master's thesis, University of Wisconsin-Madison, 1966.

Slimp, J. C. Effects of medial preoptic-anterior hypothalamic lesions on heterosexual behavior, masturbation, and social behavior of male rhesus monkeys. Unpublished doctoral thesis, University of Wisconsin-Madison, 1976.

Slob, A. K. Effects of ovariectomy on male-female interactions in the stumptail macaque (*M. arctoides*). *Acta Endocrinologica* (Suppl.), 1975, **199**, 145.

Slob, A. K., Wiegand, S. J., Scheffler, G., & Goy, R. W. Gonadal hormones and behaviour in the stumptail macaque (*Macaca arctoides*) under laboratory conditions: A preliminary report. *Journal of Endocrinology,* 1975, **64**, 38P–39P.

Stephenson, G. R. Testing for group specific communication patterns in Japanese macaques. In E. W. Menzel (Ed.), *Symposia of the Fourth International Congress of Primatology* (Vol. 1). Basel: Karger, 1973.

Stephenson, G. R. Social structure of mating activity in Japanese macaques. In S. Kondo, M. Kawai, A. Ehara, & S. Kawamura (Eds.), *Proceedings from the Symposia of the Fifth Congress of the International Primatological Society.* Tokyo: Japan Science Press, 1975.

Tokuda, K. A study on the sexual behavior in the Japanese monkey troop. *Primates,* 1961–2, **3**(2), 1–40.

Trimble, M. R., & Herbert, J. The effect of testosterone or oestradiol upon the sexual and associated behaviour of the adult female rhesus monkey. *Journal of Endocrinology,* 1968, **42**, 171–185.

Trollope, J., & Blurton Jones, N. G. Age of sexual maturity in the stump-tailed macaque (*Macaca arctoides*): A birth from laboratory born parents. *Primates,* 1972, **13**, 229–230.

Tutin, C. E. G., & McGrew, W. C. Sexual behavior of group-living adolescent chimpanzees. *American Journal of Physical Anthropology,* 1973, **38**, 195–199.

Vandenbergh, J. G. Hormonal basis of sex skin in male rhesus monkeys. *General and Comparative Endocrinology,* 1965, **5**, 31–34.

Vandenbergh, J. G., & Drickamer, L. C. Reproductive coordination among free-ranging rhesus monkeys. *Physiology and Behavior,* 1974, **13**, 373–376.

van Lawick-Goodall, J. The behaviour of free living chimpanzees in the Gombe Stream Reserve. *Animal Behaviour Monographs,* 1968, **1**(3), 161–311.

van Wagenen, G., & Simpson, M. E. Testicular development in the rhesus monkey. *Anatomical Record,* 1954, **118,** 231–251.

Wallen, K., Bielert, C. F., & Slimp, J. Foot-clasp mounting in the prepuberal rhesus monkey: Social and hormonal influences. In F. E. Poirier & S. Chevalier-Skolnikoff (Eds.), *Biosocial development among primates.* New York: Garland Publishing, in press.

Wells, L. J., & van Wagenen, G. Androgen-induced female pseudohermaphroditism in the monkey (*Macaca mulatta*): Anatomy of the reproductive organs. *Carnegie Institution of Washington Publication 603, Contributions to Embryology,* 1954, **35,** 93–106.

Whalen, R. E. Differentiation of the neural mechanisms which control gonadotropin secretion and sexual behavior. In M. Diamond (Ed.), *Perspectives in reproduction and sexual behavior.* Bloomington: Indiana University Press, 1968.

Whalen, R. E. The ontogeny of sexuality. In H. Moltz (Ed.), *The ontogeny of vertebrate behavior.* New York: Academic Press, 1971.

Wickler, W. *The sexual code: The social behavior of animals and men.* Garden City, New York: Anchor/Doubleday, 1973.

Young, W. C., & Orbison, W. D. Changes in selected features of behavior in pairs of oppositely sexed chimpanzees during the sexual cycle and after ovariectomy. *Journal of Comparative Psychology,* 1944, **37,** 107–143.

Author Index

Numbers in *italics* refer to pages on which the complete references are listed.

Subject Index

For Product Safety Concerns and Information please contact our EU representative GPSR@taylorandfrancis.com
Taylor & Francis Verlag GmbH, Kaufingerstraße 24, 80331 München, Germany

www.ingramcontent.com/pod-product-compliance
Ingram Content Group UK Ltd.
Pitfield, Milton Keynes, MK11 3LW, UK
UKHW022119190926
475702UK00013B/1536
9780898591392